Migrant Organising

International Comparative Social Studies

Editor-in-Chief

Mehdi P. Amineh (*Amsterdam Institute for Social Science Research, University of Amsterdam, and International Institute for Asian Studies, Leiden University*)

Editorial Board

Shahrough Akhavi (*Columbia University*)
W.A. Arts (*University College Utrecht*)
Sjoerd Beugelsdijk (*Radboud University*)
Mark-Anthony Falzon (*University of Malta*)
Harald Fuhr (*University of Potsdam*)
Joyeeta Gupta (*University of Amsterdam*)
Xiaoming Huang (*Victoria University Wellington*)
Nilgün Önder (*University of Regina*)
Gerhard Preyer (*Goethe University Frankfurt am Main*)
Islam Qasem (*Webster University, Leiden*)
Kurt W. Radtke (*International Institute for Asian Studies, Leiden University*)
Mahmoud Sadri (*Texas Woman's University*)
Jeremy Smith (*University of Eastern Finland*)
Ngo Tak-Wing (*Leiden University*)
L.A. Visano (*York University*)

VOLUME 54

The titles published in this series are listed at *brill.com/icss*

Migrant Organising

Community Unionism, Solidarity and Bricolage

Edited by

Emma Martín-Díaz and Beltrán Roca

BRILL

LEIDEN | BOSTON

Cover illustration: May Day demonstration in New Jersey / Unions and worker centers rally in the International Workers Day to demand rights for migrant workers in New Jersey, 2019, courtesy of Beltran Roca. Image made while conducting fieldwork among migrant activists in NYC.

Library of Congress Cataloging-in-Publication Data

Names: Martín Díaz, Emma, editor. | Roca Martínez, Beltrán, editor.
Title: Migrant organising : community unionism, solidarity and bricolage / edited by Emma Martín-Díaz, and Beltrán Roca.
Description: Leiden ; Boston : Brill, [2021] | Series: International comparative social studies, 1568-4474 ; volume 54 | Includes bibliographical references and index. |
Identifiers: LCCN 2021026812 (print) | LCCN 2021026813 (ebook) | ISBN 9789004464940 (hardback ; alk. paper) | ISBN 9789004464964 (ebook)
Subjects: LCSH: Foreign workers–Europe. | Labor unions–Organizing–Europe. | Labor movement–Europe.
Classification: LCC HD8378.5.A2 M5357 2022 (print) | LCC HD8378.5.A2 (ebook) | DDC 331.6/2094–dc23
LC record available at https://lccn.loc.gov/2021026812
LC ebook record available at https://lccn.loc.gov/2021026813

Typeface for the Latin, Greek, and Cyrillic scripts: "Brill". See and download: brill.com/brill-typeface.

ISSN 1568-4474
ISBN 978-90-04-46494-0 (hardback)
ISBN 978-90-04-46496-4 (e-book)

Copyright 2021 by Emma Martín-Díaz and Beltrán Roca. Published by Koninklijke Brill NV, Leiden, The Netherlands.
Koninklijke Brill NV incorporates the imprints Brill, Brill Nijhoff, Brill Hotei, Brill Schöningh, Brill Fink, Brill mentis, Vandenhoeck & Ruprecht, Böhlau Verlag and V&R Unipress.
Koninklijke Brill NV reserves the right to protect this publication against unauthorized use. Requests for re-use and/or translations must be addressed to Koninklijke Brill NV via brill.com or copyright.com.

This book is printed on acid-free paper and produced in a sustainable manner.

Contents

Notes on Contributors VII

Introduction: Post-Fordism, Transnationalism and Global Chains as a Context for Community Unionism and Solidarity Networks 1
   Beltrán Roca and Emma Martín-Díaz

1   Labour Activism and Organisational Bricolage among Spanish and Italian Emigrants in Germany 21
   Simone Castellani and Beltrán Roca

2   Community through Corporatisation? The Case of Spanish Nurses in the German Care Industry 59
   Mark Bergfeld

3   Cross-Border Domestic Work in Ceuta: Challenges and Alternative Organisations 81
   Emma Martín-Díaz and Juan Pablo Aris-Escarcena

4   Organising Migrant Porters of the Logistic Sector: The Italian Case of SI Cobas 104
   Giulia Borraccino

5   Migrant Worker Organisations and Overexploitation in the Garment Industry in Argentina 119
   Paula Dinorah Salgado

6   Collective Action, Experience and Identity in Global Agrarian Enclaves: The Case of Andalusia, Spain 154
   Alicia Reigada

7   Transforming Labour Law or Recurring to Grass-Root Mobilisation? The Struggles over the Empowerment of Tomato-Picking Migrant Workers in Southern Italy 181
   Giuseppe D'Onofrio and Jon Las Heras

8   Putting the Pieces Together: Post-Fordist Migrations, Community
    Unionism, Solidarity Networks and Bricolage   204
      Beltrán Roca and Emma Martín-Díaz

Index   217

Notes on Contributors

Juan Pablo Aris-Escarcena
is a PhD Candidate at the Social Anthropology Department of the University of Seville. His research is focused on the bordering process of Europe, applying an Anthropology of Law and Policy perspective in a multi-sited ethnography across some of the most importants borderlans of Europe, as Calais (UK – France border), Ventimiglia (France – Italy border), Ceuta y Melilla (Spain – Morocco border).

Mark Bergfeld
is a PhD researcher at Queen Mary University of London, School of Business and Management (the United Kingdom). His research investigates migrant workers and their forms of self-organization in Germany, Britain and the USA. He has published articles, book chapters and reviews in a number of academic books and journals as well as magazines and news outlets. He currently is the Director of Property Services and UNICARE at UNI Global Union (UNI Europa).

Giulia Borraccino
studied Sociology and Labour Policies in the University of Florence (Italy). Between 2012 and 2014 she collaborated with the Research Centre of the University of Florence "Laboris – Research on Labour Studies." In 2014 she awarded a 3 years scholarship in the University of Milan, into the PhD program "Economic Sociology and Labour Studies." She visited the Universities of Cadiz and Zaragoza, where she conducted part of the fieldwork. She graduated in 2018 with a comparative reaseach project on self-organised groups of educational workers in Italy and Spain. Her main research interest are trade unions revitalization strategies from a radical framework perspective.

Simone Castellani
is a postdoctoral fellow at the University Institute of Lisbon (Portugal) for the UPWEB/NORFACE project. He holds a PhD in Social Anthropology (University of Seville) and in Migratory and Intercultural Processes (University of Genoa). He was visiting fellow at the Wellesley College (U.S.), University of Bielefeld and University of Freiburg (Germany), FLACSO Ecuador, University of Sussex (UK) and guest lecturer at University of Bielefeld. His topics of researches focuses on the correlation between youth and international migratory processes. In the last years he has been studying the new Southern European migration flows toward Germany during the contemporary economic crisis.

Giuseppe D'Onofrio
is a PhD student in Social Sciences at University of Naples Federico II. He has been visiting PhD student at EWERC (European Work and Employment Research Center) at University of Manchester, UK. His PhD research is focused on exploitation of migrant workers in Southern Italy within global tomato value chain. His main research interests are migrations, informal work, unions and working-class conditions. He's editor of the independent magazine of social enquiry Napoli Monitor.

Jon Las Heras
is a Lecturer at the University of the Basque Country (Spain), and obtained his PhD at The University of Manchester (UK), combining the fields of IPE and Industrial Relations into the study of collective bargaining patterns in the automotive industry. His research focuses on the Political Economy of Trade Unionism, the Politics and Geographies of Labour Empowerment, Cooperative-Studies and Critical Political Economy more broadly, and he is editor of the journal *Lan Harremanak* (Industrial Relations).

Emma Martín-Díaz
is a Professor in Social Anthropology at the University of Seville. She is specialized in migration, ethnic relationships and public policies. She obtained her MA Anthropology at the University of Seville in 1985, with a thesis on migrants returning from Western Europe to rural Andalusia. Her Ph thesis (1988) focused on Andalusian immigrants in Cataluña, inter-ethnic relationships and integration policies, and won the prize "Blas Infante" for the best original research on Social Studies in Andalusia in 1991. Since 1995 she has been carrying out research on "new immigration" in Spain. The topics include immigration, agriculture and labour markets in Mediterranean Spain, (1999, 2004) immigration and citizenship (1999, 2003), immigration and domestic services, (2002) immigration and prostitution (2004) migration and transnational social networks (2007) and the 'second generation' (2009-today). She participates in several masters and doctorates on migration, ethnicity, gender, development, citizenship and human rights at different universities from Europe and Latin America.

Alicia Reigada
is an Associate Professor in Social Anthropology at the University of Seville (Spain), and member of the GEISA research rroup. She holds a PhD in Social Anthropology (University of Seville) and her studies focus on agri-food global chains, social organization of labor, class, migrations and gender relationships.

NOTES ON CONTRIBUTORS IX

She has participated in several international networks and projects, and has been as visiting scholar at the City University of New York (CUNY), University of California- Davis, Universidad Nacional Autónoma de México (UNAM), Universidad Federal Rural de Río de Janeiro (UFRRJ), among others. She has published recently in journals such as *Current Anthropology, Rural Sociology, Organization, The International Journal of Iberian Studies*.

Beltrán Roca
is an Associate Professor in Sociology at the Department of General Economics, Universidad de Cádiz. He is a member of the research group GEISA and the Institute for Social and Sustainable Development (INDESS)-Universidad de Cádiz. He has been visiting researcher at CONICET (Argentina), Yale (USA), LSE (UK) and Aix-Marseille Université (France). His research interests are trade unionism, migrations, third sector and collective action. He has coedited the book *Challenging Austerity. Radical Left and Social Movements in the South of Europe* (Routledge, 2017). He has published recently in journals such as *American Anthropologist, Critical Sociology, Transfer, Mediterranean Politics* and *Capital & Class*.

Paula Dinorah Salgado
is a Ph.D. candidate in Social Sciences at the University of Buenos Aires- Doctoral Thesis on overexploitation conditions in the garment industry in Argentina- and holds a degree in Sociology. She is currently a member of the Center for Studies in Urban Social Policy at the National University of Tres de Febrero (CEIPSU-UNTreF) in Buenos Aires. She teaches Social Research Methodology. Her main lines of research are working conditions, migration and unionism.

INTRODUCTION

Post-Fordism, Transnationalism and Global Chains as a Context for Community Unionism and Solidarity Networks

Beltrán Roca and Emma Martín-Díaz

The shift from a Fordist model of capital accumulation based on stable labour markets, inclusive welfare regimes and Keynesian regulation practices to a post-Fordist one characterized by strongly segmented labour markets, labour instability, the reduction of welfare policy and growing economic deregulation and flexibility has also affected the ambit of international migrations (Amin, 1995; Harvey, 2005). The post-Fordist model of accumulation meant not only the decline of mass production factories and the rise of high-technology production located globally, but also the replacement of mass production and consumption by flexible forms of production, customization and the growth of the service and information economy (Lash & Urry, 1987). In this sense, the post-Fordist society entails a fragmentation of identities that manifests in new forms of consumption, new forms of production and new forms of collective action (Alonso, 2002). The intensification of migration flows contribute to strengthening the dynamics of fragmentation that affect consumption, among other things, with the extension of ethnic economies within host societies.

The new model of accumulation implied a rent transfer from labour to capital; that is, a general pauperisation of the working class and growing inequalities. But this tendency has not taken place homogenously among the working class. Advanced capitalist economies have experienced a strong segmentation and fragmentation of this class. The dualisation of the labour market set the groundwork for a segmentation between a decreasing core of stable workers of the primary segment and a heterogeneous and growing secondary segment characterised by unstable and precarious jobs. Migrant labour has tended to concentrate in secondary labour markets.

Migration during the Fordist period (Martin-Diaz, 2006a) was substantially different from its counterparts under flexible capitalism (Menz 2002). There are both continuities and discontinuities between these two periods. As we have suggested elsewhere, although the organisation of labour markets is substantially different in both models, generating diverse labour and social integration strategies and policies, an articulation of national economies based on territorial imbalances persists as a structural factor (Martin-Diaz & Roca, 2017). This implies that the different European states are under a centre-periphery relationship (Wallerstein, 1974; Arrighi 1985) that is structural and, as such, remains, although with changing forms.

The following characteristics define the periphery of the world system:

> ...a region suffering from: 1) A lack of effective control over the use of resources; 2) a comparative lack of local innovation; 3) a weakness in internal linkages; 4) a weakness in information flows within the periphery and from the periphery to the center; and 5) migration outflows (Gamabarotto and Solari, 2014, p. 8).

The decline of the Fordist model after the end of the 1970s was expressed in the rise of *irregular immigration*. Multinational companies started to take advantage of the cheaper labour markets of the periphery, even when producing high-tech goods. This capitalist restructuring provoked the retrenchment of the older industrialised countries, which had high unemployment rates in the traditional industrial areas, partially compensated by areas with strong cutting-edge technology. In this context, policies oriented toward the restriction, or even blocking, of immigration have generalised in the societies of the centre, fostering vulnerability and precariousness among significant factions of the working class, especially among unauthorised migrants.

To understand these transformations, the analysis of Rousenau (1990) about the 'two worlds of World politics' can be useful. The author highlights the underlying conflict between nation-states and transnational organisations by coining the neologism post-transnationalism. The idea that under globalisation, the state is no longer the institution that concentrates most of the power is formulated in the ambit of international migrations described by Schiller, Bash and Blanc (1992), who, inspired by Bourdieu's theory of social fields, analysed post-Fordist migrations, framing them within a multiplicity of networks linked in a fragmented and unequal manner through which persons, commodities, resources and ideas flow. They proposed the concept of 'transnational social field.' In addition to the influence of the School of Manchester, it is possible to recognise the resonance of post-internationalist theory and the notion of landscapes of Appadurai (1990), among other theories on globalization. According to the authors, transnational social fields include and combine, in different ways and in different moments, social actors, networks, organisations and subjects, which transcend national containers that defined migrations during the Fordist period.

It is worth noting that most of the works in the ambit of migrations from a transnational perspective have focused more on migrants' agency than on the structure of relationships between the state and the market. Most of the authors who have adopted this perspective understand transnational social fields as spaces of relationships or webs of networks in which different types of capital move. An interesting variety of this approach is the perspective of Moser (2009). This author suggests complementing the transnational perspective by studying certain dimensions of social capital that tend to be concealed due to a lack of knowledge about the situation in the society of origin. In previous works (Martín, 2008, 2012), we have demonstrated the multifunctionality of networks, their flexible character and high adaptability. Networks facilitate the redesign of strategies in contexts of risk management. At the same time, these networks are channels by which movements of different forms of capital take place.

It is well known that transnational networks allow migrants to maintain links with their communities of origin (Kearney, 1995; Guarnizo, 2000). Research on transnationalism has pointed out that the forms adopted by contacts with social networks vis-a-vis origin mean a leap forward in contemporary migration processes because of their frequency and intensity, but also because these links are part of migratory projects themselves. Thus, whilst in previous explanatory models migrants left their localities to live a new life or exercise the role of household provider from a distance, today migratory projects, whether they are the result of individual decisions or a household strategy, acquire a collective dimension to the extent that they include members who have left or stayed. This influences and shapes the feminisation of contemporary migrations. At the same time, feminisation has a profound impact on the strategies of asset accumulation and, in particular, on the forms in which the several types of capital circulate.

Networks operate as circulation channels. Through them, not only persons and economic resources circulate, but also information, customs, social norms, relation patterns and forms of social and political participation. In other words, they are a privileged space for the circulation of physical, financial and human capital, and also social, civic and political capital (Escrivá, Bermúdez & Moraes, 2009). Within these networks of relationships, migrants can redefine their projects several times in the light of perceived advantages and disadvantages they have experienced. A change in the project will manifest in the reconfiguration of the network, both in relation to the persons who participate in it and in relation to the flow of capital and its management.

If the transnational perspective had the virtue of discrediting the prevailing methodological nationalism of the analysis of post-Fordist migrations, it is also true that the centrality inherent in the study of migrants' agency led on many occasions to excessively optimistic analysis that overestimated the ability of subjects, networks and relationships making migratory projects and designing strategies. The predominance of these variables concealed, by commission or by omission, social structures that determined the specific forms adopted by post-Fordist migratory models. The analysis of the structure implies changing the focus from individual subjects to the logic of post-Fordist accumulation, emphasising the growing processes of production segmentation and the displacement of the axis from value creation to innovation. Under post-Fordism, both phenomena are combined, generating, on the one the hand, the delocalisation of production activity and, on the other hand, a capital transfer from investment in innovation in production to investment in the innovation of the product and the technology used for its development and dissemination. Although the segmentation of production is not a new phenomenon, the development of new technologies of communication and logistics have favoured the globalization of segmentation. The analysis of global value chains provides the structural framework in which the circulation of transnational workers can be located; and within this circulation, migrants can be seen as a specific and differentiated category of transnational worker.

If production is localised, it is evident that reproductive and care work cannot be located. Sassen defines global care chains as a 'strategic research aspect for examining the organizing dynamic of globalization and for beginning to clarify how gender dimension works' (Sassen, 2003, p. 69). Whilst value chains transfer capital to product innovation and development, delocalizing production, global care chains are also transnational chains, but they work by transferring women from different countries to the areas in which they offer their services. This circulation has given new characteristics to migratory processes to the extent that it leads us to rethink the migrant subject, considering variables such as gender, ethnicity and class as determinants in the analysis of these chains.

Mass migrations have followed discernible patterns in relation to the subject's sex/gender systems (Martín-Diaz, 2006a). Hence, men and women develop different strategies both for emigration and for social inclusion in destination countries. This difference is evident both in immigration policies and in the social discourses about migration processes. As Sassen points out:

> Gender dynamics have been invisibilised in terms of their concrete articulation with the global economy. This set of dynamics can be found in alternative cross-border circuits…, in which the role of women, and especially the condition of migrant women, is essential (Sassen, 2003, p. 46).

Transnational migrations become thus a privileged place for the study of the transformation of gender patterns. The study of the formation of transnational households can shed light on women's empowerment, allowing the validation of certain hypotheses formulated by authors who developed the concept (Hondagneu-Sotelo & Ávila, 1997; Herrera, 2004, Parella, 2008). These migrations permit us to observe the creation of new forms of cross-border solidarity, but also new forms of exploitation, and the experiences of belonging and the construction of identity that represent the new female subjectivities. According to Sassen:

> Women and immigrants emerge as a systematic equivalent of the proletariat, a proletariat that develops out of the countries of origin. In addition, the demands of top-level professional and managerial labour force in global cities are such that ordinary modes of managing tasks and domestic life styles become inappropriate. As a result, we are observing the return of the so-called 'servant classes,' formed mostly by immigrants and immigrant women (Sassen 2003, p. 50).

To summarise, the study of transnational communities provides new ways of exploring migration movements and analysing migrants' participation in social, political and cultural life in post-Fordist societies. This approach suggests that the changes in the economic and cultural models should translate into a revision of the theoretical and conceptual framework that has defined the study of migratory processes (Martín-Díaz, 2006b). The reconsideration of social subjects is particularly relevant. If, in the traditional approach, the central units of analysis were the individual, on the one hand, and social class, on the other hand, the introduction of transnational communities as a unit of analysis allows us to view the complexity of the processes and the plurality of social agents involved. Thus, the studies about migration processes conducted using the neoclassical approach emphasised the individual level in decision-making, perceiving migrations as the result of rational choices based on the assessment of costs and benefits. On the other hand, the studies that focused on social class as the central level of analysis envision a world of structures that determine the action of the subjects. Both units of analysis are fundamental but insufficient for understanding the action of social subjects in the context of globalised societies. In this framework, the transnational dimension of migrations questions the definitions imposed by the states, both the sending (emigrant) and the destination (immigrant) ones. The condition of subject fits into this transnational reality, and what characterises it is a type of ubiquity that points to the suitability of the term migrant as a form of describing a model of circulation of subjects in which persons and their networks are present, but also the structures that shape and condition their circulation.

1 Trade Union Policy Toward Immigrant Workers

In a world where migrations have become one of the most compelling societal challenges, the integration of migrant workers is at the centre of political and academic debates. Since employment is a key dimension of citizenship in contemporary capitalist societies, the integration of migrant workers is connected with wider dynamics of post-Fordist capitalist accumulation, labour market transformations (including the rise of the so-called platform economy) and neoliberal ideological hegemony. Nonetheless, integration is also related to the different forms of resistance against these economic, social and cultural dynamics. Trade unions have played –and still play– a critical role in these forms of resistance, although processes of precarisation, deregulation, individualization and fragmentation of the working class have undermined their basis. Studying migrant collective responses to theses dynamics allows us to apprehend domination and resistance in contemporary capitalism.

There is abundant academic literature on migrant workers and the responses of trade unions to migration challenges. The works of Castles and Kosack (1973), Castles and Miller (1993) and particularly the comparative research of Pennix and Roosblad (2001) stand out, although the period under scrutiny is from 1960 to 1993. However, the crisis of trade union representation models promoted by globalisation has led scholars to focus more on the strategies deployed by immigrants in order to examine the obstacles faced when integrating in the labour market.

In addition, an important proportion of the current debate on trade union revitalisation refers to the strategies put forward to recruit and mobilise 'outsiders' that is, those workers who tend to be underrepresented inside unions, such as migrants, women or young people (Murray, 2017). One of the reasons for the distance between unions and migrants can be found in Silver's (2003) concept of 'boundary drawing', that describes how trade unions sometimes generate class solidarity and identity by excluding other social groups based on ethnic, gender or nationality.

As several authors pointed out for the Fordist period, trade unions have tended to perceive migrant workers as a reserve army of labour undermining the bargaining power of the national working class (Castles & Kosack, 1973). This attitude has led researchers such as Kahmann (2006) to affirm that trade unions have an ambiguous relationship with migrant workers along the continuum of inclusion–exclusion.

Effectively, trade unions have shown a great variety of behaviour toward migrant workers. Pennix and Roosblad (2001: 13) highlight four factors explaining the national differences in trade union policies toward migrant workers: the social power and structure of the labour movement; the situation of the labour market; the broader social, political and cultural context; and the characteristics of the migrant workers. The third factor—the broader context—has been underlined in many studies that have suggested that national political narratives are essential in order to understand trade union policies (Wrench, 2004). In contrast to this approach, Marino, Pennux and Roosblad (2015) underline the relevance of trade unions' internal dynamics. They stress three main factors: trade union identity; organizational structure; and internal communication processes, including decision-making procedures. These authors point out the relevance of 'extending the framework by including internal trade union variables, especially trade union identity, structure and the internal communication channels through which migrant workers' grievances might influence general union policies' (Marino, Pennix & Roosblad., 2015, p. 14).

More recently, Connolly, Marino and Martinez Lucio (2019) have developed an analytical model for the explanation of trade union policy vis-a-vis migration. According to them, trade union policy is not only the result of the interrelations between regulatory contexts and union structures, but also of trade union identities. Paying attention to union identity helps us have a better grasp of internal dynamics and debates, forms of action and organizational change. Within the tradition of comparative industrial relations, the authors share Wrench's (2004) point of view about the relevance of political ideologies and traditions of struggle in the configuration of trade union policy (beyond other factors that have tended to be more often considered, such as union structural power and national regulatory systems of labour relations). Along this line, they underscore two key factors: logics of action and strategies, both closely connected to union identities.

According to their model, which parallels the seminal work of Hyman (2001), there are three main logics of action: the *logic of class*, which consists in considering immigrants as part of the working class and puts emphasis on solidarity between native and foreign workers; the *logic of race or ethnicity*, which underlines the particular oppression suffered by migrant workers and advocates for differentiated policies and means of representation; and the *logic of social rights*, which highlights the relevance of extra-workplace citizen rights of immigrants (such as healthcare, housing and other social policies). As Connolly, Marino and Martinez Lucio (2019) argue, a full representation of migrant workers would require engagement with the three logics; however, unions experience a continuous tension among these logics.

The authors point out that the three logics tend to correspond to three different strategies for representing migrant workers. The *organizing* strategy corresponds with the logic of class, and implies promoting workers' direct participation and struggle. The second strategy, the *community* strategy, is related to the logic of race or ethnicity, and involves engaging with communities; for example, participation in wider coalitions and showing sensibility for the

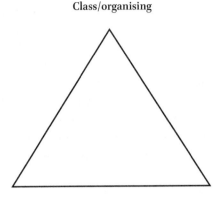

FIGURE 0.1   Trade union logics of action and strategies toward migrant workers (Connolly, Marino & Martinez Lucio, 2019, p. 20).

role of migrant activists. The third strategy, *social and institutional regulation*, is connected to the logic of social rights, and consists of engaging in regulation processes through corporatist practices of dialogue with social partners (employers and government).

In each country certain logics of action and strategies tend to prevail, although unions with different identities also tend to adopt different approaches. Although the tensions among class, race and social rights is inherent in all the cases analysed in this book, some type of community initiative is present to different forms and degrees. In this respect, the notion of community unionism is a central element in the experiences of solidarity and collective action in Germany, Spain, Argentina and Italy examined here.

2 Community Unionism and the Transformation of Labour

A good portion of the literature on trade union engagement in migration issues has focused on experiences of community unionism. Community unionism has been defined as initiatives of cooperation between unions and community groups for social change (Wills & Simms, 2004).

The political and academic debate about community-based unionism arose in the USA (Black, 2005; Fine, 2005) and later was exported to other countries, such as Canada (Tufts, 1998), the UK (Holgate, 2018), Australia (Trattersall, 2008), Japan (Suzuki, 2008; Royle & Urano, 2012), Spain (Martínez Lucio, 2012; Roca, 2016) and Argentina (Arriaga, 2018), among others; however, community-based initiatives are not a novelty for the labour movement. Wills and Simms

(2004) identify three stages in the historical development of trade unionism. They call the first one 'community-based trade unionism,' referring to the original forms of unionism that arose in the wake of industrialisation among occupational homogenous and strongly territorialised communities, in which labour unions were only a part of a wider network of mutual aid organisations that produced a dense working-class culture. The second stage is 'representational community unionism,' and corresponds with a Fordist production and social model. This type of unionism implied the delegation of political representation to left political parties, and the prioritisation of workplace issues in trade union activity. The third stage, 'reciprocal community unionism,' appears in a context of a post-Fordist and neoliberal transformation of the economy, when the previous model enters into a deep crisis (mainly manifested in the dramatic decline of union density). As an attempt to counter trade union crises, certain unions seek to build 'relationships with community groups to help improve local life as well as fostering trade union growth' (Wills & Simms, 2004, p. 66). This new model involves an emphasis on organising, building alliances and engaging in political action in the community.

Wills (2001) has underlined four reasons for trade unions to build alliances with community organizations. First, these alliances allow shaping policy-making, improving the living conditions of the workers and, hence, gaining support from working-class communities. Second, working together with community groups enables them to reach factions of the working class that have traditionally been outside the scope of trade unions (outsiders). Third, the support of community organizations helps labour unions to more effectively organise 'hard-to-organise' workers such as low-wage workers and small size firms. Fourth, community allies are also useful for success in conventional trade union campaigns.

There is a large diversity of forms of community unionism, depending on multiple variables such as socio-political contexts, organizational structures, and internal communication channels, among others (Holgate, 2009). Fine (2005) proposes a typology of community unionism: *community organization with no union partner*, in which community-based groups attempt to organise around workplaces; *trade unions with no community partner*, in which trade unions attempt to organise around extra-labour problems, asking for support from community groups but not generating bidirectional cooperation; *community-labour partnership with the predominance of community organisations*, in which both types of organisations cooperate for shared goals but there is an effective leadership of community groups; and, finally, *community-labour partnership with predominance of trade unions*. This typology suggested by Fine helps us understand the diverse characteristics and outcomes of the different cases analysed in this book.

3   Migrant Constituencies and New Forms of Labour Activism

In spite of the extension of experiences of community unionism, one of the main difficulties inherent in trade union movement is recognising the self-organization initiatives of migrant workers and connecting union structures with migrants' networks (Connolly, Marino & Martinez Lucio, 2014, p. 11). Nonetheless, migrant workers have tended to generate their own networks and organisations, and, eventually, have participated actively in trade union and political mobilisations.

In her classical study, Ruth Mikman (2006) underscores that, contrary to extended beliefs, immigrant workers are easier to mobilise that their native-born counterparts. One of the reasons for this is migrants' tendency to build dense, strong networks that, under certain circumstances, support unionisation and political mobilisation. As a result, the existence of these community networks can prove essential for successful trade union campaigns. Despite their importance, these networks have not been sufficiently studied. Issues such as its ethnic composition, types of relationships connecting members, or the conditions that activate the support of the networks, remain mostly understudied.

In a recent study about contemporary Spanish emigrant workers, the editors of this book, Roca and Martín-Díaz (2017) proposed the concept of 'interstitial trade unionism' to refer to the fact that migrants' solidarity networks tend to operate in the margins of national systems of labour relations, sometimes substituting formal trade unions and sometimes complementing them. The notion of 'improvisational unionism' also refers to these situations in which workers' networks and groups tend to develop functions that traditionally have been performed by trade unions (Oswalt, 2016).

Martínez Lucio and Perret (2009) have suggested a methodological problem in the form in which migrant communities have been studied. According to them, the approach of many academic observers that classify immigrant communities in singular terms means that the study of industrial relations, trade union strategy and race/ethnicity is reduced to a matter of institutional 'realignment'. It is meaningful that most authors underline that the scarce union organisation of migrants is not related to their social background or ethnic origin (although there is a clear lack of research focusing on gender), but to the informalisation of the jobs to which they have access (Milkman, 2000; Krings, 2007). The critique on the reification of the ethnic community of these perspectives has fuelled a debate among scholars in which the concepts of 'network unionism' (Wills, 1998) and 'community unionism' stand out (Fine, 2005, 2006; Holgate, 2009). These concepts propose to move from the space of labour relations to a wider framework that pays attention to all the spaces of social interaction, including work, community and home. This change of scope is related to the temporality of jobs and to the lack of correspondence between these jobs and workers' training (Heery & Salmon, 2000).

4 Bricolage and Diffusion as Conceptual Tools for Collective Action

Moving to all spaces of social interaction, however, demands the use of conceptual tools that have not been widely used in the study of labour relations. In particular, this book will explore the concept of bricolage and its application to the ambit of industrial relations and collective action. Lévi-Strauss' concept of bricolage refers to recombining available materials in a creative manner:

> The bricoleur can undertake a good number of diversified tasks; but, differently from the engineer, he does not subordinate any of them in order to get raw materials or tools... His rule of the game is get by always 'with what one has' (...) a set of heteroclitical materials (...) that are not related with the project of that moment (Lévi-Strauss, 1964, p. 36).

Bricolage has also been conceptualized as situational tinkering and 'making do', and is growingly used in the study of organisations and management (Visscher, Heusinkveld, & O'Mahoney, 2017). The traditional separation between migrant workers and trade unions have favoured the creative development of migrants' own networks and organisations which, at least partially, have played the role that unions fulfil for other workers.

In the sphere of trade unionism, Bernaciak and Kahancová (2017) argue that there are three dimensions of innovation, related to: organisational structure, the choice of strategies, and the selection of new target groups (including migrants, young and atypical workers). Taking self-organised migrant workers as an innovation, they can be studied as examples of trade union bricolage. This is because workers creatively combine elements from their ethnic, national and religious traditions with features of the host society, in order to adapt to new circumstances -in many cases marked by labour precariousness- and to address unsatisfied social needs (Mrozowiki & Maciewewske, 2017).

Collective action is subject to diffusion dynamics. Social movement scholars have pointed out how determinate experiences of contention have influenced other experiences located in different scales or territories (Soule, 2013; Walsh-Russo, 2014). The concepts of 'collective action cycle' or 'wave of contention' usually refer to protest movements that take place in several countries in the same lapse of time (Tarrow, 1993). The rise of social protest in different countries maybe the result of similarities in the political economy and political opportunity structures, but diffusion dynamics can also play also a key role. Castells (2012), for example, was one of the first authors to highlight the connections between the so-called "Arab Springs" and anti-austerity movements in Europe and North America. It is in this respect that the conceptual tool of *networks* comes useful to explain the interconnectivity between actors located in different spaces (Jessop, Brenner & Martin, 2008).

Romanos (2016), in his study of the Spanish movement *indignados*, identifies two processes by which social movements can be diffused: firstly, by means of indirect channels (today mainly by mass and social media); secondly, by means of third parties that act as mediators between different movements. In the second case, (migrant) activists can play the role of brokers, connecting different militant traditions from separated geographical spots. Romanos argues that, contrary to indirect channels that disseminate discourses, mediators foster the diffusion of practical knowledge and new repertoires of contention. Migrant activists are, thus, key actors in the transnational expansion of behavioural innovations.

5 The Objectives of This Book

This book focuses on a specific research area that remains mainly understudied: the creation of migrant networks, their role in industrial activism, and their complex relationship with the trade union movement. The different chapters included in this edited book address some of the following questions:
- How do trade union address the problems and needs of different segments of migrant workers? Under which circumstances do labour unions tend to be more inclusive?
- How do migrant networks attempt to respond to the needs of migrant workers and their families? Which factors favour the implication of these networks in labour issues? What types of networks do migrants tend to build?
- How do migrants' representations of work and their collective identities (across ethnic, racial, class and gender lines) shape modes of organisation, solidarity and collective action?
- What are the relationships between migrant networks and trade unions? Under which circumstances do these entities tend to cooperate or compete?
- What social innovations and dynamics of bricolage can be identified in migrant networks? What lessons can be learnt for the enterprise of trade union revitalisation?

INTRODUCTION

The originality of this book rests on four pillars: first, the use of new conceptual tools in order to shed light on migrant self-organisation, social innovation and trade union policy toward migration; second, the updating of available empirical data on recent tendencies of migrant organising; third, the development of a cross-national comparative perspective on migrant organising in Europe and America; and fourth, the systematic study of the role of social and community networks in migrant organising, and its contribution to existing debates on trade union renewal.

6 Background and Outline of the Book

This book is the result of the long lasting collaboration among a network of academics from different countries and disciplines. In particular, it is framed within the research projects 'CiviPol-Civil society organisations and policymaking in the EU' (ref. 611583-EPP-1-2019-1-ES-EPPJMO-MODULE), funded by the Erasmus+ Programme of the European Commission, and 'New intra-European mobilities. Decisions over work, family and politics among Spanish transmigrants' (ref. CSO2017-84618-P), funded by Spain's Ministry of Economy and Competitiveness. In addition, most of the authors participated in the International Workshop "Civil Society and the 'migrant and refugee crisis' in Europe: the multilevel governance of politics" held at the University of Seville in November 2017. Some authors are also members of the EC Marie Curie mobility project 'Multilevel governance of cultural diversity in a comparative perspective: EU-Latin America' (GOVDIV) (ref. 612617), which helped foster the exchange of ideas and experiences among them. The editors of the book have published previous work on this topic on the journals *Critical Sociology* and *Journal of Mediterranean Studies*. One of the editors has also employed some of the concepts explored in this book in a previous publication of the Committee on Refugees and Immigrants of the American Anthropology Association (Martín-Díaz & Bermúdez, 2017). Thus, the current volume is based on all previous and present scientific research, publications and academic exchanges.

The book consists of seven chapters that analyse cases of migrant organising in Spain, Germany, Italy and Argentina. Chapters one and two study labour activism among intra-European migrants in Germany from complementary perspectives. Chapter one, 'Labour Activism and Organisational Bricolage among Spanish and Italian Emigrants in Germany', written by Simone Castellani and Beltrán Roca, explores labour organization and collective action among Spaniards and Italians who have migrated to Germany during the last economic recession. These migrant workers have entered mostly the German secondary labour market, but when they claim social and labour rights as EU citizens they face an increasing 'welfare chauvinism'. The chapter studies practices of bricolage and innovation among migrant activists in order to counter labour and social precariousness. The authors demonstrate how migrant workers creatively combine elements from different ethnic, national and political traditions in order to develop innovative organizational forms, practices and repertoires of collective action. In addition, they pay attention to the development and use of transnational networks (both in their countries of origin and Germany) in order to carry out collective action. In this networks, trade unions and union officials play a central –though controversial- role.

In chapter two, titled 'Community through Corporatisation? The Case of Spanish Nurses in the German Care Industry', Mark Bergfeld describes the recruitment practices of Spanish nurses in Germany in order to reduce labour costs. These, together with other practices boosting language, ethnic differences and divisions within the workforce, undermine solidarities both among workers and between workers and users. Nonetheless, in this unfavourable context have risen some experiences of migrant collective action. Spanish nurses self-organised within the *Grupo de Acción Sindical* (GAS) of the 15M Berlin due to their lack of trust of existing trade unions. Within GAS they have maintained their own mobilisation lineaments importing forms of collective action and repertoires from Spanish social and labour movements, sometimes in opposition to German trade unions, but also collaborating with some organisers of the Ver.di union and members of the syndicalist FAU in other occasions. Despite their important organizational and strategic limitations, they manifest the necessity for German trade unions to take into account migrant workers' self-organisation.

Chapter three, 'Domestic Work in Ceuta: Challenges and Alternative Organisations', by Emma Martín-Díaz and Juan Pablo Aris, constitute a particular approach to the study of domestic labour in Ceuta (Spain). If the rest of the chapters of this book focus on the relationship between producers, labour organisations and native and migrant workers, in this case the authors analyse a particular situation contextualized within a Spanish national enclave (Ceuta) that is located within the Moroccan State. This particularity conditions in a clear manner a model of workers' circularity, not only, but significantly, in the domestic sector. It affects mainly Moroccan women transiting on an everyday basis through the border checkpoints, although in some cases they are *de facto* residents (not recognized by authorities) in the homes they work. The difficulties for union organisation derive from the fact that domestic labour is carried out inside home, and fromthe national policies that predominate in Spanish major trade unions. Nonetheless, this limitation has favoured the fact that this union space has been occupied by socially creative organisations that foster mutual aid and solidarity networks, and that the authors conceptualise as 'bricolage unionism'.

In Chapter four, 'Organising Migrant Porters in the Logistics Sector: The Italian Case of SI Cobas', Giulia Borraccino analyses labour organisation among migrant workers in the logistics sector in the North of Italy. It is a case of atypical employment, since workers work for cooperatives under precarious conditions. Given the lack of interest of major Italian trade unions, logistic sector workers were organised in SI Cobas, a radical political union that puts emphasis on direct participation and industrial action. This union also framed its militancy within a class-based discourse that encouraged migrant workers to join the union. In addition, it developed strong links with community organisations in order to address workers' problems in their territories and to get support for shop-floor struggles. Borraccino describes the evolution of this radical union and its main conflicts and successes. She concludes that this experience opens new horizons for workers' representation in Italy and elsewhere.

Chapter five, 'Migrant Worker Organisations and Overexploitation in the Garment Industry in Argentina', authored by Paula Dinorah Salgado, describes grassroots organisation among workers (mainly migrant) in the deregulated Argentine garment industry. The author focuses on two groups: the Migrant Workers Bloc (*Bloque de Trabajadorxs Migrantes,* BTM) and the Garment Workers and Employees Union (*Unión de Costurerxs y Empleadxs del Vestido,* UCEV). The former was formed around migrant identities, and the latter around class identity. Despite their differences, both experiences can be seen as cases of community unionism that have succeeded in recruiting and organising migrant workers. Three are the defining characteristics of these forms of community unionism. First, the strategic use of ethnic and migrant identities in contrast to the classical frames of Argentine craft and industrial trade unions. Second, the emphasis on direct action over social pacts and public policies. Third, the widening of the place of intervention from the workplace to the territory (addressing not only labour problems, but also other issues that affect profoundly the everyday lives of migrant workers and their families).

One of the labour niches in which migrant workers tend to concentrate are agrarian activities inserted within the dynamics of global value chains. Chapters six and seven analyse labour integration of immigrants in Andalusia (Spain) and Apulia (Italy). In chapter six, 'Collective Action, Experience and Identity in Global Agrarian Enclaves: The Case of Andalusia (Spain)', Alicia Reigada addresses the conflict between production/distribution and producers/working-class through the analysis of the implementation of the system of contracts in origin in the territory of Moguer (Huelva). She introduces this by first describing the socio-historical context that determined the change of class adscription of agrarian producers, from their previous position as workers and day-labourers to a new position as agrarian employers. Subsequently, she analyses the process of substitution of autochthonous agrarian day-labourers to migrant workers, and the changes that have taken place in this process of replacement (in which the gender variable had a determining dimension). These processes, she concludes, have shaped the specific strategies and forms of collective mobilisation, together with the limitations and challenges faced by class unions.

In chapter seven, 'Transforming Labour Law or Recurring to Grass-Roots Mobilisation? The Struggles over the Empowerment of Tomato-picking Migrant Workers in Southern Italy', D'Onofrio and Las Heras study tomato-picking workers in the South of Italy (Foggia), underlining the difficulties that global value chains represent for working-class organisation. In this case, contextualisation focuses on the hard living conditions of the workers in order to understand trade union strategies and their role in the conflicts in this region. Similarly to Reigada's analysis of strawberry workers in the previous chapter, here the authors discuss the possibilities and limits of the actions undertook by the two trade unions they researched, with their different goals and strategies. They conclude pointing out that the strategies of major trade unions reproduce, and even intensify, the ethnic segmentation (racialisation) of the labour market. This attitude manifests itself in what the authors understand as a profound contradiction: being part of a trade union within the socialist left and at the same time voting for a far-right government.

In sum, this book contains valuable lessons to be learnt about how migrant workers respond to labour precariousness and to situations of racial, class and gender oppression. The common thread of its seven chapters is the existence of different forms of self-organisation and the use of social innovation, bricolage and creativity. The experiences described in the book highlight the importance of migrant self-organisation for any attempts to reinforce trade unionism. Trade unions can no longer ignore migrants' own networks and groups, since any effort to recruit and mobilise them should be based on their everyday experiences, expectations and internal resources. In general terms, radical unions in different contexts have shown more willingness to bridge gaps with migrant workers. It can be explained by both a clearer internationalist ideology in its militancy and by organisational strategies to recruit membership in the secondary labour market in which mainstream unions do not have much interest. In this sense, it must be stated that trade unionism must be rethought in the light of the experiences described in the following chapters. In a time of uncertainty, precariousness and intensification of migration flows, the incorporation of migrants to trade union structures is fundamental in order to guarantee minimum standards of social justice.

References

Alonso, L.E. (2002). Postfordismo, crisis y fragmentación de la sociedad de consumo: los nuevos espacios de la distribución comercial y el comprador posmoderno. *Col·lecció Urbanitat Digitals*, 4.

Amin, A. ed. (1995). *Post-Fordism: A reader*. Oxford: Blackwell.

Appadurai, A. (1990). Disjuncture and difference in the global cultural economy. In M. Featherstone (Ed.), *Global Culture. Nationalism, Globalization and Modernity* (pp. 295–310). London: Sage.

Arriaga, A. E. (2018). Potencialidad de las Discusiones sobre Revitalización Sindical para Pensar la Historia Reciente del Movimiento Obrero Argentino. *Prohistoria*, 29, 115–133.

Arrighi, G. (1985). *Semiperipheral Development. The Politics of Southern Europe in the Twentieth Century*. London: Sage.

Bernaciak, M., & Kahancová, M. (2017). *Innovative union practices in Central-Eastern Europe*. Brussels: ETUI.

Black, S. J. (2005). Community Unionism: A Strategy for Organizing in the New Economy. *New Labor Forum*, 14(3), 24–32. https://doi.org/10.1080/1095760500245383.

Castells, M. (2012). *Redes de indignación y esperanza*. Madrid: Alianza.

Castles, S., & Kosack, G. (1973). *Immigrants Workers and Class Structure in Western Europe*. London: Oxford University Press.

Castles, S., & Miller, M. J. (1993). *The Age of Migration: International Population Movements in the Modern World*. New York, NY: Guilford Press.

Connolly, H., Marino, S., & Martínez Lucio, M. (2014). Trade union renewal and the challenges of representation: Strategies towards migrant and ethnic minority workers in the Netherlands, Spain and the United Kingdom. *European Journal of Industrial Relations*, 20(1), 5–20. https://doi.org/10.1177/0959680113516848

Connolly, H., Marino, S., & Martinez Lucio, M. (2019). Immigrants and trade unions in the European Context. The Politics of Social Inclusion and Labor Representation. Ithaca, NY: Cornell University Press.

Escrivá, A., Bermúdez, A., & Moraes, N. eds. (2009). *Migración y Participación Política. Estados, organizaciones, y migrantes latinoamericanos en perspectiva local-transnacional*. Córdoba: Consejo Superior de Investigaciones Científicas, Instituto de Estudios Sociales de Andalucía-

Fine, J. (2005). Community unionism and the revival of the American labor movement. *Politics and Society*, 33(1), 153–199.

Fine, J. (2006). *Worker Centers: Organizing Communities at the Edge of the Dream*. Ithaca, NY: Economic Policy Institute/Cornell University Press.

Gambarotto, F. & Solari, S. (2014). The peripheralization of Southern European Capitalism within the EMU. *Review of International Political Economy*, 22, 788-812.

Guarnizo, L. E. (2000). La migración internacional y el 'nuevo' orden global. La experiencia latinoamericana y caribeña. *Anuario Social y Político de América Latina y el Caribe*, 4, 113–124.

Harvey, D. (2005). *A brief history of neoliberalism*. New York: Oxford University Press.

Heery, E., & Salmon, J. (Eds.) (2000). *The Insecure Workforce*. London: Routledge.

Herrera, G. (2004). Elementos para una comprensión de las familias transnacionales del sur del Ecuador. In F. Hidalgo (Ed.) *Migraciones. Un juego con cartas marcadas* (pp. 215–231). Quito: Abya Yala.

Holgate, J. (2009). Contested terrain: London's living wage campaign and tensions between communities and union organising. In J. McBride & I. Greenwood (Eds.), *Community Unionism. A Comparative Analysis of Concepts and Contexts* (pp. 49–74). London: Palgrave.

Holgate, J. (2018). Trade unions in the community: Building board spaces of solidarity. *Economic and Industrial Democracy*. https://doi.org/10.1177/0143831X18763871

Hyman, R. (2001). *Understanding European Trade Unionism: Between Market, Class and Society*. London: Sage.

Jessop, B., Brenner, N., & Jones, M. (2008). Theorizing Sociospatial Relations. *Environment and Planning D: Society and Space*, 26, 389–401.

Kearney, M. (1995). The Local and the Global: Anthropology of Globalization and Transnationalism. *Annual Review of Anthropology*, 24, 547–565.

Khamann, M. (2006). The posting of workers in the German construction industry: responses and problems of trade union action. *Transfer: European Review of Labour and research*, 12(2), 183–96.

Krings, T. (2007). Equal rights for all workers: Irish trade unions and the challenge of labour immigration. *Irish Journal of Sociology*, 16(1), 43–61.

Lash, S. & Urry, J. (1987). *The End of Organized Capitalism*. Oxford: Polity Press.

Lévi-Strauss, C. (1964). *El Pensamiento Salvaje*. México: Fondo de Cultura Económica.

Marino, S., Pennix, R., & Roosblad, J. (2015). Trade unions, immigration and immigrants in Europe revisited: Unions' attitudes and actions under new conditions. *Comparative Immigration Studies*, 3(1). https://doi.org/10.1007/s40878-015-0003-x

Martin-Diaz, E. (2006a). De las migraciones del fordismo a las migraciones de la globalización: Europa 1960-2005. *Africa e Mediterraneo*, 54, 29–35.

Martín-Díaz, E. (2006b). Mercado de trabajo, género e inmigración. In VV. AA. *Mujeres inmigrantes, viajeras incansables*. Bilbao: Harresiak Apurtuz.

Martín-Díaz, E. (2008). El impacto del género en las migraciones de la globalización: Mujeres, trabajos y relaciones interculturales, *Scripta Nova*, 12(270–133).

Martín-Díaz, E. (2012). Estrategias migratorias de las mujeres ecuatorianas en Sevilla: Acumulación de capital social en tiempos de crisis. *Migraciones Internacionales*, 6(4), 107–138.

Martín-Díaz, E., & Bermúdez, A. (2017). The Multilevel Governance of "Refuge": Bringing Together Institutional and Civil Society Responses in Europe. In D. Haines, J.

Howell, & F. Keles (Eds.), *Maintaining Refugee: Anthropological Reflections in Uncertain Times*. Committee on Refugees and Immigrants, Society for Urban, National, and Transnational/Global Anthropology, American Anthropological Association. Retrieved from http://mason.gmu.edu/~dhaines1/CORI_2017_Final.pdf

Martín-Díaz, E. & Roca, B. (2017). Spanish migrations to Europe: From the Fordist model to the flexible economy. *Journal of Mediterranean Studies*, 26(2), 189–207.

Martínez Lucio, M. (2012). ¿Todavía organizadores del descontento? Los retos de las estrategias de renovación sindical en España. *Arxius de Ciències Socials*, 18, 119–133.

Martínez Lucio, M. & Perret, R. (2009). The diversity and politics of trade unions' responses to minority ethnic and migrant workers: The context of the UK. *Economic and Industrial Democracy*, 30(3), 324–347.

Menz, G. (2002). Patterns in EU labour immigration policy: national initiatives and European responses. *Journal of Ethnic and Migration Studies*, 28(4), 723–742.

Milkman, R. (2000). Immigrant organizing and the new labor movement in Los Angeles. *Critical Sociology*, 26(1/2), 59–81.

Milkman, R. (2006). *L.A. Story. Immigrant Workers and the Future of US Labor Movement*. New York: Russel Sage Foundation.

Mrozowicki, A., & Maciejewska, M. (2017). Bricolage unionism. Unions' innovative responses to the problems of precarious work in Poland. In M. Bernaciak & M. Kahancová (Eds.), *Innovative Union Practices in Central-Eastern Europe* (pp. 139–159). Brussels: ETUI.

Murray, G. (2017). Union renewal. What can we learn from three decades of research? *Transfer*, 23(1), 9–29.

Oswalt, M. M. (2016). Improvisational Unionism. *California Law Review*, 104(3), 597–670.

Parella, S. (2008). Aplicación de los campos sociales transnacionales en los estudios sobre migraciones. In C. Solé, S. Parella & L. Cavalcanti (Eds.), *Nuevos retos del transnacionalismo en el estudio de las migraciones* (pp. 219–243). Madrid, Observatorio Permanente de la Inmigración/Ministerio de Trabajo e Inmigración.

Pennix, R., & Roosblad, J. (Eds.) (2001). *Trade Unions, Immigration and Immigrants in Europe, 1960–1993. A Comparative Study of the Actions of Trade Unions in Seven West European Countries*. London: Berghahn Books.

Roca, B. (2016). *Transformaciones en el trabajo y movimiento sindical. Propuestas para una renovación necesaria*. Madrid: Fundación Alternativas. Retrieved from https://www.fundacionalternativas.org/public/storage/estudios_documentos_archivos/3dbb85e5f22632a0391f8ad9fa63d76a.pdf

Roca, B., & Martín-Díaz, E. (2017). Solidarity Networks of Spanish Migrants in the UK and Germany: The Emergence of Interstitial Trade Unionism. *Critical Sociology*, 43 (7–8), 1197–1212. https://doi.org/10.1177/0896920516645659

Romanos, E. (2016). De Tahrir a Wall Street por la Puerta del Sol: la difusión transnacional de los movimientos sociales en perspectiva comparada. *Revista Española de Investigaciones Sociológicas*, 154, 103–118. https://doi.org/10.5477/cis/reis.154.103

Rosenau, J. (1990). *Turbulence in World Politics*. Brighton: Harvester.

Royle, T., & Urano, E. (2012). A New Form of Union Organizing in Japan? Community Unions and the Case of the Mc Donalds 'Mc Union. *Work, Employment & Society*, 26(4), 606–622. https://doi.org/10.1177/0950017012445093

Sassen, S. (2003). *Contrageografías de la globalización. Género y ciudadanía en circuitos transfronterizos*. Madrid: Traficantes de sueños.

Schiller, N. G., Bash, L. & Blanc, C. S. (1995). From immigrant to transmigrant: theorizing transnational migration. *Anthropological Quarterly*, 68(1), 48-63.

Silver, B. J. (2003). *Forces of Labour. Workers' Movements and Globalization since 1870*. Cambridge: Cambridge University Press.

Soule, S. A. (2013). Diffusion and Scale Shift. In D. A. Snow et al. (Eds.), *The Wiley-Blackwell Encyclopedia of Social and Political Movements*. Malden, Massachusetts: Blackwell.

Suzuki, A. (2008). Community Unions in Japan: Similarities and Differences of Region-based Labour Movements between Japan and Other Industrialized Countries. *Economic and Industrial Democracy*, 29(4), 492–520. https://doi.org/10.1177/0143831X08096230

Tarrow, S. (1993). Cycles of Collective Action: Between Moments of Madness and the Repertoire of Contention. *Social Science History*, 17(2), 281–307.

Tattersall, A. (2008). Coalitions and community unionism: Using the term community to explore effective union-community collaboration. *Journal of Organizational Change Management*, 21(4), 415–432. https://doi.org/10.1108/09534810810884821

Tufts, S. (1998). Community Unionism in Canada and Labor's (Re)Organization of Space. *Antipode*, 30(3), 227–250. https://doi.org/10.1111/1467-8330.00076

Visscher, K., Heusinkveld, S., & O'Mahoney, J. (2017). Bricolage and Identity Work. *British Journal of Management*, 00, 1–17. https://doi.org/10.1111/1467-8551.12220

Wallerstein, I. (1974). *The modern World System*. New York: Academic Press.

Walsh-Russo, C. (2014). Diffusion of Protest. *Sociology Compass*, 8(1), 31–42.

Wills, J. (1998). Uprooting tradition: Rethinking the place and space of labour organization. *European Planning Studies*, 6(1), 31–42.

Wills, J. (2001). Community unionism and trade union renewal in the UK: moving beyond the fragments at last? *Transactions of the Institute of British Geographers*, 26, 465–483.

Wills, J., & Simms, M. (2004). Building Reciprocal Community Unionism in the UK. *Capital & Class*, 28(1), 59–84. https://doi.org/10.1177/030981680408200105

Wrench, J. (2004). Trade Union Responses to Immigrants and Ethnic Inequality in Denmark and the UK: The Context of Consensus and Conflict. *European Journal of Industrial Relations*, 10(1), 7–30. https://doi.org/10.1177/0959680104041194

CHAPTER 1

Labour Activism and Organisational Bricolage among Spanish and Italian Emigrants in Germany

Simone Castellani and Beltrán Roca

1 Intra-EU Mobility in the era of Platform-Capitalism and Welfare Chauvinism

The free circulation of workers within the EU has its roots in the bilateral agreements among states that, since the 1950s, regulated migration flows within Western European countries.[1] Workers' freedom of movement was first recognised in 1957 in the founding document of the newborn European Economic Community (Art. 49, Treaty of Rome), and the right of workers to freely circulate within the community was institutionalised in 1968 (Regulation EEC No 1612/68). Foreign workers coming from other EEC countries had to be assimilated with national workers in terms of wages, labour law, and social protection.[2] Foreign workers had to obey the host country's labour legislation and pay union contributions and, in exchange, they benefited from the same working schedules and conditions, insurance against accidents and diseases, unemployment benefits, and family allowances as the national workers had. The free circulation of workers was the historical seed of the right of free movement within the EU and of the residence in other member states granted to all EU member state citizens (Maastricht Treaty, 1992 and Art. 18, Treaty of Amsterdam).[3]

Following a neo-liberal push-pull frame, workers' mobility among EU states was conceived as a mechanism of systemic rebalance to appease the asymmetric shocks caused by fall in production within EU countries, and as an

---

1 E.g., the bilateral agreements signed in Rome between the Federal Republic of Germany and Italy in 1955.
2 The economic and social assimilation of migrants to national workers also existed within bilateral agreements between EEC and non-EEC countries (e.g., Spain, Portugal, Greece, Yugoslavia, Turkey, Algeria, Morocco, Tunisia, etc.) (ILO, 1999).
3 In 2000 the Charter of Nice (Article 45) extended the freedom of movement and residence to third-country nationals who are legal residents in a member state.

escape valve from unemployment (Recchi, 2015, p. 43).[4] This frame does not emphasise the systemic dynamics of dependence of the secondary economies on the economies of the centre that have historically taken place within the EU (King et al., 2016), as was clearly demonstrated by the effects of the economic recession that began in 2008. From 2008 to 2013, most of the peripheral countries (above all from Southern and Eastern Europe) displayed a negative or near zero GDP growth and high levels of youth unemployment. The central countries (Northwestern Europe) showed an opposite tendency. In Germany, for instance, the GDP, after a decline in 2009, immediately returned to growth (OECD, 2018). Looking at the unemployment data during 2008–2013, countries such as Spain and Italy registered an increase in youth unemployment rate of up to 55% and 42% respectively, while during the same period German youth unemployment fell 8% (Eurostat, 2020). The crisis affected not only young people but also those who had entered adulthood. As an example, from 2008 to 2013 unemployed people in the age range 35–39 years, has doubled in Italy (10% in 2013) and tripled in Spain (22% in 2013) (Eurostat, 2020).

Therefore, during the years of economic recession, freedom of movement within the EU represented an opportunity for citizens of peripheral countries such as the Southern EU to find employment in the countries of the centre (Lafleur & Stanek, 2017; Martin-Diaz & Roca, 2017). In the German example, that central EU country once again, as in the 1950s and 1960s, became a main destination for people from Italy and Spain. Before the crisis the Italian and Spanish residents in Germany were progressively declining. In 2007–2017, there was a significant increase: about 115,000 and 72,000, respectively, corresponding to a percentage increase of 22% for Italians and 67% for Spaniards (DESTATIS, 2020).

The literature on contemporary intra-EU mobility based on the data collected mainly before the economic crisis highlighted that most of people who moved within the EU shared a common socio-demographic profile that defined as "cosmopolitan" (Favell, 2008; Van Mol, 2013). Differently from the "proletarian" intra-Western Europe migration of the 1950s and 1970s on the south-north axis (Bade, 1987; Romero, 2001; Martín-Díaz, 2006), many people who move to another EU country today are young, have a high level of education, and fluently speak one or more foreign language. They have often earned some of their academic degrees in other European countries thanks to

---

4   Recchi pointed out that between 1970 and 1980, there was a terminological change in the EEC document that talked about international migratory flows among the community countries. In those years they began to be defined using the term mobility, trying to position the phenomenon within the semantic context of internal migration (Recchi, 2015, p. 19).

EC exchange programs such as Socrates-Erasmus or Leonardo. They usually stay in contact with other Europeans through OSNs (online social networks). Furthermore, in comparison to the emigrants of the 1950s-1960s who needed job invitations, they enjoy freedom of movement within the EU that allows them to look for a job without a work permit and to enter in the labour market of other EU countries, aspiring to medium and highly skilled positions.

One of the limitations of these studies is that they focused on the phenomenon of Europeanisation from below (Favell & Recchi, 2009), the building of a new European identity (Recchi, 2014), and on the integration of qualified migrants in destination countries (Alaminos, Albert, & Santacreu, 2010; Del Pra', 2006). Looking mainly at the mobility experience of EU people with a cosmopolitan profile (mainly coming from the EU-15 countries), these scholars did not pay much attention to, for instance, low-skilled workers who move to another EU countries, especially after the enlargement of the EU to the east that began in 2004 (Ciupijus, 2011; Brenke, Yuksel, & Zimmermann, 2009; De la Rica, 2009).

Recent studies on EU mobility that have taken into account the effects of the last economic recession highlight that the profile of those who move within the EU is changing (Raffini, 2014; Lafleur & Stanek, 2017). The phenomenon of EU mobility increasingly involves unskilled workers, as for example in the case of "posted workers" (Lillie & Simola, 2016). Furthermore, other studies have shown many young people who move to Centre EU countries with a cosmopolitan profile aspiring to enter into medium and medium-high positions in the labour market of destination sliding into the secondary market[5] working in low-skilled and unprotected jobs (Castellani, 2018).

Many mobile EU residents experience downward social mobility (Faist, 2019) when they enter a dual post-Fordist labour market (Piore, 1979). As was stressed in the case of Southern EU migrants to Germany, only a minority manage to overcome barriers (linguistic, educational, credentials, previous work experience in the domestic market, etc.) for entering skilled well-paid jobs that grant standard labour and social protection. On the contrary, many people enter secondary labour markets in the country of destination, performing unskilled and unprotected jobs over long periods of time (Castellani, 2018).

Nevertheless, in the era of the digital economy, the division between the primary and secondary labour markets has become somehow blurred. Some scholars have defined the contemporary stage of neoliberalism as "platform

---

5 According to Piore (1979), secondary labour markets are defined by unstable and low-skilled jobs, low wages, and no possibilities of promotion. They contrast with primary labour markets, characterised by regulated, stable, well-paid, and high-skilled jobs.

capitalism" (Langley & Leyshon, 2017). In their definition, the digital platforms for commencing and sharing goods and services (e.g., Amazon, Deliveroo, Airbnb, Uber, Zalando....) that have become widespread globally in the past few years aren't simply a new manifestation of informational capitalism (Castells, 1998) but a radical new feature of market and labour intermediation as well as a new means of capital accumulation. The logistic infrastructures of the digital economy (Grappi, 2017) are supported ideologically by the principles of sharing, participation, and horizontal/non-hierarchisation, which rule within enterprise organisations, especially in startups (Grohmann, 2015).[6] The horizontalisation discourse is based on a symbolic imaginary—in an enterprise, everyone should be able to do everything, experience is gained in the field, and there is no vertical decision-making. This discourse attracts young, well-educated and enthusiastic employees with little experience in the labour market who accept high-skilled jobs termed self-employed or internships that are poorly paid, marked by no social and labour protection, and are precarious. In the EU, London and Berlin are the major startup hubs. The emerging terrain of work and organisation—also defined as "crowd work" (Howcroft & Bergvall-Kåreborn, 2018) or "gig work"[7] (De Stefano, 2016)—entails new sources of conflict and social stratification that influence workers' mobility dynamics and demands new approaches to workers' agency and representation.

Speaking about EU mobility currently means also taking into consideration the question of the EU worker's mobility in countries such as Germany, Austria, the United Kingdom, Belgium, and Denmark, where political demands for limiting free movement within the EU and political demands for minimising access to welfare provisions for EU citizens are becoming stronger (Lillie

---

6 These concepts of enterprise organisation consolidated in the 1990s during the New Economy boom, especially in the Silicon Valley of California (Kunda 1992), where the largest digital corporations that now lead the world's financial economy were born. This way of thinking about enterprise management spread and was adopted in many firms, especially startups. The startups are micro enterprises that look for an investor (usually an established company or a fund) to develop an innovative idea. Many of them operate in the field of the digital economy (e.g., e-commerce, internet, MKT...) that need inexpensive infrastructure. Normally they find a joint venture capital firm or group of firms to bet on their idea for a short term period (usually two years). They usually experience a strong and rapid market expansion. Suddenly, they hire dozens of workers to quickly gain a strong market position. In most cases, they grow without a proper organisational plan and aim to achieve very ambitious objectives in a short period of time. Thus, they usually focus on young and enthusiastic employees with little experience. Most of these startups go bankrupt in the short term (Blank, 2013).

7 De Stefano (2016) differentiates the crowd economy, in which the online platform constitutes the logistic infrastructure that connects individuals and organisations employing workers (e.g., Amazon), from the gig economy, in which traditional jobs or services are organised through a platform (e.g., Deliveroo or Foodora for delivery goods or Uber for transport).

& Simola, 2016; Ghimis, Lazarowicz, & Pascouau, 2014). As a matter of fact, "welfare chauvinism" (Goldschmidt, 2015) was a core issue in the Brexit referendum campaign (Cap, 2017).

Since intra-EU mobility flows are treated as labour migration, attention must be paid to the forms in which EU migrants respond collectively to precariousness, vulnerability, and exploitation. It is worth looking at the literature on migrant workers' organisation and collective action behaviour. At the same time that transformations in global capitalism and work have intensified employers' demand for migrant workers in specific labour markets (Sassen, 1998; Castles, 2002), migrant workers have demonstrated their willingness to organise and improve their lives through collective action (Milkman, 2000). In many cases, migrant workers have tended to organise outside the margins of the trade union context. In other cases, existing unions have succeeded in organising the migrant workforce. Some studies have pointed out the potential for trade unions to respect autonomy and self-organisation among migrant workers by linking migrants' communities with labour unions (Ness 2005; Martínez Lucio and Perrett. 2009). Fine (2006), for example, described how US trade unions were reinforced by workers' centres in which ethnic minorities communities could organise. In previous research the gap between migrant workers and trade unions was studied, suggesting the term "interstitial unionism" to define the type of labour activism that migrant workers tend to produce at the borders of trade unions (Roca & Martín-Díaz, 2017). The need to create collective responses to exploitation and precariousness without the more fixed tools of national unions has favoured the emergence of creativity and innovation

Migrants are involved in transnational social spaces (Faist, 2000) within people, goods, services, artefacts, and currency, but ideas and practices also circulate (Levitt & Schiller, 2004). As the literature on political transnationalism has noted, migrants' political practices are oriented toward origin and destination localities and countries and involve both migrant and non-migrant actors, organisations, and institutions (Østergaard-Nielsen, 2003; Martiniello & Lafleur, 2008). In this sense, migrants' labour activism and collective action have to be understood as a form of political transnational practice.

In a specific context and socio-historical moment, migrant labour activists bricolage available politics and social resources (Deleuze & Guattari, 1983) within a transnational social space, combining them creatively (De Certeau, 1984; Phillimore et al., 2018). The aim of this chapter is to delve deeply into this dimension of migrant worker activism.

Looking at contemporary EU labour mobility through the theoretical and analytical frame discussed in this chapter, we want to explore the tactics that migrant workers have developed in terms of organisational forms, practices, and repertories of collective action for claiming labour and social rights and facing the dynamics of exclusion and marginalisation shaped by the market and the state. To do so, we are using the empirical case of Spanish and Italian migrants in Berlin.

2   Spanish and Southern EU Migration to Berlin

As was highlighted above, the number of Spanish and Italian residents in Germany has constantly grown during the crisis periods following 2008, especially since 2011. The majority of Spaniards and Italian in absolute terms is concentrated in the *Länder* of Baden-Württemberg, Nordrhein-Westfalen, Bayern, and Hessen. Historically, these were the industrial Federal Republic of Germany (West Germany) destinations of Southern EU migration flows during 1950–1970. If we pay attention to the geographical distribution of those who arrived in the last ten years from Southern EU countries, we noticed that Berlin[8] has registered the major influx of these migrants. Data show that a quarter of the Italians and Spaniards who arrived in the past decade lived in the German capital. A fifth of the Italians and Spaniards who arrived in the past 12 years lived in Berlin. Since 2007, Italian and Spanish populations tripled: from 12,000 in 2007 to 34,000 in 2018, and from 5,000 in 2007 to 17,000 in 2018, respectively (DESTATIS, 2020).

Berlin was not among the historical destinations of Spanish and Italian migration flows because during the Cold War West Berlin was isolated and did not undergo the industrial reconstruction of other West Germany cities destroyed during WW2 such as Munich, Stuttgart, Cologne, etc. On the contrary, to avoid depopulation the city was kept afloat economically and socially by welfare policies and tax benefits. In East Berlin, the productive facilities were partially rebuilt, but after reunification they were dismantled, as were those in all the former German Democratic Republic (East Germany).

During the past two decades the economy of Berlin started to grow slowly thanks to the hostelry sector linked to tourism and the construction sectors due to strong property investment. Moreover, the completion of the capital transfer from Bonn to Berlin created numerous jobs linked to public administration. Finally, there was an expansion of the IT and communications sector thanks to the numerous startups that choose Berlin as their headquarters (Osservatorio degli Italiani a Berlino, 2015).

---

8   The city of Berlin enjoys the status of city-state, having the same powers and competences of the other *länder* of the German Federal Republic.

The large majority of jobs in Berlin are concentred in the tertiary sector, consisting mainly of small and medium-sized enterprises. The increase in labour supply has led to a gradual lowering of the unemployment rate from 20% in 2007 to 5.5% in 2019. Nevertheless, it remains one of the highest within Germany, which has an unemployment rate of 3,1% (Eurostat 2020).

Many German and multinational companies chose to move to Berlin because the cost of labour is lower than other German cities (up to 30% less than München, Hamburg, or Frankfurt). The average rent price is still low compared to the average in other large German cities, even if prices have been growing fast due to the increase in housing demand and property speculation (DESTATIS, 2020).

Alongside the economic data, we have to take into consideration the cultural factors that attract people from all over the globe who works as figurative artists, actors, musicians, etc., to Berlin. For this reason Berlin, especially among younger people,[9] is considered a place where there are economic, social, and cultural opportunities to experiment creatively as people with different lifestyles and new youth cultures try to develop their own business ideas or experiment with new political practices (Landau 2016). Nevertheless, this migration experience often tends to be temporary, and there is a lack of opportunity in the Berlin labour market for these individuals.

3 Methodology

This chapter draws on two studies carried out in Berlin with Spanish and Italian migrants (aged 18–39 years) who moved to the German capital for work and with their migrant organisations. The first study is based on a doctoral thesis that focuses on new migratory flows of Italian and Spanish young adults (18–39) who emigrated to Germany for work starting in 2008. The study is based on ethnographic and qualitative techniques such as participant observation, virtual ethnography, and in-depth interviews. Fieldwork was conducted between 2014 (July-December) and 2015 (March-July) in the cities of Berlin, Freiburg, and Mannheim. The participant observation was conducted in the aggregation and leisure spaces of migrants as well as in educational spaces as well as blogs, forums, and Facebook groups of Italians and Spaniards in Germany. In addition, 60 in-depth narrative-type interviews were carried out with Italian and

---

9 In the German capital 40% of the population is under 35; it has increased in the past 10 years of about 150,000 people representing the 87% of the 10-years total growing population (Eurostat, 2020).

Spanish migrants and key informants: members of Italian and Spanish historical and recent associations and organisations, migrants who arrived before the beginning of the economic recession, migrants from the Fordist era, and documentary filmmakers. In Berlin, 12 in-depth interviews with Spaniards, 10 with Italians and 4 with key informants were carried out. Moreover, in 2018, the field was re-visited during a 3-month period to understand the evolution of an Italian migrant workers' organisation that had participated in the study in 2014.

The second study is framed within postdoctoral research carried out during 2015 on political activism among Spanish migrants that consisted of 15 in-depth interviews with Spanish migrants (30 percent of them located in Germany) and the analysis of documents from websites, social media, and press notices of the 15M movement out of Spain. In addition, this study connects with a new research project that began at the end of 2017 in which seven Spanish activists were interviewed in Berlin to analyse the ways in which they frame their militancy, and how it is entangled with family and work decisions.[10]

The analysis carried out in this paper will focus mainly on these new Italian and Spanish migrant workers' organisation, looking at how members of this new flow started to organise themselves to respond to the specific context of the Berlin labour market, bricolaging resources of the context of origin with the context of destination, understanding this combination not as a simple assemblage but as a conflictual process carried out in this social and political field in a specific socio-historical framework that changes with time.

4   Spanish Migrants' Activism

4.1   *15M Diffusion to Berlin*

The rise of the 15M movement in Madrid took place when Spanish emigration was at its peak. In 2011, at the same time that activists undertook demonstrations and protest camps in Spain, Spanish emigrants organised actions in the main cities of a wide array of destination countries. Spanish migrants and local activists gathered at symbolic spots on key dates. Mimicking their counterparts in Spain, they began to organise assemblies in public places. The role of the new information and communication technologies, and especially

---

10   This chapter shows partial results of the ongoing project titled "New intra-European 'mobilities': Decisions over work, family and politics among Spanish 'transmigrats'," ref. CSO2017-84618-P, funded by the R&D plan of the Ministry of Economy and Competitiveness of Spain.

social media, in the spread of collective action throughout Spain and across the globe was essential (Castells, 2012). As time went on, Spanish activists built stable networks and began to hold meetings in locations such as social centres and pubs.

Berlin was no exception. On May 15, 2011, approximately 200 demonstrators gathered at the Spanish Embassy and later at the Brandenburg Gate. They carried placards with slogans such as *"Ladronazos basta de bipartidismo"* (Big thieves, no more bi-party system), *"Democracia real ya. Echte Demokratie jetzt"* (Real Democracy Now), *"No hay pan para tanto chorizo"* (There is no bread for so many *chorizos* [crooks in English]), and *"Si no nos dejáis soñar no os dejaremos dormir"* (If you do not allow us to dream, we will not allow you to sleep). Some of these slogans were copied from the slogans of protests taking place in Spain at that time.[11]

They initially organised three working groups. The first, *Berlin*, was in charge of coordinating the 15M group with local social movements, 15M groups in Spain, and on an international scale. The second, *Press*, was in charge of relations with the German and Spanish media, the use of the Internet, audio-visual productions, and written statements and releases. The third group, *Demonstration*, was in charge of organising protests.

In following months, people keep on attending the demonstrations and participating in assemblies in public spaces such as Babelplatz. Spanish migrants and German activists from a diversity of leftist groups attended these events. It must be said that Berlin is an exceptional city in Germany in relation to leftist politics: it has a long tradition of leftists and autonomous movements (Katsiaficas, 2006). Activists of these movements, as will be shown below, have given significant support to many of the initiatives of Spanish 15M activists in Berlin.

In Spain, the 15M changed over the following months. Protest camps and demonstrations declined and the militant energy was translated into new organisational forms (Roca & Diaz-Parra, 2017). From 2012, 15M local and neighbourhood assemblies began to disappear or to substantially lose their power to mobilise. Other organisational formulas, in turn, began to acquire relevance in the field of citizen protest. Outside Spain, several 15M assemblies also disappeared or lost much of their initial impulse. Gaspar explains his experience of the Berlin 15M, which, after its initial success suffered a stage of

---

11   "Berlin se une al movimiento 15 M" of Lucas Rubio-Albizu in *Heraldo* 20 May 2011. https://www.heraldo.es/noticias/suplementos/elecciones2011/autonomicas/berlin_une_movimiento_m.html

decline, although it was later revitalised due to the integration of new people with militant backgrounds:[12]

> When I arrived a year and a half ago the 15M was consolidated. It was created at the same time as the 15M in Spain, in 2011. Here it formed an assembly. According to what they have told me, it had a peak and then it went down to the point of being a discussion group of four of five people. But anyhow it resumed a year after the beginning of 15M. When I arrived it was a group which worked very well, with an assembly of 20 or 25 people, with different working groups. It was clear that it was a group of people who had been organised previously. There were comrades from the United Left and from feminist groups, which invigorated the assemblies a lot [Gaspar, male, 25 years old, commerce worker in Berlin, interview conducted 30 January 2015].

In effect, the elevated geographic mobility of the people involved in migration dynamics, especially in Berlin, together with the instability of a movement such as 15M, meant that many groups of Spanish workers outside Spain disappeared or experienced periods of withdrawal in which their activity was reduced to meetings with very small attendance and to providing information through social networking sites. In specific cities, however, where the activists were able to recruit people with a militant background, the 15M assemblies succeeded in maintaining or intensifying their activity. This was the case for 15M in Berlin.

4.2 The Creation of the Precarious Office

In 2012, following the example of the "Precarious Offices" organised by other Spanish autonomist organisations, 15M Berlin launched the initiative *Berlin Wie Bitte*. They offered free legal counsel to Spanish workers on a variety of issues such as housing, health care, language, legal, and labour. The fact that one of the 15M local leaders was a lawyer became a central asset for providing consultation services to Spanish migrants.

In February 2013, the Spanish group *Juventud Sin Futuro* (Youth without a Future). an autonomous organisation formed by university students of Madrid who participated in the origins of the 15M and, later, Podemos (Juventud Sin Futuro, 2011; Díaz-Parra, Jóver & Roca, 2017), launched the campaign *No nos*

---

12 In order to preserve anonymity and confidentiality, we have used pseudonyms. We have only used their original name when using their declarations in public documents, such as interviews to the media or articles published with their names.

vamos, nos echan (We are not leaving, we are being expelled). The campaign highlighted the situation of thousands of young Spanish workers who had to emigrate in order to get a life. It also denounced the lack of opportunities for the young generation and made visible the problems of hundreds of thousands of young people who were forced to emigrate for economic reasons. They used the expression "labour exile" rather than "emigration" or "territorial mobility" to emphasise the fact that the decision to emigrate was imposed by political and economic powers. The precarious situation of the emigrants, they argued, was not something temporary. Precariousness had turned into the labour norm:

> Against those who speak of temporary exile, of emigration as a transitory stage which allows young people to obtain knowledge and experience with which to return, the reality is very different. The only alternative to unemployment is precariousness: the government opted for a flexibility and temporality of contracts, but temporality is no longer temporary, and the young people are chained by this type of contract as a norm.[13]

The campaign made the situation of Spanish workers abroad visible by publishing an interactive map of the world on the Internet in which each point was linked to particular witnesses of exploitation and the lack of rights experienced by Spanish emigrants.[14] The campaign caught the attention of the mass media and many migrants joined Youth without a Future. In the following months the emigrants felt that they had specific needs, so many of them decided to create their own network, which they called Maroon Tide. They also used the metaphor of the tide following the example of the Green Tide and the White Tide, networks of citizens and workers who were very active in defending public education and health care in Spain after 2011 (Béroud, 2014). They selected the colour maroon because it is the colour of Spanish passports.

The Maroon Tide managed to create nodes (local or regional groups) in more than 30 territories that connected more than 200 activists, influenced the Spanish population and media, and targeted economic and political powers. The 15M group of Berlin became the local node of the transnational network.

In 2015 the 15M sub-group *Berlin Wie Bitte* adopted the name Precarious Office after the group split. Those who wanted to continue the initiative of providing counselling for other Spanish emigrants created the structure of the

---

13   Available at http://www.nonosvamosnosechan.net/p/exilio-labroral.html [Retrieved 27 February 2015].

14   Available at http://www.nonosvamosnosechan.net/ [Retrieved 27 February 2015].

Precarious Office, which was being replicated by Spanish activists groups in other countries.[15] These groups were inspired by, among other sources, the Italian autonomist movement No Global, which in 2001 started to organise independently of political parties and trade unions as a space of self-organisation for precarious workers. From this perspective, the needs and conditions of precarious workers are different from those of other workers, so they need to generate their own organisations. In 2004, this movement acquired more visibility, linked at that time to the new anti-globalisation movement, and organised a protest called Euro May Day in Milan, with an original movement following "Saint Precarious" as a liturgical pilgrim. This movement, which had its intellectual roots in the *operaismo* of Toni Negri and others, did not achieve great popularity, but continues in Italy and appears in other territories reformulated according to their contexts and traditions, being generally integrated within wider social movements such as those of squatters and housing in the Spanish case.[16]

The different work groups of 15M Berlin have had an unstable life. They have had very active groups on feminism, on connecting *Vernetzung* with local struggles and social movements, on training, and on the study of Marx's *Capital*, among others, although today the most active groups are The Precarious Office and the *Union Action Group* (GAS in Spanish).

The Precarious Office provides consultation service in Spanish to migrants once a week in a community organisation located at Mehlinplatz (in the district of Kreuzberg), although they also provide online consultation on their website

---

[15] The Precarious Office of Madrid was created in January 2012 by militants from 15M. Its main goal was the defense of the labor rights of temporary and unemployed workers, carrying out a type of parallel trade unionism, providing legal advice on a multiplicity of problems (mainly involving labor, but also housing, health care, immigration, etc.), and launching direct actions such as the precarious *escraches* (public protests in the target's private life) against employers who abuse their workers. In 2012, new precarious offices were created in other Spanish cities such as Vigo, Valencia, and Sevilla. 15M assemblies in several European cities also adopted this kind of organisation and used it as work groups within the general assembly. In September 2012. a precarious office was founded in Vienna; in November 2013, in London; in January 2015. in Paris; and in February 2015, in Berlin (although, as mentioned above, in Berlin the 15M work group *Berlin Wie Bitte* had carried out these types of actions for several years).

[16] In Spain there are antecedents to the autonomist movement in the 1970s. There was a parallel movement to trade unions that defended horizontalism, unity, and direct action against the model of labor relations imposed during the political transition with the complicity of the main workers' organisations (Espai en Blanc, 2008; Florido, Roca, & Gutiérrez, 2013). These autonomous currents declined during the 1980s, and they did not enter the arena again until the end of the 1990s, this time reformulated by the inspiration of the new global social movements that were emerging in several areas of the world.

(publishing, for example, a complete list of forms of several German public bodies translated into Spanish) and by email and their Facebook account. They have created a protocol for responding to the many requests for information emails that they receive. They provide counselling for free, although they accept voluntary donations from the users in order to cover their meagre expenses, such as the €20 monthly rent they pay to the association for using their premises once a week and in their monthly meetings.

A good proportion of the people who demand their service are newly arrived migrants who need orientation in order to adapt to the host country. The Precarious Office provides counselling on a variety of issues, all of them related to the precarious condition of emigrants in Berlin: social benefits such as the *Arbeitlosengeld2*, popular known as *Hartz IV*;[17] accompaniment when attending a meeting with the local administration; registering at the city administration; getting a VISA for non-EU migrants; language; housing; fines (for example, for not paying public transport tickets); problems with taxes, such as the tax for having a TV at home; and health insurance, among others.

They have translated a wide number of administrative documents and have collected and adapted a large number of documents, leaflets, and informational brochures from other institutions and groups. They usually refer people to local lawyers, institutions (such as the consultation services of the Spanish Embassy), and other organisations (such as German trade unions).

4.3 *The Union Action Group*

In 2014, due to the high demand for labour consultations, Jorge, who had just arrived from Seville and was a union organiser for the Andalusian Workers Union (*Sindicato Andaluz de Trabajadores*, SAT), a radical Andalusian union (Roca, 2014), proposed the creation of a specific group within 15M Berlin in order to focus on labour problems. They called it the Union Action Group (*Grupo de Acción Social*, GAS). They provide periodic labour counselling in Spanish to individuals or groups of workers, hold meetings, and undertake collective action in order to defend labour rights and combat employers' abuses.

The group does not have formal membership; it is formed by a network of Spanish activists interested in labour struggles. It is organised around the

---

17   *Arbeitlosengedl2* or *Hartz IV* is a subsidy that can be requested by unemployed people (who don't have a right to the unemployment subsidy *Arbeitlosengeld1*) or part-time workers (*Minijobbers*) who not reach what is considered the minimum subsistence level for their particular situation. It covers housing rent and their (and their family's) basic needs The Hartz IV social aid takes its name from Peter Hartz, coordinator of the German parliamentary committee that in the early 2000s redrew social protection for unemployed people.

principles of horizontalism, gender balance, rotation of speakers, distribution of internal work, and training in labour activism (Sanz, 2016). GAS members get support from a network of German activists by means of an email distribution list. Their knowledge of labour law, language, institutions, graphic design, and communication is an important asset for GAS militancy. These German activists are mostly from Trotskyite and anarcho-syndicalist local organisations.

GAS members used to hold twice-monthly meetings, generally on Saturday. They used to meet at the *Cafe Commune*, a bar of the Berliner left located in the district of Kreuzberg. Between meetings, they make decisions by an email distribution list. The GAS has had an irregular trajectory. They have had moments of intense activity and social projection and moments of withdrawal. However, they have managed to maintain their activity (meetings, consultation) with a core of activists.

According to members' testimonies, they have attended or organised two types of young workers (something that reflects the dualism of the German labour market and, consequently, the working conditions of Spanish migrants). On the one hand, precarious workers in the retail, logistic, e-commerce, and hospitality industries and delivery platforms generally have individual labour problems. On the other hand, stable workers, mainly nurses in the healthcare industry, have been able to organise collectively. The most common labour problem with Spanish nurses concerns what they called the "fine," a kind of compensation that Spanish workers are forced to pay if they leave a job after signing certain clauses in their contracts.[18] According to GAS members, this clause leads to many cases of abuse and tends to be used as an instrument for suppressing workers' rights. In addition to these cases, they have also organised some older workers who have emigrated from Spain to Germany with their families in the logistics and construction sectors.

GAS members believe that trade unions are fundamental for the defence of labour rights. GAS is not conceived as a substitute to trade unions, but as a complement that aims at reinforcing them. They refer many cases to the lawyers of trade unions, they foster union membership among the workers, and they try to work in cooperation with German trade unions.

GAS activists reflect constantly about their actions, looking to improve their power to mobilise workers and improve their performance. Although they receive numerous individual claims, in some cases they are able to collectively organise workers from a given workplace or industry. In addition, they perceive

---

18   This fine is connected to the German language course (normally 2 months) and the relative accommodation costs which the enterprise offer in the contract when they recruit nurses through an agency in Spain.

that the temporary character of Spanish migration makes it extremely difficult to develop effective strategies against labour precariousness. On the contrary, the fact that many Spanish emigrants were familiar with the radical democratic values of the 15M is seen by GAS activists as a factor that has facilitated their organising drive:

> The key issue is that we have realised that Spanish people are easier to organise thanks to the 15M. That is, the first meetings that we organised with nurses, I noticed that convening an assembly, writing the minutes or formulating demands was not something new for them. I think it is because of the 15M. This makes the difference between Spanish emigrants and other emigrants, such as the Greeks and the Italians of our same age [Jorge, male, 35 years old, GAS militant. Interview conducted online, 30 January 2015].

4.4 Framing Militancy: Innovation, Transnational Bricolage, and Brokerage

The testimonies of activists interviewed for this research can be examined in order to study the ways in which they frame their migrant experience and their militancy. They also contain valuable information about the roles played by brokerage, bricolage, and innovation in the design of collective action.

Similarly to the Spanish 15M (Flesher-Fominaya, 2015), the Berlin 15M group defined itself as an organisation autonomous from political and economic powers. They advocate for self-organisation. One of the characteristics of the Precarious Office and GAS is that they reject state subsidies. Representatives of the Spanish Embassy have offered them grants to support their activity, but they have always refused such proposals. They think that they could lose their autonomy, and that this distinguishes them from other emigrant organisations:

> They [the Spanish Embassy] give you grants or whatever, but we, the Precarious Office, don't want any grant, and less if it comes from the Ministry of Work [laughs]. Anyway, we can go through without grants, but of course we don't have hired professionals working on counselling. We are the only ones who don't have it [Federica, female, 60 years old, member of the Precarious Office, interview conducted in Berlin, 8 December 2017].

The defence of autonomy is one of the benchmarks of the 15M. A GAS activist even defined other associations of Spanish emigrants as clientelist because they are focused on getting subsidies from public authorities.

The organisational model derived from the principle of autonomy, nevertheless, entails certain shortcomings. They depend exclusively on volunteers, and sometimes they have difficulties helping the people who demand their services. For example, one of the main difficulties of the Precarious Office is the important demands of people who need accompaniment to do certain tasks (generally having to do with public administrations) because they do not know German, whilst only a limited number of volunteers know German and are available to undertake such work. During the interviews with workers, they had the support of a German volunteer who used to be in charge of the most urgent cases.

Another defining feature of 15M groups is horizontalism—every member has the same formal decision-making power, and decisions must be adopted by direct democratic means (mainly assemblies and voting using the email distribution list), and they try to rotate representation roles.[19]

Training is another important hallmark of the 15M Berlin organisational model. In this sense, this social movement organisation can be viewed as a learning organisation. Knowledge and skills come from two practices: training and experimentation. In order to provide counselling to other emigrants, they have to acquire knowledge of German and Spanish laws, labour regulations, or social services. They also have to know to which administrative entity, expert, or organisation they have to refer emigrants depending on their particular needs. Interviewees and documents point out that they constantly update their knowledge and participate in training sessions from a variety of entities. A common topic in most of the Precarious Office meetings is the constant training actions activists participate in in order to improve their performance. Federica, for example, says that she is about to be retired, and she was registered at a three-day workshop of a German trade union. She also suggests that attending these events contributes to expanding networks with trade unions in order to strengthen mutual cooperation:

> They explain how to do consultancy. And apart from explaining the labour law and what measures can be made in order to prevent certain situations at work, I will take advantage of being there to try to do things together. In this sense, we have to look forward to their lawyers accepting our people. We have tried this before, but if they don't join the union they don't have access to the lawyers [Federica, female, 60 years old, member of the Precarious Office, interview conducted in Berlin, 8 December 2017].

---

19   This principle connects with defining characteristics of previous international and autonomous Spanish social movements (Graeber, 2009).

Melina also highlighted the importance of training for the Precarious Office:

> In the Precarious Office, every time we have a meeting we point out that we have to organise workshops. We have to keep on collecting information in order to improve. We do an analysis of what comes to us. Yes, this is one of the goals of our meetings: to see how things are evolving and how to incorporate the new activists [Melina, 33 years old, member of the Precarious Office, interview conducted in Berlin, 8 December 2017].

Migrants' frames also relate with narratives about their socioeconomic and political situations. In this sense, 15M activists are aware of the benefits that their emigrant condition implies for German employers. They explain it in Marxist terms:

> German employers have very clear [knowledge] that the immigrant workforce has to be used in order to increase general levels of surplus extraction by means of the recruitment of cheaper workers, and using them in order to lower salary and labour conditions of the native workforce (Sanz, 2016, 54).

15M members, in particular GAS militants, understand their struggle in connection not only with emigrants of other nationalities, but also with German workers. They promote the enrolling of emigrant workers in German trade unions (both radical unions such as *Freie Arbeiterinnen-und Arbeiter Union* (Free Workers' Union-FAU) and major unions such as Ver.di and other unions of the general confederation DBG). Jorge explains their affinity with the FAU and certain militants in major unions such as Ver.di:

> With the FAU we have a special relationship because there are a lot of similarities in the way in which we work. That is, we practice revolutionary unionism. It is a grassroots struggle. There are comrades of GAS that have close relations with FAU. They send us their calls, we attend their activities, and we plan to start a campaign together in the hospitality industry. And we also have a very good relationship with Ver.di, which is the big union. When a worker from Bavaria, the other part of Germany, calls us, we have a telephone number of Ver.di that we can call and we ask them to assist that worker. And she can have access to a lawyer in order to address her labour problems [Jorge, 38 years old, GAS member, interview conducted in Berlin, 10 December 2017].

During additional fieldwork in Germany at the end of 2017, we noticed that many GAS members had joined the FAU. This was not the case for Jorge, who belonged to a Trotskyite organisation, and to several leftist Spanish and German political organisations such as Die Linke and Podemos. Several members of the Precarious Office were also members of Podemos, although they refrained from engaging in electoral politics within the 15M group. In addition, some of the founding members of 15M Berlin were members of the Spanish United Left, the political coalition of the Communist Party of Spain.[20] The political background and double militancy of many 15M members contributed to giving consistency, stability, and effectiveness to their structure and activities. Jorge described his experience in the following manner:

> When I arrived [in 2014] it was a group that worked very well, with an assembly of 20–25 people and with different work groups. It was evident that there was a group of people with a political background. There were comrades of United Left and from feminist groups. They facilitated the assembly very well (…) and the assembly was so well prepared that people who had just arrived would enrol directly in any group or activity [Jorge, 38 years old, GAS member, interview conducted in Berlin, 10 December 2017].

Spanish migrant activists also perceive the precarious condition of emigrants as a source for galvanizing workers. This is, they have argued, why the 15M have persisted out of Spain whilst it disappeared in Spanish cities:

> There are many factors that affect you individually because when your life is economically secure, stable, close to your family and everything, you don't have to worry, nor be active. You just let things flow. You have your space, your comfort zone. But when you go abroad, anger and a willingness to struggle appears. And that is the reason why I think that the people are more active [out of Spain] than inside [Melina, 33 years old, member of the Precarious Office, interview conducted in Berlin, 8 December 2017.]

In order to address many of the problems derived from the precariousness affecting emigrants, GAS members follow organising techniques attempting to unify workers regardless of their nationality (trying to join Spanish and German

---

20   For a deep analysis of the radical left and social movements in contemporary South European countries, see Roca, Martín-Díaz, and Díaz-Parra (2017).

workers). They attempt to apply the methodology of union organising of Andalusian radical unionism to the German context. Jorge explains their protocol:

> We meet the workers. They make an assembly. Decide their demands. They prioritise the demands. They decide how they want to conduct the conflict. We help them in these first assemblies, and we make some proposals. But we end up using trade unions. That is, we help the people to organise a conflict, but we also tell them, depending on the situation and depending on the union, we drive them to join the union. And then what we do is pressure the union to take care of them [Jorge, 35 years old, GAS member, interview conducted 30 January 2015].

GAS methodology also includes an approach to the spaces of Spanish migrants' sociability. They organise parties at their homes or meet at pubs in order to be in the private sphere of Spanish workers. This contributes to strengthening the relationships between workers and activists. In this sense, they follow some procedures of the Anglo-Saxon organising model (McAlevey, 2014).

Therefore, GAS and Precarious Office collective actions are a transnational bricolage of consolidated practices coming from different political groups and traditions, improvisation, training, and self-learning through experience. Activists need to innovate not only for adapting to a new context but also to answering new challenges created by platform capitalism and migrant conditions.

Union bricolage is related to the position of migrants as "brokers" (Faist, 2014), who connect emigrants with other migrants and non-migrants as well as with other organisation and institutions, both in Germany and abroad. The activists of the Precarious Office have formalised networking among their common duties. In one of their first meetings, activists made the decision to foster collaboration with other entities, and that such a task was fundamental for their mission. We have mentioned that they refer people to other institutions, organisations, or professionals. They maintain periodical contact with these entities in order to strengthen collaboration and cooperation and share materials and information. The debate that took place at the assembly of 9 April 2015 reflects the criteria followed by the activists of the Precarious Office in order to cooperate with other organisations. They discussed cooperation with the association Cisne, linked to the Catholic Church, which focuses on solidarity with migrant people. They made this decision about cooperation with other groups:

> In relation to the cooperation with other groups, we must bear in mind their values and the work that they do, and depending on this decide

whether to collaborate or not, and to what extent. First of all, we have to clarify that this association does not ask us to join them, since we do not share the same values. We are a grassroots movement, self-organised, assembleist and horizontal, and that [other] association is not like us (minutes of the assembly 9 April 2015 of the Precarious Office).

Following this criterion, they decided to revise the Cisne materials and use them if they did not contain religious content. Although they cooperate with a plurality of institutions and organisations, they show more affinity with certain groups with which they share common ideas, values, and goals. This is the case for other migrant associations and groups, in Berlin and abroad, that provide consultation and promote collective action such as Berlin Migrant Strikers, Basta!, the Centre for Counselling Immigrants of the German Union DGB in Germany, and the Precarious Offices of other cities and countries, the Brighton Solidarity Federation or platforms like People in Movement.[21]

GAS members also think of themselves as brokers between Spanish emigrants and German labour unions. Nevertheless, they recognise that trade unions entail serious contradictions. In some cases, the trade unions have played a de-mobilising role and GAS members have opposed them. One activist explains it in an interview to the media:

> Today German and Spanish trade unions are very similar in the sense that they have two ways of defining themselves: as structures for mobilisation and defence, or as spaces for management and bureaucracy. As can be expected, we prefer the first one. These two ways are clear when one works with unions, but until now we have been lucky with the people with whom we have cooperated. They were not only union officials, but also very involved politically, who understood that labour conflict always implies a political conflict at a wider scale (Carlos Aparicio, GAS activist,[22] quoted in Ruiz del Arbol, 2014).

One interviewee exemplifies this conflict with a struggle with truck drivers. The representative in the *Betriebsrat* (Works Council)[23] from Ver.di signed

---

21 The permanent links in their website include those groups with which they have more affinity. For a complete list, see: http://oficinaprecariaberlin.org/ (Retrieved 19 July 2018).

22 It is quoted in "Trabajar en Alemania" interview of Diego Ruiz-del-Arbol to GAS activist Carlos Aparicio. On-line at: http://trabajar-en-alemania.es/entrevista-carlos-aparicio-del-grupo-accion-sindical-gas (Retrieved 15 July 2018).

23 In the German labour relations system, *Betriebsrat* is the name of shop-floor workers representation structures, elected for four-year periods among the workers, and that used to

an agreement with conditions that were below the standards of the regional agreement. The employer imposed on the drivers the obligation of paying 30 per cent of the damages that they might accidentally cause the trucks from their salary instead of covering this totally with insurance. According to GAS members, this point was used by the employer to have the workers work for free. They denounced this to Ver.di leadership, but they ended up realising that a member of the *Betriebsrat* was a close friend of the Ver.di regional leader. In this situation, GAS was in clear conflict with the union leadership and carried out the campaign in an autonomous way.

In contrast, in the struggle of Spanish nurses in several work centers, the Ver.di leader of the healthcare industry in Berlin was also a member of a leftist autonomist group, *Interventionistische Linke* (Interventionist Left). In this case, the union and GAS developed a symbiosis that contributed to enhancing union membership and to achieve some of the goals of the workers. Nonetheless, the trade union bosses of this union activist also attempted to attenuate the conflict, originating contradictions with GAS. For GAS members, the key point for fostering their mobilisation line before the moderate line of major unions is having previously organised the workers at the shop floor.

5   Italian Migrants' Activism in Berlin

5.1   *The Reconstruction of Political Activism in Emigration*

The experience of the new Italian migrant workers' organisations in Berlin is quite different from the Spaniards'. The economic crisis in Italy did not boost a social movement like 15M in Spain (Castellani & Queirolo, 2017). As Antonio, one of the activists of the first Italian migrants' political collective, explained in 2014:

> We participated in the Italian political context for many years. We left it discouraged, and arrived here looking for a different perspective. I mean, maybe in my personal imagination: "Here I'm going to work. I'm going to make a full life under certain points of view and the political issues are going to be partially put aside." I mean, I'm going to help other people in a mutual way and my level of action is going to be this one. Nevertheless, it is not like that because the migrant condition forces you to undertake political practice. So, our political background automatically becomes useful for what we are doing here. Life is strange. Italy kicked

---

carry out firm bargaining in order to make concrete what labour unions have previously negotiated on an industrial-national scale.

us out, rejecting us from a certain point of view. We moved within the European Union, finding another place and looking for a different way of acceptance, also a different line of action. But it is not like that! Here the radicalisation starts [Antonio, gastronomy worker, 31 years, male, in Berlin since 2011, interviewed on 19 August, 2014].

Many of the new Italian migrants who constituted the first *collettivo* in Berlin named *Berlin Migrant Strikers* (BMS) were people who militated in the extra-parliamentary left and the squatters in Italy who have politically grown up in the wave of non-global movements. Most of them arriving in the German capital during the economic crisis, experienced the exploitation of the secondary labour market in the intra-ethnic labour market niche: Italian gastronomy (there are about 4,000 Italian restaurants in Berlin), Italian workers who recently arrived in Berlin without a job offer and without speaking German and did not have the opportunity to enter a company where English was used as a vehicular language, without an amount of money to subsist on, learning German and looking for a job, can find employment very quickly in this market niche. Entering this ethnic labour market permits them to solve the principal bureaucratic and housing difficulties[24] that most EU migrants have to face.

Sometimes restaurant owners offer employees an accommodation room in a house they own (many times without a rent contract), discounting the rent from the salary. On the one hand, this help, provided by the Italian networks, helps cover the basic needs and overcome barriers that migrants face when they enter a new place. On the other hand, migrants are exposed to the risk of blackmail: accepting working for a poor salary and contractual conditions compared to German standards, agreeing to work in the black or waiting a long time to get a regular contract that allows them to look for other accommodations. In this sense, the intra-ethnic network can become toxic (Di Falco & Bulte, 2011), hindering the socioeconomic inclusion of Italians who arrive in Berlin. Enrico, one of the founders of the BMS, spoke about employment in the Italian gastronomy industry:

> On average, the pay is between €4 and €5.50 per hour for dishwasher and assistant cooks.[25] There is no standard wage salary in the gastronomy

---

[24] As an example, for having a job contract in Germany, among other documents an *Anmeldung* (registered domicile) is needed that you can get by showing a rental contract. However, for renting a house, among other documents, you have to show pay checks from the past three months and a job contract. In many Italian restaurants, employers hire people without this documentation if they accept working without a contract.

[25] For the first time after the second World War, in Germany in 2015 a minimum wage €8.50 (in 2017 €8.84) per hour (gross) was introduced. This meant an improvement for many

industry in Germany. They give you a contract of 450 euros a month, a *Minijob*. The worker must pay *Krankenkasse* (health insurance) and a pension contribution. In many cases, the only solution is going to the *Jobcenter* and asking for an income integration. The *Jobcenter* can pay three things. It gives you 300 euros for the house, 400 euros to live, and it pays your *Krankenkasse*. But the *Jobcenter* tells you: "You have to work more. We cannot give you 400 euros for the rest of your life. So, my dear, find another job. Even better, we find it for you and if you refuse we reduce your minimum income." We found some cases, such as the one of an Italian who already worked 40 hours in a restaurant, even if his contract was only 20 hours, and he has to work as a cleaner in a McDonald's, working about 70 hours a week [Enrico, male, 29 years, self-employed, in Berlin since 2011, interviewed on 19 August, 2014].

Minijobbers can apply for the Hartz IV subside. Nevertheless, as was reported by many Italian and Spanish migrants in Berlin, especially after 2011, they face increasing difficulties in applying for this subsidy.[26] On the one hand, there was a diffuse lack of knowledge of the system and its requirements (deadlines, documents) as well as a linguistic barrier in dealing with the bureaucracy. On the other hand, many practices of dissuasion implemented by front office Jobcenter employees were reported, with the goal of managing the candidates who apply for benefits: i.e., rude treatment or misinformation about the application requirements. This situation seemed to worsen by 2014, when in the politic-media discourse the welfare chauvinist narrative against "social tourisms" and "welfare shoppers,"[27] in particular against Rumanian and Bulgarian people, became prevalent—a narrative, in fact, that has been refuted by official data (Fernandes, 2016).

Within Italian FB groups and blogs articles about Italians who were expelled from Germany because they gained the minimum income

---

minijobbers (who can earn a maximum of €450 per month), a reduction of monthly hours at parity with income.

26   Beginning in October 2016, Germany imposed the requirement of a minimum five years of job contributions for applying for *Arbeitlosengeld2* and other welfare benefits such as a family allowance. Nevertheless, if migrants work only with a *Minijob* or are self-employed it is still possible to apply for an integration of the salary (for covering rent, health insurance, etc.).

27   Before the EU election of 2014 (far before the actual populist wave), Merkel declared "The EU union is not a social union" (http://www.spiegel.de/politik/deutschland/bundeskanzlerin-angela-merkel-cdu-eu-ist-keine-sozialunion-a-970956.html). An example of an article on the political debate on social tourism: http://www.spiegel.de/politik/deutschland/hartz-iv-fuer-zuwanderer-csu-wettert-gegen-eu-kommission-a-942810.html

> started to circulate. Bullshit! In the Italian community urban legends often circulate (...) At some points, my partner and I had a sort of small union at home because people knew that we were squat militants and we fought for the introduction of the minimum income. We were identified as knowing a little more about the topic, and people knocked on our door, terrorised by a media campaign that said that Germany wants to send the Italians back because they gained the minimum income [Enrico, male, 29 years, self-employed, in Berlin since 2011, interviewed on 19 August 2014].

Enrico and other people, before founding the BMS, started to help as volunteers in *Sozialberatung* (social consulting) at the squat Basta!, giving support in different languages to unemployed people or *Minijobbers* for applying to *Arbeitlosengeld2*. In this manner they have become familiar with German labour legislation and with the system of welfare benefits in Germany, learning from the German volunteers at Basta! and through self-learning (going to the *Jobcenter* and submitting applications for themselves and other people). Currently, a couple of members of BMS still offer support in Italian once a week at Basta!, giving information and helping prepare documentation for the *Jobcenter*. Moreover, from time to time they go the *Jobcenter* with applicants to help them with translation.

5.2 Berlin Migrant Strikers: An Experience of "Bio-Unionism"

In the summer of 2014 Italian migrant activists decided to organise themselves into a migrant *collettivo,* named "Berlin Migrants Strikers" (BMS). The impulse for formalising the group was given by the *Rote Hilfe* network.

> We understood that we have to implement mechanisms of conflict, that we cannot only let the battle against the system here exist on the plan of testimony. We needed to equip migrants with legal systems and solidarity-based solutions for escaping the crazy mechanism in which Italian masters are one pillar, the German welfare is another, and your subjective existential condition of migrant is what legitimates all of this [Enrico, male, 29 years, self-employed, in Berlin since 2011, interviewed on 19 August, 2014].

Initially, BMS collaborated with FAU, which was the only union in Berlin with counselling for migrants. They found that FAU practices, focusing on collective actions targeting singular firms, in many cases did not met the Italian workers' needs, marked by temporary jobs, black jobs, precariousness, etc. In addition, from the beginning the structure of the union hindered collaboration.

> They are unionists in the true sense of the term. The affiliation, the organisation. Surely, it must be recognised that the FAU is the only one that tries to address certain problems. The problem of German trade unionism from the '50s is that they are made to be corporativist in the literal sense of the term [Giuseppe, male, 27 years, PhD student, in Berlin since 2016, interviewed on 16 August, 2018].

The experience of the BMS with other German unions and leftist parties[28] was that even if they seem interested in the discourse on the migrants' worker issues, they tend to ignore in practice the problems of migrant workers.

> To receive legal assistance from a union, you must be registered in the union for more than three months. This means that many precarious workers not have time, do not have money, often renounce their job because it is a shitty job (...) the German union system is thought to exist for a certain type of worker [Giuseppe, male, 27 years, PhD student, in Berlin since 2016, interviewed on 16 August, 2018].

The large unions seem to go along with welfare chauvinism (Van der Waal et al., 2010), especially in a highly ethno-stratified labour market such as contemporary Berlin, where migrant labour is concentrated mainly in the lower fractions of the working class and there is "ethno-specialisation": the sub-Saharans working in logistics (i.e., Amazon), the Eastern EU members in the construction or cleaning sectors, the Southern EU workers in the call centres and as "riders" for digital platforms such as Foodora and Deliveroo. In this sense, labour protection seems to affect only German workers who mostly occupy regulated jobs and have the right to access welfare benefits.

> They do not even have the idea that there is Amazon in Berlin.[29] We made flyers written in a thousand languages, and we distributed them at 6 a.m. out of the firm. We did it. We moved to try to understand their situation. Nobody speaks to them. They are Africans, they have a visa problem, they

---

28　Very few Italians (and southern EU workers) are unionised, with the exception of the Greeks.
29　Amazon acts in Berlin as Amazon Prime and Amazon Fresh.

are kicked in the ass as soon as they try to complain. Ver-di doesn't care to represent these workers (...) The question of the "riders" demonstrates how traditional unionism, with a certain idea of work, fails. It is not really capable of and does not want to organise labour struggles in the middle of an epochal transformation. This doesn't mean that all is new because they work on piecework, which is something that exists since the 1800s, but the digitalisation, the logisticisation of work relations, the hyper-flexibility, the algorithm (...) all these factors became central. The traditional trade unions have made a huge effort to understand this change and it reminds me a little, if I can make a historical comparison, given all the differences in the case, of the time when the Italian unions had an enormous difficulty in organising the labour fights of the mass workers in '69 [Giuseppe, male, 27 years, PhD student, in Berlin since 2016, interviewed on 16 August, 2018].

From the beginning, BMS carried on another idea of unionism that they define as the bio-unionisation of workers:

We worked with the instrument of the inquiry with which we tried to identify the critical points of the subjective migrant condition and give the subjects a series of opportunities. (...) At this moment we have a labour market, a life, no longer connected to the Fordist labour tool. At this moment your whole life is commodified: from being on Facebook, to your consumption, to the same welfare. How do you organise this precarious multitude, which also has desires that should be taken into consideration? Because the migrant condition has to deal with needs to be realised, it has much to do with the sphere of desire: subjective ambitions, needs, hopes, existential designs. How do you unionise them? Yes, we can start a dispute with the single asshole boss, we can appeal to German law, but this is not enough, because sometimes you win, sometimes you lose, but we talk about lives, we talk about a much more intense political scope. We do not pretend to represent or to be an avant-garde, but we try to question ourselves about this process [Enrico, male, 29 years, self-employed, in Berlin since 2011, interviewed on 19 August, 2014].

Doing inquiry into some topic for discussion in the assembly, as well as an exercise of reflection (Bourdieu & Wacquant, 1992), is part of the practice of self-learning. Many members of BMS had a theoretical-political Marxist foundation and, as in the case of GAS, some of the more active members were pursuing a PhD in social or political sciences and experiencing in person the downgrading of the secondary labour market when they arrived in Berlin.

5.3 Framing Militancy: Innovation, Transnational Bricolage, and Brokerage

Differently from the GAS, the BMS didn't focus their actions on collective disputes. When they found a problem with a single enterprise they looked for support from volunteer lawyers who were connected to the squat collectives. In the same way, they collaborated with FAU, as in the case of the dispute that some Amazon workers who contacted first with the *collettivo* started against the firm. They acted in these case as a broker between migrant workers and the union.

The BMS practices of giving voice and self-subsistence solutions to migrant workers has to be connected again to the widespread presence of Italian migrants in the ethnic environment of Italian gastronomy as well as to some exit tactics from the situation of exploitation that they found in this labour market. As we have analysed in other works (Castellani, 2018), some Italian migrants who were employed in the Italian gastronomy industry found, in their micro entrepreneurship, a way out of their situation. Because it is very easy and cheap in Germany to register a VAT number and there is a tax regime that exempts self-employers from a tax burden up to a certain threshold of revenue, many Italians who worked in Italian restaurants in Berlin began to manufacture and sell food or handicrafts, trading them in the flea markets of the German capital.

Even if renting a stand in the markets is affordable (about 30 euros a day), it is difficult to be accepted into the markets and rent the stands in the best positions because demand is very high. The market in Berlin is a niche monopolised by a Turkish entrepreneurs. In fact, even if the markets are formally self-organised by the sellers, they are de facto managed by Turkish employers, who for decades have specialised in this type of trade. Helping other new migrants (mainly Italians, but also Spanish) get into the Berlin markets business and exchanging information about the dues, rights, and rules within the different markets, some sellers founded a closed Facebook group. The use of a social network makes the exchange of information easy and the group's members can do lobbying to address the people who manage the markets.

Among these market sellers were the founders of the future *collettivo*, who interpreted the micro-entrepreneurship not only as a tactic of emancipation from the dynamics of exploitation and social downward movement caused by market dynamics and the migrant condition, but also as collective financial and social self-support. In other words, it was interpreted as a political tool within the frame of bio-unionism:

> You cannot only start a dispute, you must also invent a way to guarantee subsistence to a person that is a mechanism of labour protection outside

the mechanism of exploitation. We invented it because it seemed a fun idea to sell *panzerotti* [stuffed pizza pockets] at the market. (...) Then we refined the idea by putting it in a system with other comrades and other people (...) according to your need. If you need money and you are in deep shit, for avoiding entering a exploitation system, work in my place! You take the money that I have to earn because I'm in a more stable situation, I can do it another day. Or someone else has the *Hartz IV* at the *Jobcenter*. This create a rotation. We build a solidarity mechanism that goes from coaching for welfare benefits, to micro-entrepreneurship, even to hospitality at home (...) We also have a processing laboratory and we make sausages according to German law. We sell them to restaurant owners, invoicing everything. We make a fairly interesting policy because we sell them to private concerns for a lower price than for the restaurant owners so that they have a profit. (...) We put an experienced guy in the system. He came from Bari, working 12 years in a black job. We said: "Well, we invest some money on this thing, we buy two machines, the license (...) total investment 500 euros." Absolutely affordable. "You have know-how and we invest in this thing." Now he has found his professional way out of the exploitation mechanisms, inside the gastronomy industry but above the gastronomy industry [Enrico, male, 29 years, self-employed, in Berlin since 2011, interviewed on 19 August, 2014].

This innovative experiment of micro-entrepreneurship is a product of a creative combination between their know-how in preparing food with an active position against the dynamics of exploitation and precariousness that many of them experienced at first hand.

Nevertheless, criticism of the distortions of the Italian ethnic labour market in Berlin was also carried out through open denunciation of labour violations. It is interesting to dwell on one of the protest against a well-known historical Italian chain of pizzerias in Berlin, which based their brand on a leftist imaginary.[30] Despite this, they were reproducing the same conditions of exploitation and precariousness toward new Italian migrant workers.

Members of the BMS, together with the workers, organised an online and off-line protest directly involving two famous bands close to the Italian squat environment who were going to play in Berlin in an event sponsored by these

---

30   Many Italian restaurant owners in Berlin are part of the post-wall migration flow. People who came to Berlin right after 1989 were mostly politically engaged in the critical and extra-parliamentary left. Some of them decided to establish themselves in Berlin and opened restaurants.

pizzerias. The workers and ex-workers wrote an open letter to the bands denouncing the conditions of exploitation, abuses, and violence that they suffered in their workplace. The protest acquired resonance both in social media and in an important newspaper in Italy. The bands declared solidarity with the protesters and invited a delegation of workers to read a letter on stage with their requests to the pizzerias' owners for improved working conditions. This protest was understood as a trigger for denouncing the conditions of exploitation in many other Italian restaurants in Berlin.

An important evolution of BMS after its foundation was the internationalisation of the group. One of the crucial moments in this sense was the demonstration against the politics of the European Central Bank in Frankfurt in March 2015 by Blockupy. This European "hub of movements," similarly to the anti-globalisation movement of the end of the millennium, is a network of activists, migrants, unemployed people, precarious workers, parties, and unionists from different European countries. The idea is to link critical reflections, experiences, and practices to embrace the old and new challenges in contemporary EU society: financial crisis, gig economy and on-demand economy, border control, restriction of mobility, and cuts in welfare. Another large demonstration that followed this wave was organised by the international network "transnational social strike" on 1 March 2016. In between, there was the so-called "refugee crisis," in which Berlin received almost 80,000 asylum-seekers (Katz, Noring & Garrelts, 2016).

Since 2016, the BMS has aimed to open the *collettivo* to non-Italian people. Even if the majority of activists are Italians, some Greeks, Spaniards, and Germans have started to participate in the weekly assembly at Fritto in Neukölln. The BMS also began to embrace the struggle of non-Southern EU migrant workers such as the Sub-Saharan Africans who work for the Amazon shipping warehouse.

Moreover, BMS members were among the founders of the Critical Workers' activist hub in Berlin together with other leftist political activist and unionist groups that focus on the fight for rights for precarious workers. Critical Workers is understood as a space for critical reflexion on the changes connected to work in the context of Berlin and elaborating practices to emphasise workers' difficulties in the era of platform capitalism. Moreover, they aim to spread a collective conscience among workers regarding their conditions and boost the process of collective action. They meet once a month in the BMS location and once a month they offer a *Sozialberatung* service carried out by a volunteer lawyer at Infoladen Lunte, a squat in Neukölln, for workers who cannot access the union's workers' services. The majority of people who look for counselling are migrant workers. However, members of BMS stressed the necessity of always combining theoretical reflexion with providing solutions to the urgent problems that many migrants face (housing, having a minimum income, social support). Many BMS activists experienced first-hand these degrading conditions as migrants and precarious workers, and this facilitates communication with the workers who are looking for their help.

> We try to go beyond individuality, creating networks. One of the big problems is loneliness. Finding an environment that is supportive with people that understand what you're talking about, it's very important. I've worked a lot in the gastronomy sector. When people who work in this sector come and tell me this and that, I understand immediately because I lived that [Giuseppe, male, 27 years, PhD student, in Berlin since 2016, interviewed on 16 August, 2018].

For this reason, BMS members also organise many socialisation moments where individuals can gather together and new people can learn about the group, as for example the monthly Soli-Pizza evening that they organised in a squat in Schönenberg. Thanks to the volunteers, during these evenings they enjoy pizzas and drinks at a nominal price, and a DJ plays music.

BMS is also connected with activists in Italy. They participated in the network *Sconnessioni precarie*, a platform that was started in Bologna for promoting transnational theoretical debate focusing on the transformations of work and capitalism. Furthermore, many BMS members still keep in contact with the squats and associations in Italy in which they participated and try to maintain transnational cooperation. For example, some of the people who followed the first big protests of the Turin Foodora riders[31] in the EU went to Berlin to share the experience of delivery workers' actions and the tactics they put into place. BMS tried to connect Berlin delivery riders to create a network, acting as brokers with Berlin and abroad as well as with FAU. Moreover, they gave support for organising a riders' encounter where EU riders could share their experiences of actions for demanding better labour conditions. Even with large difficulties because of the heterogeneity of the context in which the delivery workers operate, these exchanges continue:

> There is a WhatsApp chat for the riders for coordination at the transnational level. They share strategies and tactics of struggle through Skype calls, with enormous difficulties because they move in totally different contexts of labour law [Giuseppe, male, 27 years, PhD student, in Berlin since 2016, interviewed on 16 August, 2018].

---

31   *Vid.* Tassinari and Maccarrone (2017)

They also are close to the new party *Potere al Popolo* (Power to the People) a political party that arose before the 2018 general election in Italy and where there is a consistent presence of an Italian emigrant community.

The boost for the transnationalisation of BMS is led by the reflection within the group that it is necessary to create transnational instruments and platforms for fighting against the dynamic of a transnational capitalism. This is one of the main deficits that they found in the traditional national unionism in Germany and in Italy. Moreover, they think that the work that they did in these years, together with the work of other activists, started to have some direct or indirect consequences. For example, in one firm 900 migrant workers are unionised; in one of the big call centre companies in Berlin, SAIX, the migrant workers organised themselves and are the majority in the company *Betriebsrat*.

As was demonstrated above, the BMS innovated creating new types of worker protection, doing transnational bricolage within a clear radical left ideological and political frame, combining improvisation, self-reflection, training, and self-learning. They have used this bricolage to act as brokers for migrant workers, connecting it with other organisation and institutions.

6   Final Remarks

Throughout this chapter, Spanish and Italian activist labour networks operating in Berlin have been described. These new forms of labour activism attempt to respond, on the one hand, to contemporary changes in capitalism and the spread of the platform economy, characterised by precariousness, informality, self-employment, subcontracting, and increasing alienation. On the other hand, they answer the dynamics of the intra-EU migrations on the south-north axis in a context of economic recession as a result of centre-periphery dynamics. The pattern of insertion of Spanish and Italian migrant workers into the Berlin labour market, with a large presence in the secondary market, engenders situations of precariousness and vulnerability that traditional trade unions (including radical unions such as the FAU), are not able or willing to address.

The existing trade unions in Berlin are perceived as insufficient for these activists. Consequently, Spanish and Italian workers have created their own networks and organisations, such as GAS and BMS, which cooperate with more or less frequency and closeness with mainstream unions such as Ver.di or radical unions such as FAU, opting to build their own structures and strengthen collaboration with other networks for worker mobilisation and representation in parallel. In addition, they have widened the repertoires and services that used to be provided by trade unions, providing counselling on a variety of issues related to the special vulnerability of migrant workers (translation services, administrative support, housing, etc.). Italian activists framed this type of activism as bio-unionism. From our point of view, this type of activism is better grasped with the concept of interstitial trade unionism. Addressing issues related to the living conditions (housing, social benefits, etc.) of the working class has historically accompanied salary and workplace issues in a great part of the trade union movement. In this sense, migrant labour activism has a different nature and is a means of recovering historical unionist functions and practices. The difference, however, rests on the fact that consolidated union representation, structures, and devices for collective action are not designed for migrant workers in the era of platform capitalism, a segment of the labour force with special needs. For this reason, Spanish and Italian migrants have created their own networks in the margins or interstices of the German labour relations system.

Trade unionism also plays a central role in self-positioning in the political field of this type of activism. At this point there is a difference between GAS and BMS. In the first case, the most actives members were involved in a radical union in Andalusia (SAT). For this reason they defined themselves as a union complementary to German unions and tried to create synergies with them when they found willing collaboration with native unions. BMS, whose core group referred to the squatting tradition, presented themselves as an alternative structure created by migrant workers from below, compared to traditional unions, which they described as institutional organisations not aware of and not interested in the labour conditions of the ethno-stratified labour market.

The history of the two groups' creation is also meaningful for understanding their differences. People who founded 15M Berlin, Oficina Precaria, and the GAS modelled it on 15M forms of participation and organisations. Moreover, in the early years, they recruited union and political activists who were familiar with German labour rights and conflicts, generating a flywheel effect on the evolution and legitimacy of the organisation, both in the social and political fields. This organisational model was also crucial for appealing to Spanish migrants, who knew the format because they were familiar with the 15M practices of participation and a-ideological narrative (Roca & Díaz-Parra, 2017; Cuberos, 2016).

BMS members came to Berlin with previous experiences in Italy of militancy or closeness to collectives that have the heritage of non-globalist movements. They couldn't find a political hub like the 15M, which works as transnational aggregator of people who want to have a political voice. The Italians who founded BMS initially got in contact with and collaborated with their German comrades of the radical left and squat collectives in Berlin. After several years, they decided to create an Italian migrants' collective clearly ideologically oriented to the model of what they were familiar with. Horizontalism and autonomy from the state, which was the flag of 15M, was already part of their political tradition and didn't need to be reinvented. Moreover, while the Spanish migrants were more transnationally connected with 15M and Podemos groups in Spain and abroad, the BMS followed the line of transnationalisation with other radical left groups.

The end of the recession and the return of many migrants to Spain, particularly of those who became militant in unions or political parties, and the lack of a clear political project, weakened the Spanish workers' organisation. On the contrary, Italian migrant workers, being ideologically based, seemed to better support the temporary nature of their members as well as changes in the socioeconomic context.

Nevertheless, as we observed above, the tactics adopted by the two groups are very similar. For both Spanish and Italian workers' collectives, the organising model and repertoire of collective action is the result of creative innovation (Oswalt, 2016), transnational bricolage (Phillimore et al., 2018), and brokerage (Faist, 2014). Being conscious of playing in a conflictual social and political field in order to give innovative responses to the precarious and vulnerable situations of migrant workers, GAS and BMS bricolaged their available resources. Their backgrounds of political and labour activism in Spain and Italy, together with their networks with German, Spanish, Italian, and international organisations, are the basis from which they creatively found solutions to everyday problems migrants experience. They bricolaged their resources through improvisation, self-reflection, training, and self-learning through experience. This bricolage is partly a result of the migration process and partly a result of dissemination via information and communication technologies. Finally, they acted as a broker, connecting migrant workers; referring people to other institutions, organisations, or professionals both in Germany and abroad; maintaining periodical contact with these entities in order to strengthen collaboration; and connecting to share materials and information and to cooperate.

References

Alaminos, A., Albert, M. C., & Santacreu, O. (2010). La Movilidad Social de Los Emigrantes Españoles En Europa. *Revista Española de Investigaciones Sociológicas*, 129, 13–35.

Bade, K. (1987). *Population, Labour and Migration in 19th and 20th Century Germany.* Leamington/Spa: Berg.

Béroud, S. (2014). Crise Économique et Contestation Sociale en Espagne : Des Syndicats Percutés par les Mouvements Sociaux ?. *Critique internationale*, 65, 27–42.

Blank, S. (2013). Why the Lean Start-up Changes Everything. *Harvard Business Review*, May 2013. Retrieved from https://hbr.org/2013/05/why-the-lean-start-up-changes-everything

Bourdieu, P., & Wacquant, L. (1992). *Respuestas: Por Una Antropología Reflexiva.* Mexico D. F.: Grijalbo.

Brenke, K., Yuksel, M., & Zimmermann, K. F. (2009). EU Enlargement under Continued Mobility Restrictions: Consequences for the German Labor Market. In *EU Labor Markets After Post-Enlargement Migration* (pp. 111–29). Berlin, Heidelberg: Springer. https://doi.org/10.1007/978-3-642-02242-5_4

Cap, P. (2017). Immigration and Anti-Migration Discourses: The Early Rhetoric of Brexit. In P. Cap (Ed.), *The Language of Fear* (pp. 67–79). London: Palgrave Macmillan UK. https://doi.org/10.1057/978-1-137-59731-1_6

Castellani, S. (2018). Scivolando Verso Il Basso. L'inserimento Lavorativo Dei Nuovi Migranti Italiani e Spagnoli in Germania Durante La Crisi Economica. *Sociologia Del Lavoro*, 149, 77-93. https://doi.org/10.3280/SL2018-149006

Castellani, S., & Queirolo Palmas, L. (2017). When the spring is not coming. Radical left and social movements in Italy during the austerity era. In B. Roca, E. Marín-Díaz & I. Díaz-Parra (Eds.), *Challenging Austerity. Radical Left and Social Movements in the South of Europe* (pp. 133–151). London/New York: Routledge.

Castells, M. (1998). *La Era de La Información: Economia, Sociedad y Cultura. Vol I, La Sociedad Red.* Madrid: Alianza Editorial.

Castells, M. (2012). *Redes de indignación y esperanza.* Madrid: Alianza.

Castles, S. (2002). The International Politics of Forced Migration. In L. Panitch & C. Leys (Eds.), *Fighting Identities: Race, Religion and Ethno-Nationalism* (pp. 172–92). London: Merlin.

Ciupijus, Z. (2011). Mobile Central Eastern Europeans in Britain: Successful European Union Citizens and Disadvantaged Labour Migrants? *Work, Employment and Society*, 25(3), 540–50. https://doi.org/10.1177/0950017011407962

Cuberos, F. (2016). Lo Que Diga La Asamblea. El Ritual Político Como Fetiche En Tiempos de Crisis. *Nómadas. Revista Crítica de Ciencias Sociales y Jurídicas*, 48(2), 61–75. http://dx.doi.org/10.5209/NOMA.53291

de Certeau, M. (1984). *The Practice of Everyday Life.* Berkley: University of California Press.

de la Rica, S. (2009). The Experience of Spain with the Inflows of New Labor Migrants. In M. Kahanec & K. F. Zimmermann (Eds.), *EU Labor Markets After Post-Enlargement Migration* (pp. 131–44). Berlin: Springer.

Deleuze, G., & Guattari, F. (1983). *Anti-Oedipus: Capitalism and Schizophrenia. Substance.* Minneapolis: University of Minnesota Press. https://doi.org/10.2307/3684887

Del Pra', A. (2006). Giovani Italiani a Berlino: Nuove Forme Di Mobilità Europea. *Altreitalie*, 33, 103–26.

De Stefano, V. (2016). The Rise of the «Just-in-Time Workforce»: On-Demand Work, Crowdwork and Labour Protection in the «Gig Economy». *Comparative Labour Law & Policy Journal*, 37(3). 471–504.

DESTATIS. (2020). *Migration & Integration.* Wiesbaden: Statistisches Bundesamt. https://www.destatis.de

Díaz-Parra, I., Jover, J., & Roca, B. (2017). Del 15M al Giro Electoralista. Proyectos Espaciales y Fetiches Políticos en las Estrategias de Acción Colectiva. *Cuadernos Geográficos*, 56(1), 344–364.

Di Falco, Salvatore, and Erwin Bulte. 2011. A Dark Side of Social Capital? Kinship, Consumption, and Savings. *Journal of Development Studies* 47 (8): 1128–51. doi:10.1080/00220388.2010.514328

Espai en Blanc. (2008). *Luchas Autónomas en los Años Setenta. Del Antagonismo Obrero al Malestar Social.* Madrid: Traficantes de Sueños.

Eurostat. (2020). *Database Eurostat.* European Commission. Retrieved from http://ec.europa.eu/eurostat/data/database

Faist, T. (2000). Transnationalization in International Migration: Implications for the Study of Citizenship and Culture. *Ethnic and Racial Studies*, 23(2), 189–222. https://doi.org/10.1080/014198700329024

Faist, T. (2014). *Brokerage in Cross-Border Migration: From Networks to Social Mechanisms.* Bielefeld: COMCAD.

Faist, T. (2019). *The Transnationalized Social Question. Migration and the Politics of Social Inequalities in the Twenty-First Century.* Oxford: Oxford University Press.

Favell, A. (2008). *Eurostars and Eurocities.* Oxford. Oxford: Blackwell Publishing.

Favell, A., & Recchi, E. (2009). *Pioneers of European Integration: Citizenship and Mobility in the EU.* Cheltenham: El Colegio de la Frontera Nord.

Fernandes, S. (2016). Access to Social Benefits for EU Mobile Citizens: 'Tourism' or Myth? 168. Policy Paper.

Fine, J. (2006). *Worker Centers: Organizing at the Edge of the Dream.* Ithaca: Cornell University Press.

Flesher-Fominaya, C. (2015) Debunking Spontaneity: Spain's 15-M/Indignados as Autonomous Movement. *Social Movement Studies*, 14(2), 142–163.

Florido, D., Roca, B., & Gutierrez, J. L. (2013). Tightening the Screws. Autonomy, Collective Action and Violence in the Shipyard of Puerto Real During the Second Shipbuilding Restructuring. *Anthropological Quarterly*, 86(3), 891–921.

Graeber, D. (2009). *Direct Action: An Ethnography.* Oakland: AK Press.

Ghimis, A., Lazarowicz, A., & Pascouau, Y. (2014). Stigmatisation of EU Mobile Citizens: A Ticking Time Bomb for the European Project. Brussels. Retrieved from http://www.epc.eu/documents/uploads/pub_4096_stigmatisation_of_eu_mobile_citizens.pdf

Goldschmidt, T. (2015). Anti-Immigrant Sentiment and Majority Support for Three Types of Welfare. *European Societies*, 17(5), 620–52. https://doi.org/10.1080/14616696.2015.1088959

Grappi, G. (2017). *Logistica*. Roma: Ediesse.

Grohmann, R. (2015). Faça o Que Você Ama ? O Consumo Do Trabalho Adjetivado e a Startup 99Jobs. In *Comunicon2015*. Sao Paulo.

Howcroft, D., & Bergvall-Kåreborn, B. (2018). A Typology of Crowdwork Platforms. *Work, Employment and Society*. https://doi.org/10.1177/0950017018760136

ILO. (1999). Migrant Workers, Report III(1B), 87h Internationa Labour Conference. Geneve.

Juventud Sin Futuro. (2011). *Juventud Sin Futuro*. Barcelona: Icaria.

Katsiaficas, G. N. (2006). *The Subversion of Politics: European Autonomous Social Movements and the Decolonization of Everyday Life*. Chico, CA: AK Press.

Katz, B., Noring, L., & Garrelts, N. (2016). *Cities and Refugees—The German Experience*. Washington DC.

King, R., Lulle, A., Conti,F., & Mueller, D. (2016). Eurocity London: A Qualitative Comparison of Graduate Migration from Germany, Italy and Latvia. *Comparative Migration Studies*, 4(1), 3. https://doi.org/10.1186/s40878-016-0023-1

Kunda, G. (1992). *Engineering Culture*. Philadelphia: Temple University Press.

Lafleur, Jean-Michel, and Mikolaj Stanek, eds. 2017. *South-North Migration of EU Citizens in Times of Crisis*. Springer.

Landau, F. (2016). Articulations in Berlin's Independent Art Scene: On New Collective Actors in the Art Field. *International Journal of Sociology and Social Policy*, 36(9/10), 596–612. https://doi.org/10.1108/IJSSP-11-2015-0129

Langley, P., & Leyshon, A. (2017). Platform Capitalism: The Intermediation and Capitalization of Digital Economic Circulation. *Finance and Society*, 3(1), 11–31. https://doi.org10.2218/finsoc.v3i1.1936

Levitt, P., & Schiller, N. G. (2004). Conceptualizing Simultaneity: Social Field on Society. *International Migration Review*, 38(3), 1002–39.

Lillie, N., & Simola, A. (2016). The Crisis of Free Movement in the European Union. *Mondi Migranti*, 3, 7–20.

Martín-Díaz, E. (2006). De Las Migraciones Del Fordismo a Las Migraciones de La Globalización. Europa: 1960–2005. *Africa e Mediterráneo*, 54, 29–35.

Martin-Diaz, E., & Roca, E. (2017). Spanish Migrations to Europe: From the Fordist Model to the Flexible Economy. *Journal of Mediterranean Studies*, 26(2), 189–207.

Martínez Lucio, M., & Perrett, R. (2009). Meanings and Dilemmas in Community Unionism. *Work, Employment and Society*, 23(4), 693–710. https://doi.org/10.1177/0950017009344916

Martiniello, M., & Lafleur, J. M. (2008). Towards a Transatlantic Dialogue in the Study of Immigrant Political Transnationalism. *Ethnic and Racial Studies*, 31(4), 645–63. https://doi.org/10.1080/01419870701784471

McAlevey, J. (2014). *Raising Expectations (and Raising Hell). My Decade Fighting for the Labor Movement*. New York/London: Verso.

Milkman, R. (2000). *Organizing Immigrants : The Challenge for Unions in Contemporary California*. ILR Press.

Ness, I. (2005). *Immigrants, Unions, and the New US Labor Movement*. Philadelphia: Temple University Press.

OECD. 2018. *OECD.Stat*. OECD.

Osservatorio degli Italiani a Berlino. (2015). Web Page. Retrieved from https://osservatoriodegliitalianiaberlino.com/

Østergaard-Nielsen, E. (2003). The Politics of Migrants' Transnational Political Practices. *International Migration Review*, 37(3), 760–86. https://doi-org/01989183/03/3703.0143

Oswalt, M. M. (2016). Improvisational Unionism. *California Law Review*, 104(3), 597–670.

Phillimore, J., Bradby, H., Knecht, M., Padilla, B., & Pemberton, S. (2019). Bricolage as Conceptual Tool for Understanding Access to Healthcare in Superdiverse Populations. *Social Theory and Health*, 7(2), 231–252.

Piore, M. J. (1979). *Birds of Passage: Migrant Labour and Industrial Society*. Cambridge: Cambridge University Press.

Raffini, L. (2014). Quando La Generazione Erasmus Incontra La Generazione Precaria. La Mobilità Transnazionale Dei Giovani Italiani e Spagnoli. *OBETS. Revista de Ciencias Sociales*, 9:, 139–65. https://doi.org/10.14198/OBETS2014.9.1.05

Recchi, E. (2014). Pathways to European Identity Formation: A Tale of Two Models. *Innovation: The European Journal of Social Science Research*, 27(2), 119–33. https://doi.org/10.1080/13511610.2013.873709

Recchi, E. (2015). *Mobile Europe : The Theory and Practice of Free Movement in the EU*. London: Palgrave Macmillan.

Roca, B. (2014). Izquierda Radical, Sindicalismo y Acción Colectiva en Andalucía (1976–2012). *Cuadernos de Relaciones Laborales* 32 (2): 439–468.

Roca, B., Martín-Díaz, E., & Díaz-Parra, I. (2017). *Challenging Austerity. Radical Left and Social Movements in the South of Europe*. London/New York: Routledge.

Roca, B., & Díaz-Parra, I. (2017). Blurring the Borders between Old and New Social Movements: The M15 Movement and the Radical Unions in Spain. *Mediterránean Politics*, 22(2), 218–37.

Roca, B., & Martín-Díaz, E. (2017). Solidarity Networks of Spanish Migrants in the UK and Germany: The Emergence of Interstitial Trade Unionism. *Critical Sociology*, 43(7–8), 1197–1212. https://doi.org/10.1177/0896920516645659

Romero, F. (2001). L'emigrazione Operaia in Europa. In P. Bevilacqua, A. De Clementi, & E. Franzina (Eds.), *Storia Dell'emigrazione Italiana. Vol I - Partenze*, (pp. 397–414). Roma: Donzelli.

Sanz, M. (2016). Organizándonos en el Exilio Económico. *Laberinto*, 46, 47–55.

Sassen, S. (1998). *Globalization and Its Discontents. Essay on the New Mobility of People and Money*. New York: The New Press.

Tassinari, A, & Maccarrone, V. (2017). The Mobilisation of Gig Economy Couriers in Italy. *Transfer: European Review of Labour and Research*, 23(3), 353–57. https://doi.org/10.1177/1024258917713846

Van Mol, C. (2013). Intra-European Student Mobility and European Identity: A Successful Marriage? *Population, Space and Place*, 19, 209–22. http://onlinelibrary.wiley.com/doi/10.1002/psp.1752/full

Van der Waal, J., Achterberg, P., Houtman, D., de Koster, W., & Manevska, K. (2010). 'Some Are More Equal than Others': Economic Egalitarianism and Welfare Chauvinism in the Netherlands. *Journal of European Social Policy*, 20(4), 350–63. https://doi.org/10.1177/0958928710374376

CHAPTER 2

Community through Corporatisation? The Case of Spanish Nurses in the German Care Industry

Mark Bergfeld

1   Introduction

In the wake of the crisis in Spain, German private care companies have been recruiting Spanish nurses to work as care workers for private companies, clinics and care homes in Germany. This study analyzes how Spanish nurses are recruited into the German care regime, how employers seek to save labor costs by employing them, and the way in which this situation produces the conditions for Spanish workers' organisation in the German care sector. Previous studies have highlighted migrant care workers' capacity for self-organisation and trade unions' responses to care work migration (Hardy, Eldring, and Schulten 2012; Schilliger 2016). This study aims to show how the "corporatisation of care" (on which more below) creates the conditions for worker solidarity and organisation, locates where solidarity and organisation can potentially arise within the care chain and what it means for the transformation of social relationships. In doing so, this study seeks to contribute to the debates around the commodification of care, care chains and corporate care. In conclusion, this study finds that solidarity and community-building between care workers and care-users, as well as carers of different origins is obstructed through different managerial mechanisms; yet I maintain that these mechanisms can produce new forms of workers' organisation among Spanish migrant care workers themselves.

In her article, *Social Politics and the Commodification of Care*, Clare Ungerson (1997) questions whether the commodification of the care relationship vis-à-vis payments to both caregiver and care-user facilitates "post-traditional" forms of (micro-)solidarity and community, as Adalbert Evers had argued elsewhere (Evers, 1994). According to Evers, these forms of (micro-)solidarity and community lie beyond "the polarities of state, family, and market", "consumerist individualism" and "service-oriented collectivism" (Ungerson, 1997, p. 377). Writing at a time when the commodification of care manifested itself in the process of moving from the remit of "unpaid work" to "paid work", Ungerson rejects the assumption that social relationships would move into "a single and particular direction". It remains open whether the commodification of care work can engender both privatisation and individualism, as well as new forms of (micro-)solidarity and community. Clare Ungerson writes:

> It seems to me that the social, political, and economic contexts in which payments for care operate and the way in which payments for care are themselves organised are just as likely to transform relationships as the existence of the payments themselves (Ungerson, 1997, p. 377).

The changes to the social, political and economic contexts are likely to change the relationship between care-giver and care-user, in as much as the existence of payments creates a transactional relationship. As care work moves into the remit of "paid work", it raises the question whether these changes only affect the care-giver-user relationship, or whether carers – now considered workers – start to engage in community-building and solidarity on an occupational basis.

As the care context has changed within the last 15 years, a growing body of research emphasises the exploitative labor relations and working conditions in care work (Williams, 2010; Bauer & Osterle, 2013). Care work has not only moved from the remit of "unpaid work" to "paid work" but has been outsourced to migrants from poorer countries, creating what authors refer to as a "global care chain" or "nanny chain" (Hochschild, 2000; Murphy, 2014). For the purposes of this study, I will focus on the former, in which individuals from poorer countries frequently choose to become health care professionals because of the migration possibilities that the career offers (Connell 2008, 2). Insofar as that states stand in competition with one another to attract workers, employment regimes are shaped and shape the global care chain and care work migration (Glinos, 2015; Lutz & Palenga-Möllenbeck, 2012, p. 29; Schellinger, 2015). Such care work migration engenders a "care drain" in migrants' sending countries as well as a "brain gain" in receiving countries regardless of whether the state follows state-led, market-led policies or a mix of the two (Fedyuk, Bartha, & Zentai, 2014; Lutz & Palenga-Möllenbeck, 2012). Accepting that inequities are reproduced within the care chain, Glinos's research suggests that the mobility of healthcare professionals and care workers within the European Union disproportionately benefits wealthier EU member states, despite there being positive and negative effects for sending and destination countries alike (Glinos, 2015).

Nicola Yeates, amongst others, has criticised this care chain analysis and the global commodity chain framework from a feminist perspective. She posits that such a chain analysis requires further theorisation and gendering as well as empirical work to distinguish it from the economic determinism of the global commodity chain. While it is a valid analytical tool to analyze the globalisation-migration-care nexus, it reduces care work to production of goods for market consumption and does not account for the service nature of this type of work as well as omitting gender concerns. She draws attention to the diversity and specificity of migrant workers and the care contexts, as well as the unpaid labor that goes into care work (Yeates, 2005a; Yeates, 2005b).

The debate on global care chains helps one to understand the transformation of the social, political, and economic context, which Clare Ungerson foreshadowed in 1997. It is in this context that the "corporatisation of care" can make a useful theoretical contribution.[1] Hence, the question whether the pervasiveness of such business rationale in care provision prompts the conditions for the development of worker agency and solidarity.

In answering this question this study draws on 30 semi-structured interviews with three groups of people: Spanish nurses, members of the Spanish activist group Grupo Accion Sindical (GAS), and trade union staff. I recruited the Spanish nurses by joining a Facebook group that resembles a professional association and through contacts with the GAS. I chose to interview trade union staff based on whether they had directly worked with Spanish nurses or indirectly with the GAS. I drew on interviews from activists of the GAS because they organise, represent, and provide mutual aid to fellow Spanish-speakers in Germany. The interviews were conducted in German and English between September 2015 and January 2016. The interviews were based on an interview guide, which contained the following topics: the workplace, the community, discrimination, power and relationship with trade unions. The quotes used in this paper have been translated from German into English by myself and then have been translated back again into German to see whether it matched. This method allows me to establish that these are accurate in form and content and wholly represent what the interviewee told me at the time of the interview. The interviews were transcribed and coded per new emergent themes (reason to migrate, labor movement in sending countries, agency work, interns, deskilling, language, racism and discrimination) in NVIVO.

2   The German-Spanish Care Context

Germany's labor shortage facilitates corporate and business-like approaches to the recruitment of foreign nurses and care workers. Following World War II,

---

1   Sara Farris and Sabrina Marchetti have argued that the corporatisation of care manifests itself in both for-profit and non-profit care providing contexts insofar as they employ management and business rationales primarily through saving on labor costs and increasing productivity.

the German state imported Korean nurses to fill the labor shortage in the health sector (Choe and Daheim, 1987). At present, the German government has a bilateral trade deal with the Philippines – a country which 'produces' care workers and nurses for the global market – and continues to recruit care workers and nurses with the assistance of its development agency (GIZ) in 'Third States' such as Vietnam and Tunisia (Güllemann & von Borries, 2012; Ramm & Güllemann, 2013). Other programs such as these are in hiatus: the costs of devising, planning, and running them are substantial yet they have not been able to tackle Germany's shortage of skilled care workers and health personnel. As inequities in the care chain have led to insufficient numbers of health and care workers in many regions of the Global South, the World Health Organisation's (WHO) new regulatory framework recommends equitable and sustainable recruitment practices of care and health personnel (WHO, 2010). Consequently, private care companies and recruitment agencies have refocused on recruitment within the European Union where these regulatory framework agreements are over-ridden by the European Union's principle of freedom of movement for services and labor.

Germany's insistence on informal and private provision as well as the lack of state control of care services created an unregulated market and a growth of private for-profit providers since the 1990s (Anderson, 2012, p. 140). Before that, large non-profit welfare organisations associated with the Catholic/Protestant Churches and other charitable organisations were responsible for long-term elderly care provision with local municipalities overseeing and monitoring their work (Theobald, 2012a). Through the introduction of a long-term care insurance (LTCI) system,[2] the state pursued the goal of increasing efficiency of care provision, with measurable standards, market mechanisms and competition being introduced into long-term care under the guise of personal choice (Winkelmann, Rodrigues, & Leichsenring, 2014, p. 2–3). At present, private for-profit and not-for-profit providers compete in a market primarily by saving on labor costs (Theobald, 2012b; Winkelmann, Rodrigues, & Leichsenring, 2014). Germany's care regime has been subject to both commodification and corporatisation, insofar as care work has moved from the remit of unpaid work to paid work, and business rationality shapes different care actors. According to

---

[2] Helmut Kohl and his government introduced the German long term care insurance in January 1995. It is part of the social security system in Germany and makes financial provision for long-term care. The insurance covers some part of home and residential care costs for sick or old people in need for the duration of up to six months. Consequently, this person is not dependent on social assistance but can live an independent and self-determined life under the given circumstances.

Juliane Winkelmann et al., (2014, p. 7) this has a "positive effect" on prices of private providers, yet their study does not consider the specific effects on a predominantly female and migrant workforce.

At present, an estimated 115,000–300,000 Eastern European carers work in Germany. Many of them are recruited by international placement and recruitment agencies and work without professional recognition or a fixed contract, twenty-four hours on call (Knaebel, 2015; Wilde, 2014; Kniejska, 2014). Since the enlargement of the European Union (EU) in 2004, employers use these legal loopholes to pay below the minimum wage, pay them less than German workers and do not pay social security or insurance contributions by having them work in bogus self-employment (Ver.di, 2011). This has been possible because A8-citizens from Eastern Europe (Poland, Romania, Bulgaria etc.) did not have access to the German labor market following the EU enlargement and circumvented the ban by working as posted workers or illegal workers in both private homes and care homes for three months on a rotation basis (Lutz & Palenga-Möllenbeck, 2010; Goździak, 2016; Leiber & Rossow, 2016). Helma Lutz and Ewa Pallenga-Möllenbeck show that this grey market and the continued dependence on migrant labor constitutes "an integral part of German welfare state policies" (Lutz & Palenga-Möllenbeck, 2010, p. 419; Lutz & Palenga-Möllenbeck, 2012, p. 30), possibly explaining why the German government continues to ignore these practices.

Despite these measures, Germany continues to experience a shortage of care workers. Germany's labor shortage amounts to 70,000 full-time care workers and a total of 162,000 care workers, with the current unemployed worker to open vacancy ratio standing at 38/100 (Bertelsmann-Stiftung, 2015). The services union ver.di - the main union representing workers in care - meanwhile, claims that more than 50,000 jobs have been slashed in the sector since 1997 (Ver.di, 2015), highlighting how private care companies, public hospitals and other providers have increased labor productivity and increased margins by saving in labor costs. A government report states that this has led to a significant number of workers deciding to work part-time or leave the job altogether (Afentakis, 2009). While demographic changes account for part of this trend the German trade union confederation's study on care underlines that it cannot be reduced to this (DGB, 2012). Accordingly, labor conditions account for a significant part of the labor shortage as 92 percent of care workers identify with their job but only 3 percent believe their working conditions are good; 79 per cent of care workers think that they are unfairly remunerated and 20 percent believe that they will be able to keep on working until retirement age.

The state-facilitated recruitment of Spanish nurses shows the extent to which Germany's care regime is shaped by corporate logic. Through the theoretical framework of the care chain one can see how inequities are reproduced in the care work migration from Spain to Germany. As Eastern European care workers and bilateral agreements with Third States have not been effective in tackling the care sector's labor shortage, private care companies look to crisis-ridden countries elsewhere within the European Union. Spain has an unemployment rate of 25 per cent and the budget for its public health care system has been cut by 13 per cent(Legido-Quigley et al., 2013), so its university-educated nurses have been recruited to come and work in Germany. While there are no definite numbers on this form of migration (Faraco Blanco et al., 2015; Barslund & Busse, 2014), this policy has been endorsed by the EU, and the respective German and Spanish governments. EU-led initiatives such as *MobiPro-EU* have moved from tackling the financial barriers involved in European mobility to targeting qualified Spanish workers (Barslund & Busse, 2014, p. 122–23). German chancellor Angela Merkel and Finance Minister Wolfgang Schäuble have argued that Spanish youth unemployment will only be solved if young people are willing to move to Germany (Evans, 2013). The Spanish Minister for Employment and Social Security Fatima Bañez has labelled the current wave of emigration as *movilidad exterior* (exterior mobility), claiming that these young people have displayed the "ability and willingness to be mobile, to master foreign languages and expand their professional horizons. This can never be considered a negative phenomenon [*own translation*]." (*quoted in* Galindo, 2014).

3 The Recruitment of Spanish Nurses

Commercial recruitment practices epitomise the extent to which Germany's care system is guided by a business rationale. There are two main routes through which Spanish nurses enter the German care industry and labor market: They either are recruited by private clinics, care homes, commercial recruitment agencies or, they receive stipends from one of several EU-state-financed projects and web platforms set up to broker jobs for Spanish qualified workers abroad. By tailoring the message directly to Spanish care workers and nurses need for work, commercial agencies and German care companies can encourage them to migrate to Germany despite them not being able to speak German. The following example illustrates care companies' use of business practices to recruit care workers.

> I saw it on public television. Something about this clinic. And then I looked a bit more and got in touch. I applied online. In many cities in Germany: Freiburg, Hamburg etc. Also in London, not only Germany.

Even in Brighton. The first ones who answered was this clinic. After that there was a job interview in Spain. They talked a bit superficially about the project and then we immediately started to work.

The use of television commercials to recruit Spanish qualified workers such as this nurse is so widespread that it even has been featured in the Spanish mainstream film *Perdiendo El Norte* (engl. *Off course*), in which an engineer and a business graduate migrate to Berlin after seeing an advert on television for highly qualified jobs but end up working in a Turkish falafel shop. Other interviewees recount being recruited online by targeted Facebook ads in Spanish featuring detailed information about starting salaries and income. Time and time again, Spanish nurses emphasised that the German language constitutes a mobility barrier and that they would have preferred to work in the UK. But one of the reasons why Spanish nurses decide to migrate to Germany is the quick reply they receive from these agencies. This is repeated across the interviews. Through using private recruitment companies and agencies, clinics advertising at universities, television ads and social media and a high and fast response rate to applications they are able to generate a sense of German efficiency and professionalism which corresponds to Spanish nurses' need for a job. One Spanish nurse received a call for a job interview in Britain once they had already started their job in Germany.

For Spanish nurses, commercial web platforms and agencies are indistinguishable from platforms such as EURES - the European Commission's Job Mobility Portal - as they advertise the same kind of jobs and draw on official state discourses on migration. By employing signifiers such as, "Europe", "EU", "work and travel", "job of my life", *Euro Rail, Erasmus*, or "mobility" they inspire a sense of trustworthiness in the agency and the jobs on offer. Such discourses appeal to the European outlook of young Spanish nurses, as well as serve the Spanish and German governments' agenda of solving youth unemployment through emigration and produce a flexible workforce.

By looking at a state-led initiative and what jobs are advertised, we can see how pervasive business practices have become. A Spanish nurse from Murcia signed up to work in Germany via *Job of my life*, an online platform launched by the German Federal Employment Agency (BA) and German government. Only once she arrived she discovered that she would be working below her skill-level as a care assistant in a staffing agency in the Hannover area. This was a distant world from when her father had come to work in Germany as a guest worker in the 1970s, as she had to pay for her own air travel to Germany, the first three months of rent and even the transport to move between different care homes for work.

Private care companies specializing in 24-hour mobile care use deceptive tactics to recruit Spanish care workers to fill the German labor and care shortage. An activist from the Grupo Accion Sindical (GAS) which organises Spanish care workers recounts one company's recruitment practices:

> [This company] organises informational events in Spain and they also have a website which no longer exists because they branded it "work and travel". The idea was that you can get to know different German cities and you can work flexibly in different deployments: In Munich, the beautiful city! Berlin, the party city! Hamburg! And the 'work and travel'-part consists in the fact that you have an apartment in Berlin but you work in a small village in the Ruhr area, after that a week in Berlin, then a week in Brandenburg, then two weeks in Berlin, and then three weeks in a small village in Bavaria. That's what they call "Work and Travel". Total flexibility, so to speak.

These recruitment practices are the product of the labor shortage and the primacy of private care provision. They are facilitated by the EU as well as the discourse of Spanish and German governments on migration, who present recruitment as a way of solving the unemployment crisis. The question is whether such pervasive business practices on behalf of state-led initiatives and private companies engender the conditions for worker solidarity and community-building.

These interviews suggest that these recruitment practices can foster community and worker solidarity insofar as they engender a common experience of migration. The commercial recruitment practice plays a role in creating bonds of solidarity between different Spanish workers. As one interviewee recounts:

> We were a group but we didn't know each other. We were 30 nurses, we arrived at the same time. We needed to stay in touch because [the company] didn't do anything for us once we arrived.

Working in a care home alongside 30 other Spanish nurses, the interviewee states: "we needed to stay in touch". This is not so much a choice as a product of not being given adequate preparation before coming to Germany. It is facilitated by workers' common language being Spanish and their lack of German. This form of community and solidarity is based on the common experience of commercial recruitment and a collective experience of migration. As we will see in the following section, it does not, however, imply solidarity with German co-workers or care-users.

4   Saving Labor Costs

Sara Farris and Sabrina Marchetti (2016) argue that the corporatisation of care primarily occurs through the application of business logics to care management and the business imperatives of saving on labor costs. In the case under focus here, this is achieved in two ways: Employers produce difference between groups of workers by employing Spanish nurses on lower wages despite having a university-degree and German co-workers only having vocational training. Furthermore, they externalise the costs associated with the reproduction of labor power. The author's interviews, various newspaper articles, union reports (Kunkel, 2015; Stern, 2014; Kellner, 2013; Nessler, 2015) show that German employers depend on paying foreign nurses less, yet force them to work the same unsociable hours and perform the same tasks as fully qualified care workers. One care worker states that "we do the same work. Here in Germany carers and care assistants do the same". However, when it is convenient, employers and co-workers point out that they are care assistants or interns and task them with non-contractual work, including mopping floors, cooking meals or taking dogs for walk.

As care companies prioritise early entry into the labor market, Spanish nurses enter workplaces as interns or care assistants with insufficient German skills. The company provides them with basic language training for two hours a week with a private tutor, with one nurse reporting that the company owner's spouse teaches them German in their breaks. One care worker waited six months to have his first German language class and at another care company "there are people that continue to wait for their B2 course for two and a half years", continuously working as care assistants. According to another interviewee, they are often only given three to six months to pass their German Level B2 test, which allows them to gain their professional recognition. If they fail, they remain employed as care assistants or interns.

These labor-cost saving mechanisms are, of course, to the detriment of careworker and care-user alike. "We couldn't understand anything and we work with people…not with plants or so", a Spanish nurse reports. Others reiterate this point in a different way:

> […] I'm a bit sad for these people, the patients. I can't do everything I can actually do. And I see it. These people can't communicate well with us because we don't speak German well enough. That makes it stressful.

Corporate care further undermines the emergence of community and solidarity between care-user and care-worker. It is not the payment which shapes the relationship between care-user and care-worker, but rather the fact that they cannot communicate. Occurrences of community and solidarity between patients and staff were not observed or recorded in interviews. Furthermore, the interviews reveal that companies seemingly do not want to teach their Spanish staff German, as they appear to be more interested in saving labor costs. Spanish nurses' lack of German means that they cannot even communicate with the care-user in an adequate fashion. While the interviews indicate that the Spanish nurses feel for the care-users and patients, their situation of moving between different care homes, working around the clock and being isolated from other colleagues contributes to care workers' inability to build bonds of solidarity with care-users. Another factor which obstructs community-building and solidarity between care-users and care-worker is the way in which different companies (recruitment agency, private company, staffing agency) mediate the relationship. Thus, the corporatisation of care does not only blur the lines in regards to the employment relationship, but also affects the care-users' ability to build a connection with a care-worker, ultimately undermining the very task of care.

This leads to a sense of frustration because it clashes with their expectation of care work transmitted through their university studies.

> A1: We think we have one of the best university studies in care work in Spain. But yeah, we knew about it. We came here and knew that we might have to wash a patient but not clean floors.
> B2: Yes, basic care such as washing, hygiene. Normally, that's done
> A1: Normally, you don't have to do that.
> B2: Only the care assistants and helpers do that in Spain

Another care worker confirms this:

> I didn't know what work would be like here in Germany. [...]. In Spain, we do more technical work, here it's more care. More maintenance, more washing, more serving food and make the bed. We don't do any of these tasks in Spain. [...]. Here it is an apprenticeship, in Spain you go to university. But I don't feel like I'm more qualified than the Germans. No. I must understand that it's different and that there are things I can't do now. If that's not clear in your head, you can't work well and you feel terrible.

By referring to her university education, she reveals that she expects more from her work. The same applies to the other two nurses above. The interviewee previously worked as a nurse in a Spanish public hospital. Now she finds herself in a 24-hour mobile care service where she is employed to fill labor shortages in up to five care homes a week. As care work in Germany and Spain differ, she gives them the labels "technical" for Spain and "care" for Germany, indicating that not only the institutional setting differs but also the national context in which care is provided and the labor process as such. In other words, particular tasks are deemed care tasks in Germany are considered auxiliary tasks in Spain. Despite freedom of movement in the EU, different educational and professional standards apply along the care chain. Thus, Spanish care workers' labor process is marked by them losing their professional recognition and their autonomy. The corporatisation of care contributes to the devaluing of labor and care, as it treats labor like any other input into the care chain.

The question is whether occupying this position within the care chain facilitates solidarity and community within the workplace. Commenting on the issue, one ver.di trade union secretary states the following.

> They didn't somehow say 'we have a better qualification' but they wanted to be treated as equals. That was their central theme. But I think it played a role that their education and qualifications are academic.

Thus, their university education is used to demand equal treatment and at the same time leveraged to receive language classes. One of the interviewees and her Spanish colleagues collectively approached management and demanded language classes which they refused. Another group of care workers approached their labor union in Spain which in turn contacted the Spanish Labor Ministry. Others approached the Grupo Accion Sindical (GAS), a group of migrant activists associated with 15M movement, to assist them in their demand for language classes. However, all the routes facilitate separate organisation rather than solidarity and community-building with care-users or co-workers as the national context, the institutional setting and their experience of the labor process come to dominate.

German care companies depend on producing difference between different groups of workers in the workplace, by having Spanish care workers work below their education and skill-level in Germany and paying them less than their German colleagues.

Further, management fosters divisions between groups of foreign and non-foreign workers to manage the workforce. This undermines the prospect of community-building and solidarity between care workers of different origin. An interviewee recalls:

> On some stations[German] colleagues were mean to the foreign ones because they see 30 foreign new colleagues arrive. These people didn't want to work with foreigners - with the new ones - or train them because

it's difficult. Some were just really mean. [...]. So, I asked 'can I do something?' 'No, but you can mop the floor'....*That was nice of them*...But at the beginning you can't do anything, so you do it.

The interviewee describes a division between German and Spanish care workers - those who are new on the job and those who have been already working there - within their workplace. In other cases, German co-workers do not distribute work tasks, insult them as "lazy Spanish" and make them perform non-contractual work such as mopping the floors. This produces resentment between the two groups and forecloses the possibility of solidarity. Management, on the other hand, creates a division of labor by using Spanish care workers to fill labor shortages in partner clinics, care homes or domestic services, jobs which German workers refuse to do.

A ver.di trade union organiser says: "That became part of the conflict because the companies sent them to the places where the German colleagues didn't want to go either".

A Spanish care worker recounts:

For example, I had my shifts scheduled for three days and then I had planned a day off. They said: 'No, you got to work.' At the beginning, I couldn't believe that this is normal. [...]. I worked in four or five different elderly care homes in a month without knowing the city, without knowing anything. [...]. [The people you work with], they're not your real colleagues because you're outside of the company. You come from a different company. You're there for a day and then tomorrow you're elsewhere. You can't build any relationships or contacts.

This division of labor in the company serves the purpose of filling staff shortages, as well as isolating Spanish workers from one another.

Companies' high demand for mobile domestic work and the lack of a geographically fixed workplace leads to an individualised experience of work and, consequently, produces an individualised workforce. The fact that the nurse says "they're not your real colleagues" displays the lack of community and collegiality between workers of different origin, which corporate care comes to depend on. As employers can draw on a steady supply of workers who will perform these tasks, work those jobs at the same or lower wage, community and solidarity become difficult to construct within the workplace. Consequently, Spanish nurses are inhibited from building sustainable contacts and collegial relationships with German co-workers, which might bring them into discussions over pay, conditions or possibly a union. One can argue that the division of labor within private companies and the different experiences of work rule out the potential of spontaneous manifestations of worker solidarity against the employer.

5 The Externalisation of Costs

Private companies save labor costs by passing on the costs of reproducing labor power to the Spanish state or the individual Spanish nurse. Thus, inequalities are reproduced both up- and downstream within the care chain.

Based on the care chain analysis, one can argue that labor costs are externalised upstream to the Spanish state insofar that the Spanish state and respective individuals bear the costs associated with training, education and language. This chimes with the view that:

> reproduction costs, social risks, and the responsibility for investing in human capital are shifted from the receiving to the sending countries and from society as a whole to the individual (Lutz & Palenga-Möllenbeck, 2012, p. 30).

The German state and the private care companies, which employ Spanish nurses depend on Spanish universities to educate and train Spanish nurses. Furthermore, private companies receive money from the state, the European Union or European Social Fund so that Spanish nurses can learn German and work as fully recognised nurses in Germany. Private companies, though, externalise the costs associated with learning German on to the individual. A nurse working at a staffing agency recounts that she received money for a language course through the EU-financed project *Job of my life* while at the same time the company claimed money from the European Union for German language training. In turn, the Spanish healthcare and care system experience a "brain drain" and "care drain", reproducing inequities and inequalities in the care chain. The German state thus saves costs by not paying for vocational training and companies save money by employing qualified nurses as care workers below their skill and qualification level and pay them less than German workers.

The inequalities reproduced in the care chain and carer migration are felt most strongly by those who have migrated to Germany as the company demands that nurses pay a penalty fee in case of a breach of her work contract. So, the company saves money twice. Once, by receiving money from the European Social Fund to train workers and, secondly, by including it as a penalty fee in the contract in the likelihood that employees breach the contract. In doing so, employers undermine workers' labour mobility power and the opportunity of moving on to better jobs, which has been a strategy used by many workers in the sector as the cited government report above documents. The penalty fee shows that employers find a strategy necessary to prevent workers from leaving their jobs. One could argue that better working conditions and high pay could stop care workers from leaving. However, this would mean that private care homes and companies would not be competitive against forms of informal provision. The penalty fee is a means to discourage the Spanish workforce from leaving in the face of difficult labor conditions and unequal treatment. It epitomises another way employers isolate Spanish workers, yet as discussed in the final section it also has galvanised Spanish care workers to organise for their rights, as having a penalty fee in one's contract is not an isolated occurrence. The case of a nurse working in Hamburg epitomises this:

The company argues they paid for a German course, coaching and a psychologist which he never made use of. They asked for 4,950 euros in case he left his job. In other cases, companies demanded up to 8,000 euros. This systematic externalisation of costs takes place despite the EU stipends covering the costs and the move to Germany.

> For example, how much does my professional recognition cost? 250 euros. Paid by the stipend. My B2 language course was financed by the European Social Fund. And the company claims that they paid 2000 euros for the course. My question is why should I pay them 2000 euros if they never paid anything?

By externalising the costs associated with high labor turnover and labor shortage on to individual workers, companies save money. Inadvertently, we also see how the penalty fee creates the conditions among Spanish care workers to move beyond solidarity and community toward organisation.

6   From Community and Solidarity to Organisation

The previous sections show how corporate care seeks to undermine solidarity between care-user and careworker as well as care workers of different origin. Spanish nurses are not able to build community and solidarity with their German co-workers due to the division of labor at a workplace level and the hostility they face from German colleagues. This is exemplified by the fact that Spanish workers are not able to mobilise German or Polish workers despite working to organise with them through the ver.di union and distributing multilingual flyers, which address that they do not want to be played off against their co-workers. Neither did the author observe any indications of solidarity and community-building between care-users and workers as language skills are insufficient and staffing agencies and recruitment companies mediate the employment relationship. The business practices discussed above, though, do not only generate the basis for community and solidarity to emerge among Spanish care workers themselves, but also for worker organisation to emerge in the German care sector.

At a workplace level, Spanish nurses have engaged in a myriad of collective tactics to improve their working conditions. In one case, Spanish nurses collectively approached the company demanding language classes. As soon as they approached their employer he retaliated by firing the workers or reduced the number of hours. Arguably, this is a disproportionate response as workers wanted to improve their work, which one would think might fit with their employers' business goals. In another case, Spanish nurses started to organise dinners to discuss work-related issues. These would lead to the formulation of collective demands such as planned scheduling, so that workers could organise their work and free time. Again, one would think that this was in the interests of the private care company as it is a more efficient way to manage the workforce. Workers' letters and grievances to employers, management, the Spanish Labor Ministry and their professional associations at home were to no avail. While Spanish nurses develop collective demands, interviews reveal that they first and foremost want to leave their job. Given the penalty, individual flight is impossible. That is why many nurses decided to build pressure collectively and make "trouble" within the company so that employers would let them leave their jobs. This proved to be a successful tactic insofar as workers could leave the job without having to pay the penalty fee because employers were happy to no longer have them in the company. As Irene Glinos's research points out that return migration and a "cycle of brain gain, waste and drain" is the likely consequence if foreign trained health professionals are de-skilled, face inadequate working conditions and lack appropriate structures (Glinos, 2015, p. 1532).

The organisational forms that Spanish nurses choose underlines the extent to which their experiences as Spanish migrants needs to be featured in the analysis. To understand the work of the GAS and the Spanish nurses and their collaboration it is necessary to focus on forms of organisation which have emerged upstream in the care chain, as well as the failure of traditional forms of trade union representation within the care chain in Germany.

The GAS and Spanish nurses draw upon the collective experience of the 15M movement, which saw more than 200 towns and city squares occupied in

May 2011. In the wake of this movement, new forms of solidarity and organisation emerged in Spain's healthcare sector, with campaigning and direct action being taken against cuts and privatisation. In particular, the GAS draws on the activism and organisational forms of networks such as the *Marea Blanca* which moves between new forms of unionism and an open peer-to-peer network in which everyone is allowed to use the logo, name and identity (Gutierrez, 2014). Thus, activists who agree with the principles of the GAS can start their own group. Unlike the initial indignados protests, which rejected trade unions, health activists in Spain built alliances with traditional labor organisations as the UGT and CCOO (Stobart and Sans, 2012). The case of the GAS and Spanish nurses show that migrants can transport such forms of organisation into their new host society. My research shows collaboration with ver.di, as well as collaboration with the syndicalist Freie Arbeiter Union (FAU) and Spanish unions, which have an interest in maintaining a membership base among young people below the age of thirty-five. There is no evidence which suggests that the Marea Blanca in Spain has organised around the issue of care work migration. But groups such as the GAS attack the EU, Spanish and German government discourses on migration and mobility discussed earlier in this study. Spanish activist groups frame their migration as a collective process of being "kicked out", "in exile" or even "forced migration". These slogans are also confirmed in the stories of my interviewees, none of whom studied to become a nurse in order to migrate as John Connell (2008) might suggest. Instead, structural issues such as the cuts in health care and political situation explain their migration. It is on that basis that nurses and activists challenge the dominant discourses, and use their common experience of migration as a basis for collective organisation.

It is not only the dominant migration discourse they attack, but they also turn private companies' and recruitment agencies' practices on their head by placing targeted Facebook ads to Facebook users in Germany and Spain who post or mention anything related to nursing and care work. In doing so, they employ the very same corporate practices to organise care workers by which private care companies recruit Spanish nurses. On that basis, they built a contact list of 138 nurses affected by the penalty fee, and it resulted in two new groups being founded, both with the aim of organizing care workers.

The forms of organisation developed by the GAS and Spanish necessarily need to move beyond the traditional forms of servicing encountered in traditional trade unions due to their individualised experience of the labor process and the organisational weakness of trade unions in the sector. Workers' experiences with the works councils, which are not convened by the trade union but are elected by the entire workforce to represent their interests, illuminate the need for separate organisation:

A1: I tried to go to the works council. But all my colleagues told me it's better not to. Because he's from the company.[...]

B2: The works council's office is directly next to the employer's office. What are you going to do when he asks: 'What are you doing here? Do you want to discuss something with me?'. 'No, no. I'm just going next door.' 'What do you need to discuss with the works council?' That's what's going to happen. I haven't spoken to anyone from the works council.

A1: And then the works council representative will just tell the employer and manager: 'He said this, and this, this, this." Then I might as well tell him directly.

B2: I just don't trust the works council in my company so I have looked for different support.

Distrust of works councils and the lack of support from the trade union due to its organisational weakness leaves a space for GAS activists to step in an organise workers on a collective basis. As Jane Hardy et al. (Hardy, Eldring, & Schulten 2012, p. 354) highlight the union has prioritised the introduction of a statutory minimum wage for all care workers, possibly creating a further barrier to organizing workers in the care sector.

Their successes in improving terms and conditions at workplace level are limited: most Spanish nurses either have insufficient language skills or are not committed to staying with their employer, let alone in Germany.

This leads to problems for the GAS in convincing ver.di to invest resources into organizing this group of workers. Nonetheless, they have built sustainable relationships with responsible trade union organisers and embed themselves in wider campaigns for more care personnel in hospitals.

> But this is the thing, because the German model is so based on the *Betriebsrat* [*works council*], and so less based on unions, that when the union perceive there is nothing to do with the *Betriebsrat*, there is nothing to do in the clinic. All their activity goes through the *Betriebsrat*. If you can't access the *Betriebsrat*, there's nothing you can do. [...].

By connecting individual workers to the union, identifying conflicts that can be fought collectively, leafleting actions at care companies, the GAS provides a space to Spanish workers across different companies to group together and build community and worker solidarity under difficult circumstances. Thus far, the GAS fulfils a similar function to the Polish Church as a center of mobilisation for Polish nurses working in home care in Switzerland (Schilliger, 2016).

7 Conclusion

This chapter finds that the corporatisation of care in Germany is the product of the country's labor shortage. It manifests itself in the recruitment practices of private agencies and is facilitated by the EU, German and Spanish states' discourses on migration and mobility. These recruitment practices by state-led initiatives and private companies exacerbate inequities in the care chain, as companies rely on the Spanish state and individuals to bear the costs associated with education and training. In doing so, German care companies save costs.

Furthermore, this chapter has highlighted that corporate care practices seek to undermine solidarity and community between the care-user and careworker as well as care workers of different origins. The case of Spanish nurses exemplifies the wholesale commodification of care, and the shift from care-giver to care worker, which has consequences for the debates on the commodification of care (Ungerson, 2003; Ungerson, 1997). Solidarity and community between care-user and careworker are obstructed insofar as Spanish nurses are not given adequate language training to communicate with care-users. The insistence on Spanish nurses' early entry into the labor market and working below their level of qualification and skills highlights private care companies' primary motive of using Spanish nurses to save labor costs. In doing so, this study contributes to a better understanding of the mechanisms of labor exploitation and the working conditions of health and care workers. This study also reveals that management draws on German employees' hostility toward new Spanish care workers to control the workforce. These cost-saving mechanisms lead to unequal treatment. This situation is reinforced by creating a division of labor and tasks within the company, with Spanish workers performing the role of care assistant or intern and being used to fill labor shortages in mobile care or being given tasks that German workers are unwilling to do. This labor market segregation with immigrant women working in care services on sub-standard wages in jobs that native workers will not accept is also observed by Olena Fedyuk et al. (Fedyuk, Bartha, & Zentai, 2014, p. 2). However, in the case of Spanish nurses they are observable within the same workplace. These divisions obstruct a development of community across racial and national divides and means that Spanish nurses forge a sense of community only among themselves even though the squeeze on labor effects all workers. Thus, Clare Ungerson's emphasis on the care context and its changes remains an important pointer when analyzing the emergence of solidarity and community within the care sector.

Inadvertently, the very business practices discussed in the above sections create the basis for community and solidarity to emerge among Spanish nurses working for German private care companies. This chimes with Clare Ungerson's claim that solidarity and community are multi-directional. The commercial recruitment practices foster a mutual dependence on one another, creating bonds of solidarity and community. Spanish nurses' insufficient German skills means that they are used for similar jobs which are experienced as degrading and are subject to a loss of professional autonomy and professional recognition. This establishes a commonality between Spanish nurses. Management uses Spanish workers for the jobs that Germans refuse to do and draws on German workers' hostility to their Spanish colleagues in order to control the workforce; the result is that Spanish workers collectively demand equal treatment. But solidarity between the Spanish workers is primarily expressed through opposition to the penalty fee that prevents them leaving their jobs. It takes the organisational form of being organised in the Grupo de Accion Sindical which draws on forms of activism and trade unionism imported from Spain, as well as using communication techniques and messages to undermine the dominance of business in the sector. The lack of union representation and the complicity of works councils with management therefore opens the space for new forms of activism to emerge within the German care sector.

The forms of community and solidarity that emerge among Spanish nurses represent a challenge for unions as does the corporatisation of care itself. This research contributes to a better understanding of where labor unions and activist organisations can draw on already existing forms of solidarity and community up- and downstream in the care chain and potentially integrate them into their organizing and campaigning work.

References

Afentakis, A. (2009). Krankenpflege - Berufsbelastung Und Arbeitsbedingungen. *Statistisches Bundesamt, STAT Magazin,* 46, 56–59.

Anderson, A. (2012). Europe's Care Regimes and the Role of Migrant Care Workers Within Them. *Journal of Population Ageing,* 5(2), 135–46. https://doi.org/10.1007/s12062-012-9063-y

Barslund, M., & Busse, M. (2014). Too Much or Too Little Labour Mobility? State of Play and Policy Issues. *Intereconomics,* 49(3), 123–28. https://doi.org/10.1007/s10272-014-0495-x

Bauer, G., & Osterle, A. (2013). Migrant Care Labour: The Commodification and Redistribution of Care and Emotional Work. *Social Policy and Society,* 12(3), 461–73. http://dx.doi.org.libproxy.wlu.ca/10.1017/S1474746413000079

Bertelsmann-Stiftung. (2015). *Internationale Fachkräfterekrutierung in Der Deutschen Pflegebranche Chancen Und Hemmnisse Aus Sicht Der Einrichtungen*. Retrieved from https://www.bertelsmann-stiftung.de/fileadmin/files/Projekte/28_Einwanderung_ und_Vielfalt/Studie_IB_Internationale_Fachkraefterekrutierung_in_der_deutschen_ Pflegebranche_2015.pdf

Choe, J., & Daheim, H. (1987). *Rückkehr- Und Bleibeperspektiven Koreanischer Arbeitsmigranten in Der Bundesrepublik Deutschland*. Retrieved from http://pub .uni-bielefeld.de/publication/1914440

Connell, J. (2008). *The International Migration of Health Workers*. London & New York: Routledge.

DGB. (2012). *Arbeitsethos Hoch Arbeitshetze Massiv Bezahlung Völlig Unangemessen*. Retrieved from http://www.verdi-gute-arbeit.de/upload/m51d11e5e1fb38_verweis1.pdf

Evans, S. (2013). Merkel Tells Young Europeans to Move to Find Work. *BBC*. http://www .bbc.com/news/world-europe-22906820

Evers, A. (1994). Payments for Care: A Small but Significant Part of a Wider Debate. In A. Evers, M. Pijl & C. Ungerson (Eds.), *Payments for Care: A Comparative Overiew* (pp. 19–41). Aldershot: Averbury.

Faraco Blanco, C., Kraußlach, M. Montero Lange, M., & Pfeffer-Hoffmann, C. (2015). *Die Auswirkungen Der Wirtschaftskrise Auf Die Innereuropäische Arbeitsmigration Am Beispiel Der Neuen Spanischen Migration Nach Deutschland*. 002. Düsseldorf: Forschungsförderung. Retrieved from http://www.boeckler.de/pdf/p_fofoe_WP_002_2015.pdf

Fedyuk, O., Bartha, A., & Zentai, V. (2014). *The Role of Migrant Labour in Meeting European Care Demand*. Retrieved from http://pdc.ceu.hu/archive/00007222/01/ cps-working-paper-role-of-migrant-labour-2014.pdf

Galindo, J. (2014).La «movilidad Exterior», O Cómo Nos Fuimos de España. *Jot Down: Contemporary Culture Magazine*. Retrieved from http://www.jotdown.es/2014/08/ la-movilidad-exterior-o-como-nos-fuimos-de-espana

Glinos, I. (2015). "Health Professional Mobility in the European Union: Exploring the Equity and Efficiency of Free Movement. *Health Policy*, 119(12), 1529–36. https:// doi.org/10.1016/j.healthpol.2015.08.010

Goździak, E. (2016). Biała Emigracja: Variegated Mobility of Polish Care Workers. *Social Identities*, 22(1), 26–43. https://doi.org/10.1080/13504630.2015.1110354

Güllemann, H., & von Borries, B. (2012). *Tauziehen Um Pflegekräfte - Gesundheitspolitik Verschärft Globale Krise Um Fachkräfte*. Retrieved from www.venro.org

Gutierrez, B. (2014) El 15M Como Una Arquitectura de Acción Común. *Redes, Movimientos y Tecnopolítica*. Retrieved from http://tecnopolitica.net/sites/default/files/ bernardogutierrez.pdf

Hardy, J., Eldring, L,, & Schulten, T. (2012). Trade Union Responses to Migrant Workers from the 'New Europe': A Three Sector Comparison in the UK, Norway and Germany. *European Journal of Industrial Relations*, 18(4), 347–363. https://doi.org/ 10.1177/0959680112461464

Hochschild, A. R. (2000). The Nanny Chain. *American Prospect*. Retrieved from http://web.stanford.edu/group/scspi/_media/pdf/key_issues/globalization_journalism.pdf

Kellner, H. (2013). Spanische Pflegekräfte Sind Deutsche Hilfskräfte. *Deutschlandfunk*. Retrieved from http://www.deutschlandfunk.de/erfahrungen-einer-spanierin-krankenpfleger-sind-in.795.de.html?dram:article_id=264297

Knaebel, R. (2015). The Invisible Workers Caring for the German Elderly. *Hesa-Mag*. Retrieved from https://www.etui.org/content/download/20639/169053/.../Hesamag_11_EN_26-29.pdf

Kniejska, P. (2014). Polnische Pflegekräfte In Deutschland: Eine Möglichkeit Zur Behebung Des Pflegenotstands? *Heinrich Böll Stiftung*. Retrieved from https://www.boell.de/de/2014/03/04/polnische-pflegekraefte-deutschland-eine-moeglichkeit-zur-behebung-des-pflegenotstands

Kunkel, K. (2015). Absahner Des Pflegenotstands - Migrantische Pflegekräfte Organisieren Sich Gegen Knebelvertäge Bei GiP. *Express-Texte Zur Care Debatte*, 18(23), 35–38.

Legido-Quigley, H., Urdaneta, E., Gonzalez, A., La Parra, D., Muntaner, C., Alvarez-Dardet, C., Martin-Moreno, M., Mckee, J., & McKee, M. (2013). Erosion of Universal Health Coverage in Spain. *The Lancet*, 382 (9909), p1977. https://doi.org/10.1016/S0140-6736(13)62649-5

Leiber, S., & Rossow, V. (2016). Self- Regulation in a Europeanized 'Grey Market'? The Role of Brokering Agencies in the (Informal) Care Market between Germany and Poland, paper Presented at the *Third ISA Forum of Sociology (Vienna, July 10–14, 2016) to the RC02 Economy and Society Session: The Regulation of Cross-Border Labor Mobility*, 1–16. Vienna.

Lutz, H., & Palenga-Möllenbeck, E. (2010). Care Work Migration in Germany: Semi-Compliance and Complicity. *Social Policy and Society*, 9(3), 419–30. https://doi.org/10.1017/S1474746410000138

Lutz, H., & Palenga-Möllenbeck, E. (2012). Care Workers, Care Drain, and Care Chains: Reflections on Care, Migration, and Citizenship. *Social Politics*, 19(1), 15–37. https://doi.org/10.1093/sp/jxr026

Murphy, M. (2014). Global Care Chains, Commodity Chains, and the Valuation of Care: A Theoretical Discussion. *American International Journal of Social Science*, 3(5), 191–99.

Nessler, S. (2015). Schwerstarbeit in Der Fremde. *Deutschlandfunk Radio Kultur*. Retrieved from http://www.deutschlandradiokultur.de/spanisches-pflegepersonal-in-deutschland-schwerstarbeit-in.2165.de.html?dram:article_id=310590

Ramm, W-C., & Güllemann, H. (2013). *Health Workers for All - Case Studies*.

Schellinger, A. (2015). *Brain Drain – Brain Gain: European Labour Markets in Times of Crisis*. Retrieved from http://library.fes.de/pdf-files/id/ipa/12032.pdf

Schilliger, S. (2016). Self-Organised Struggles of Migrant Care Workers. *Open Democracy / ISA RC-47: Open Movements*, 1–5. Retrieved from https://www.opendemocracy.net/sarah-schilliger/self-organised-struggles-of-migrant-care-workers

Stern. (2014). Wie Spanische Pflegekräfte in Deutschland Schuften. Retrieved from http://www.stern.de/wirtschaft/news/knebelvertraege-in-heimen-wie-spanische-pflegekraefte-in-deutschland-schuften-3959612.html

Stobart, L., & Sans, J. (2012). Spain: A Spiral of Crisis, Cuts and Indignacion. *Socialist Review*. Retrieved from http://socialistreview.org.uk/370/spain-spiral-crisis-cuts-and-indignacion

Theobald, H. (2012a). Combining Welfare Mix and New Public Management: The Case of Long-Term Care Insurance in Germany. *International Journal of Social Welfare* 21 (SUPPL.1): 61–74. https://doi.org10.1111/j.1468-2397.2011.00865.x

Theobald, H. (2012b). Home-Based Care Provision within the German Welfare Mix. *Health and Social Care in the Community*, 20(3), 274–82. https://doi.org10.1111/j.1365-2524.2012.01057.x

Ungerson, C. (1997). Social Politics and the Commodification of Care. *Social Politics*, 4(3), 362–81. https://doi.org/10.1093/sp/4.3.362

Ungerson, C. (2003). Commodified Care Work in European Labour Markets. *European Societies*, 5(4), 377–96. https://doi.org/10.1080/1461669032000127651

Ver.di. (2011). *Grauer Pflegemarkt« Und Beschäftigung Ausländischer Pflegehilfskräfte*. Retrieved from http://gesundheitspolitik.verdi.de/++file++507fb6e06f6844 06d6000008/download/Argumentatsionshilfe-Grauer-Pflegemarkt.pdf

Ver.di. (2015). Mangel Bekommt Gesichter. *Ver.di News* 9, June 27. Retrieved from http://www.der-druck-muss-raus.de/sites/default/files/seite_3_aus_news_09_2015_0.pdf

WHO. (2010). *The WHO Global Code of Practice on the International Recruitment of Health Personnel*. Retrieved from http://www.who.int/hrh/migration/code/WHO_global_code_of_practice_EN.pdf

Wilde, W. (2014). The Plight of Germany's Foreign Careworkers. *Deutsche Welle*. Retrieved from http://www.dw.com/en/the-plight-of-germanys-foreign-careworkers/a-17489055

Williams, F. (2010). Migration and Care: Themes, Concepts and Challenges. *Social Policy and Society*, 9(03), 385–96. https://doi.org/10.1017/S1474746410000102

Winkelmann, J., Rodrigues, R., & Leichsenring, K. (2014). *To Make or to Buy Long-Term Care II: Lessons from Quasi- Markets in Europe*. Policy Brief 10/2014. Vienna: European Centre.

Yeates, N. (2005a). Global Care Chains: A Critical Introduction. *Global Migration Perspectives*, 44. Retrieved from http://www.refworld.org/docid/435f85a84.html

Yeates, N. (2005b). A Global Political Economy of Care. *Social Policy and Society*, 4(2), 227–34. https://doi.org/10.1017/S1474746404002350.

CHAPTER 3

Cross-Border Domestic Work in Ceuta: Challenges and Alternative Organisations

Emma Martín-Díaz and Juan Pablo Aris-Escarcena

1   Introduction

As noted in the introduction of this book, the crisis of trade union representation models originated by globalisation has lead scholars to focus more on the strategies deployed by the migrants in order to examine the obstacles faced when being integrated in the labour market. In addition, an important proportion of the current debate on trade union revitalisation refers to the strategy of trade unions to recruit and mobilise "outsiders" - that is, those sectors of workers that tend to be underrepresented by unions, such as migrants, women or young people (Murray, 2017). In this sense, and for the case of Spain, we find examples of trade union organisations that, having played the role of fundamental pillars of the negotiation for the labour markets regulation during the period of the Fordism, encounter difficulties defending the groups whose jobs do not fit within the framework of formal employment, where the overrepresentation of young people, women and migrants is a fact. But, on the other hand, we also find union organisations that have a significant entrenchment among these groups. We refer to radical unions such as the CNT ("Confederación Nacional del Trabajo" - National Confederation of Labour), the CGT ("Confederación General del Trabajo" - General Confederation of Labour) and, for the Andalusian case, the SAT ("Sindicato Andaluz de Trabajadores" - Andalusian Workers' Union). Along with these examples of union organisations, we find a variety of organisations, some promoted by the immigrants themselves, others emerged as initiatives of civil society and the Third Sector. Those have - at least partially -played the role that trade unions have had for other workers. These organisations can be studied as examples of trade union bricolage.

With this objective, we focus on cross-border domestic workers.[1] In particular, our focus is on the challenges of the exercise and development of union

---

1   We are using the terminology of ILO. e.g.: https://www.ilo.org/actrav/info/pubs/ WCMS_115035/lang--en/index.htm and for cross-border domestic workers: https://www.ilo

actions in a work environment marked by informality, migratory pendularity, multiplicity of exploitation relationships, and migrants' claims directed primarily against non-labour exploitation.

2 Gender and Migration: Transnationalism and Global Care Chains

The study of migratory processes is undergoing an important transformation in a twofold direction. Firstly, in relation to the unprecedented expansion of exchanges and flows of production and goods, of finance and communication, as well as of people and ideas characterizing the current moment of global capitalism. Secondly, the emergence of new theoretical approaches in the social sciences that attempt to provide explanations of varying scope for this historic moment. The current social phenomena, although not entirely new, do take on new forms that force researchers to rethink the world which we live in. The growing interconnection between the different societies of the planet has not been accompanied neither by greater levels of wealth and well-being for all individuals, nor by greater solidarity between the producers of different nations. In spite of this reality, wealth creation has experienced a dizzying rise as it has been disengaged from its dependence on production and taking advantage of the contraction of space and time allowed by new technologies for the expansion of financial capital. At the same time, these processes have facilitated the trans-territorialisation and re-territorialisation of production by taking advantage of the difference in wages, working conditions and social protection among different areas of the planet for labor dumping, generating significant conflicts of interest between workers in different countries. However, the expansion of the new information and communication technologies allows workers to benefit from this contraction of space-time categories, giving rise to the appearance of massive displacements on a planetary scale that attempt to take advantage of this new reality for their own benefit. In summary, we can point out that while it is true that inequalities in terms of income are on the rise as a result of the new economic models, the responses - whether adaptive or refusing - to this situation have also multiplied. The result is a constant increase in the flow of people who move in search of a place that offers the opportunities to develop their projects denied in their places of origin. It results also in a significant increase in the number of professionals and technicians who carry out their activities in the opposite direction: from the rich

---

.org/global/topics/labour-migration/publications/WCMS_436343/lang--en/index.htm (p. 33: *"They exclude however cross-border domestic workers who are not residents…"*).

areas of the planet to the less favoured ones, exercising solidarity, or looking for a place to invest (Inda & Rosaldo, 2002). Overall, these processes emphasize two key trends that characterize the current model of globalization: the increase of all flows (Appadurai, 1990), and, consequently, the growing interconnection between people and societies (Martin, 2003).

In the specific field of the study of international migration, the theories grouped around the concept of transnationalism stand out. Glick Schiller et al. (1992), based on Bourdieu's social field theory, analysed post-Fordist migrations by framing them in a set of multiple networks linked in a fragmented and unequal way through which people, goods, resources and ideas circulate. They thus coined the concept of the transnational social field. For the authors, the transnational social fields include and combine, in different forms and at different times, social actors, networks, organizations and subjects that transcend the national social container that characterized the migrations of the Fordist stage.

It should be noted that most of the work that has been done in the field of migration from a transnational perspective has focused on the agency of migrants rather than on the structure of relations between the State and the market. Most authors who have adopted this perspective understand transnational social fields as spaces of relations or networks between which different types of capital circulate. In our work (Martín, 2008, 2012) we have been able to verify the multifunctionality of networks, as well as their flexible nature and high adaptability, facilitating the reformulation of risk management strategies in uncertain/unstable contexts. At the same time, these networks are the channels through which the circulation of the different forms of capital takes place.

If the transnational perspective had the virtue of taking the analysis of post-Fordist migrations out of the prevailing methodological nationalism, it is also true that the centrality acquired by the study of migrants' agency processes led on numerous occasions to over-optimistic analyses of the subjects' capacity, their networks and their relationships to shape migration projects and design their strategies. The predominance of the variables cited has concealed - by decision of the researchers or by omission - the structure that determined the specific forms that post-Fordist migration models take. The structural analysis implies changing the focus of the individual subjects to the logic of post-Fordist accumulation, emphasizing the processes of growing segmentation of production and the displacement of the axis of value creation towards innovation. In post-Fordism, both phenomena combine to generate a delocalization of productive activities and a transfer of capital. The investment in innovation of the productive process shifts to the investment in innovation of the product and the technology necessary for its development and diffusion. Although the segmentation of production is not a new phenomenon but the development of new communication and distribution technologies has led to it reaching a global dimension. The analysis of global value chains builds the structural framework in which to insert the movement of transnational workers, and within this movement, migrants as a specific and differentiated category.

If production is relocated, the same cannot be done for reproductive and care work. Sassen defines global care chains as "a strategic aspect of research to examine the organizing dynamics of globalization and to begin to clarify how the gender dimension operates" (2003: 69). While value chains transfer capital to innovation and product development by delocalizing production, global care chains are also transnational chains, but they function by transferring these activities to women from countries other than those in which they provide their services. This circulation has given new characteristics to migratory processes insofar as it forces us to rethink the migrant subject by introducing the variables of gender, ethnicity and class as determinants in the analysis of these chains.

Mass migrations have followed different patterns in relation to the subject's membership in the sex/gender systems (Martín, 2006a). Thus, men and women develop different strategies for both emigration and social insertion in the host countries. This difference is clearly perceptible as much in the immigration policies as in the social representations that originate on the migratory processes. As Sassen indicates, (2003: 46) *"the dynamics of gender have been made invisible in terms of their concrete articulation with the global economy. This set of dynamics can be found in alternative cross-border circuits..., in which the role of women, and especially the condition of migrant women, is crucial"*. Transnational migrations appear to be a privileged place to study the transformation of gender patterns. In this regard, the study of the formation of transnational domestic units provides enlightening data on the empowerment of women, allowing for the validation of certain hypotheses formulated in this regard by the authors who have developed this concept (Hondagneu-Sotelo and Ávila, 1997; Parella, 2008). They allow us to observe the creation of new forms of cross-border solidarity, but also of new forms of exploitation, and the experiences of belonging and the elaboration of identity that the new female subjectivities represent. Returning to Sassen (2003: 50) "women and immigrants emerge as the systematic equivalent of the proletariat, a proletariat that develops outside the countries of origin. Moreover, and on the other hand, the demands of the labour force at the highest professional and managerial level, in global cities, are such that the current ways of handling domestic tasks and lifestyles become inadequate. As a consequence we are seeing the return of the so-called 'bonded classes' composed mostly of immigrants and immigrant women".

In short, the study of transnational communities offers us new ways of exploring migratory movements and analysing the participation of migrants in social, political and cultural life in post-Fordist societies. This approach emphasizes that changes in economic and cultural models must be translated into a revision of the theoretical and conceptual framework that has characterized the study of migratory processes (Martín, 2006b). Particularly relevant is the reconsideration of social subjects. If in the traditional approach the central units of analysis were the individual, on the one hand, and the social class on the other, the inclusion of the transnational communities as unit of analysis allows to draw the complexity of the processes and the plurality of social agents involved. Thus, the studies on migratory processes carried out from the neoclassical approach emphasized the individual level of decision-making by positing the process as the result of a rational analysis articulated on the evaluation of costs and benefits. On the other hand, studies focused on social class as the central level of analysis draw a world of structures that determine the action of the subjects. Both units of analysis are essential but insufficient to understand the action of social subjects in the framework of globalized societies. In this context, the transnational dimension of migration calls into question the definitions imposed by the sending (emigrant) and receiving (immigrant) states. The condition of the subject fits this transnational reality, and what characterizes it is a kind of ubiquity that points to the suitability of the term migrant as a way of describing a model of circulation of subjects in which people and their networks are present, but also the structures that shape and condition their circulation.

3   The Constrictions of Domestic Work in Ceuta

The city of Ceuta is marked by contrast. It is the province of Spain with the higher unemployment rate and where the poverty rate is highest,[2] with 35.6%; it also has the lowest economic growth and is at the bottom of the list for a number of social and economic variables (from the access to the internet of companies to the average life expectancy). However, the GDP per capita in Ceuta exceeds the average of the autonomous communities of Andalusia and Extremadura (as well as Melilla).

---

2 In fact, in the last report on the socioeconomic and labour situation in Spain (2017), where these data come from no reference has been made to the unemployment rate of the autonomous cities of Ceuta and Melilla, arguing that there is too great variability between the different sources and surveys (Consejo Económico y Social, 2018).

Despite all this, Ceuta is a focus of attraction for Moroccan citizens living in the border environment of the city. For those who live on the other side of the world's most unequal border, accessing a job in Ceuta represents a substantial improvement in their purchasing power. As Cristina Fuentes Lara points out in the Report Frontera Sur 2016 (APDHA), the socioeconomic differences between the Tetouan area and Ceuta, Morocco and Spain, Africa and Europe, are evident through macro-indicators such as the Human Development Index (where Morocco ranks 156 and Spain the 26th) or in terms of the level of economy in the IMF world ranking (56th and 16th respectively). The minimum wage, officially, in Morocco is € 220 while Spanish is € 735.9.

But the relationship is symbiotic. The city of Ceuta depends economically on the small cross-border trade and the daily entry of people from Morocco, whose estimate varies more than considerable according to the sources consulted, always exceeding 30,000 daily entries (La Frontera de Ceuta: Vidas al Límite, 2018). In 2011, the last report presented by the Economic and Social Committee of Ceuta (before its disappearance in the middle years of the economic crisis), recognised the economic dependence that the city manifested towards cross-border trade (Ciudad Autónoma de Ceuta, 2012). As Ferrer Gallardo points out: *"The enclaves* (referring to Ceuta and Melilla) *are total border areas, the border serves as their main resource, the preservation of which requires the simultaneous deployment of meticulous and contradictory smoothing policies and fortification"* (2008: 144). In May 2018, the groups of Entrepreneurs, Hoteliers and Merchants of Ceuta and Melilla called a demonstration under the theme "For the present and the future of Melilla and Ceuta", to demand more fluidity, better conditions, more personal and greater permissiveness to the cross-border trade in the passes with Morocco (Europa Press, 2018).

In this border zone, cross-border female domestic workers are not considered as migrants for practical purposes. Their legal situation is governed by the "Ley Orgánica 4/2000", on rights and freedoms of foreigners in Spain and their social integration; regulated in article 43 in its consolidated version (BOE, 2000; whose last amendment was made on August 2018). This law is applied according to the "Real Decreto 557/2011", approving the Regulation of the "Ley Orgánica 4/2000", on rights and freedoms of foreigners in Spain and their social integration, after its amendment by the "Ley Orgánica 2/2009" (BOE, 2011, whose last amendment was made on November 9, 2015), in particular by the provisions of Title X, Articles 182, 183 and 184. However, the situation of Moroccan women workers who carry out this activity is based on the exemption of visa on small border transit of residents in the areas of Nador (towards Melilla) and Tetouan (towards Ceuta) according to point III of the final act of the Agreement on the Accession of the Kingdom of Spain to the Convention implementing the Schengen Agreement (European Union, 1985). Cross-border workers can carry out work for others and their own, whose taxation is determined on the basis of the Agreement between the Kingdom of Spain and the Kingdom of Morocco to avoid double taxation on income and property taxes (BOE, 1985; BOE, 2016).

Thus, the legal framework regulating this situation is strongly segmented. To what has been illustrated up to now, we must add the segmentation of the normative frameworks regarding access to the social security system, and the exclusion suffered by cross-border workers. As we will see later, this has important consequences for people who carry out this type of cross-border economic activity.

In general terms, the migratory model is pendular, based on the possibility of accessing Ceuta without a visa. The daily round trip across the border involves a large cost in travel, both economic and time wise. Since migrant workers are not resident in Spain, there are a whole series of rights to which they do not have access. In addition, as noted in the report 03/2013 of CCOO drafted by José Antonio Moreno Díaz *"Limits on freedom of movement and cross-border workers in Ceuta and Melilla"* (*"Límites a la libertad circulatoria y trabajadores transfronterizos en Ceuta y Melilla"*), there is a specific problem regarding the authorisations of cross-border work and its renewal. The period of validity of this permit is only one year, with the possibility of another year extension after its expiry. This represents an important difference from the general scheme of work permit renewal, which has a biannual duration for the first two extensions and can have the duration of five years after its third renewal. This also generates significant expenses in time and economic resources, as it requires the submission of documents from Morocco, as well as their translation, to which must be added the administrative fees charged by Spain.

Beyond these costs, the difficulty in obtaining and, above all, renewing these permits creates another obstacle in the normalisation of the work situation of these workers, accentuating their vulnerability. The latest regulation (Royal Decree 557/2011) modified the maximum duration of permits for cross-border workers, reducing it to one year. In addition, it increased the cost of administrative procedures in Spain and the volume of documentation requested.

On the other hand, the lack of legal residence in Ceuta does not prevent a part of the women who carry out the activity in Ceuta from residing in the city as well. The impossibility of regularizing this situation is based on several factors. The main cause highlights the absence of employment contracts. Since the reform of the domestic employment law, effective as of 2012 by Royal Decree 1620/2011, there was a significant increase in hiring in this sector, although less than expected in the first instance (Andreo Tudela, 2013).

However, as Nuria Galán Pareja points out in her doctoral thesis (Galan Pareja, 2012), a huge majority of these jobs are carried out without effective regulation: 82.5% of the 4,000 jobs that unions estimated at that time were not governed by contract. Bearing in mind that the data it provides are from 2011 and that after the reform it went from 700 contracts of this type to almost 1,300, a figure in which contract growth stagnated, there is still a large and majority sector that operates without a contract and that has no option to regularise its settlement in Spanish territory. On the other hand, even in the case of obtaining a stable employment contract, there is an administrative tendency to reject applications for residence permits in the autonomous cities of Ceuta and Melilla. This has been proved by the judgments against the State for having denied the residence permit to people who met all the requirements. One example was sentence 975/2013 of the Superior Court of Justice, Litigation Room; in this instance the court ruled in favour of the plaintiff, considering that the decision not to grant him a residence permit on the basis of "covert family reunification" lacked arguments (TSJM, 2013).

In this socio-economic context, cross-border domestic work as an economic activity acquires a new dimension. On the one hand, it is a comparatively profitable economic activity for Moroccan women despite the low wages, since in Morocco the jobs at that level of training have much lower salaries (Belhorma, 2017). It is an alternative to the "atypical trade", which although it can provide higher income as an economic activity, supposes a much greater physical and mental cost and excludes in any case any possible regularisation of the labour activity. On the other hand, it supposes an offer of services at a reduced cost and that allows certain sectors of the Ceuta community to cover ample needs of the work in the home.

In a logic that goes beyond this context, we must specify that domestic service must face a situation of clearly negative departure for recognition as a work activity. An essential occupation for the production and reproduction of the labour force, and therefore, for social reproduction, which, however, has to face the widely widespread consideration of non-work. In this activity, sex / gender relations are determinant, since domestic service is perceived as a "natural" activity of women, who have the field of reproduction as their own domain of sociability. The identification between the biological fact of reproduction and domestic work implies the acceptance that women are endowed, by the simple fact of belonging to the female sex, of a series of knowledge and skills that enable them to perform the tasks of the home.

Since the nineties, a series of transformations have taken place in Spain within the family units, which represent an increase in the demand for wage labour in this sector: incorporation of women into labour markets, re-composition of homes through the increase of reconstituted families, increased life expectancy, and, consequently, the number of dependent elderly. These transformations affect the increase experienced in the domestic sector, and make it one of the fields of employment with the most future, although in conditions of precariousness and social non-recognition.

It can be concluded that domestic service lacks social recognition, insofar as its development in the private sphere ensures its labour dimension. Several results derive from this situation:
- Low wages.
- Work conditions of great hardness and enormous ambiguity, which affects the schedule, holidays, and the performance of specific tasks.
- The lack of real comparison to other work activities: the inclusion in the general Social Security scheme is not effective.[3]

For women workers, social non-recognition means that domestic work is not considered by women workers as a profession, but rather as an activity carried out to the extent that other, better paid and socially considered jobs cannot be accessed. It is this lack of connection with work that affects the lack of interest in professionalisation, and, consequently, the recognition of labour rights.

On the other hand, two factors are decisive for this situation to occur: a) The fact that it is an activity primarily carried out by women; and b) The consideration of the workplace - the home - as a private sphere, and, therefore, the difficulty of ensuring compliance with the law in labour relations.

The separation between public and private space, far from being a universal and timeless reality, is materialised in a historical moment that marks the development of the model of industrial capitalism, and, in particular, the triumph of the aspirations of the working class. In order for women to be able to dedicate themselves exclusively to household chores, men had to become the only winners of family support, which, when acquiring production relations, a salary form of recognition of work should be carried out outside the home, in spaces specifically designed and built for that purpose. The sexual division of work that is established in the bosom of the contemporary family presents a very marked dichotomy between the figure of the head of the family and the housewife. Although this is the ideal model, and therefore, hegemonic, reality shows a wide variety, and implies aspects that have remained veiled by the ideological predominance of this pattern of behaviour.

The ethnography developed in Ceuta shows us that for the majority of domestic workers the main supporters of their household are their salaries.

---

3   The assimilation to the general regime of social security was postponed until 2024.

Despite this, many even understand this as a temporary situation that should not last. A woman explained to us that she kept her house and her children because her husband could not find work, when we asked her how long her husband was not working, she answered us, "Almost two years now, buff! The work is really bad nowadays..." Even so, she saw her salary as a contribution to cover the lack of her husband's salary. Other cases contradicted this situation. For several women, salaried work in Ceuta has allowed them to separate from their husbands by relying on family networks.

The link between domestic work and the labour market is therefore twofold. In the first place, this type of work is thought of as something alien to it from the cultural construction that we have described. Second, the rise in salaried domestic work depends on the expansion of the market and the incorporation of more women into the non-domestic work environment. However, it would be inaccurate to consider that this labour incorporation is the only determining factor. There are other factors that should be highlighted.

An important part of the female population that works outside the home resides outside the place where their extended family lives, which makes it difficult to recur to kinship networks in domestic tasks, particularly with regard to the care of children. Contrary to what happens in other EU countries, in Spain the labour legislation that protects the rights of the family, guaranteeing the possibility of combining domestic and extra-domestic work, is scarcely developed. This reality also generates a greater demand for domestic service.

On the other hand, the increase in the number of elderly people living alone also affects the increase of this demand. The responsibility involved in caring for dependents has led to its consideration as a full economic and employment activity when it is waged outside the domestic sphere. However, this recognition has not served to improve the assessment of domestic workers. In the current legislation (in the mentioned RD 1620/2011), the "care" is understood to belong to a different work nature and those kinds of services are excluded from this model of employment relationship. That is, the contract as "domestic worker" is not applicable for people who carry out care activities. In practice, this means that these jobs are carried out without due guarantees and that the fundamental need for this type of services as well as the importance of domestic workers for social reproduction are ignored.

The increase in the demand for domestic work does not come to be covered by native workers, especially when it is necessary to alleviate the need for full-time work. The arrival of immigrant women, and the increasingly significant feminisation of migrations, has been causing a series of changes in this sector, with a substitution process taking place in some fields, particularly in the inmates' sector. Progressively, this incorporation is extended to other sectors of the activity, such as external employees or part-time employees. The report made by the Claver Association in collaboration with the ODS (Villalba Ferreira, 2015) highlights this characteristic even after the effects of the 2008 economic crisis.

In Ceuta, there is a more acute effect of this general trend. The vulnerability of cross-border workers makes them "attractive" to employers. The feminisation of economic activities based on cross-border mobility has been very significant, becoming visible in the domestic work sector and in the "atypical trade". The incorporation of migrant women into this labour market has had as one of its results a process of "ethnification" of the activity. In Ceuta, the popular qualification received by domestic workers is illustrative of these processes. When they are named in informal conversations, they are often referred to in terms such as "mi Fatima" (my Fatima) or "mi Mora" (my Moor). These are designations that show, in a subtle but profound way, the cultural construction of these workers as feminised subjects, with a clear ethnic and racialised determination, and as an inserted part within the domestic structure, as a possession of it.

The difference in roles that is marked by the hegemonic development of the social representations of the sex-gender systems in that historical moment determines the symbolic devaluation of the economic activities that take place within the household, to the point of denying their recognition as such. Work then becomes work outside the home, while domestic activities are naturalised, to the point of being considered inherent to sex: the famous phrase "sus labores" (their duties), indicating the "occupation" in the National Identity Documents of the Spanish women of the Franco era. Even today, the debate about the recognition of domestic activities is fraught with difficulties, since - as has happened recently - social measures to support families have been focusing on subsidies for working mothers out of the home.

The special characteristics that define domestic work and that, in broad strokes, we have developed, are clearly illustrated in the legislation that regulates this activity. It should be remembered here that, although we found some men -both native and immigrants - working in this sector, we are dealing with a basically feminine activity, and that the gender variable is very present, although rarely explicitly, in the legislative development.

Domestic service legislation is a tangible proof of the difference between the economic activities that take place in the private and public spheres, and that only labour that takes place in the latter is worth social recognition. In the current regulation of domestic work this link between home and non-work is produced explicitly. The "Real Decreto 1620/2011", of November 14, regulating the special nature of the employment relationships in the domestic work service, states that this type of activities deserve a differentiated regulation because they take place in *"the family home, thus linked to personal and family intimacy and completely outside and strange to the common denominator of labour relations, which are developed in productive activity environments presided over by the principles of the market economy"* (Preamble).

This cultural construction and its normative expressions have very specific effects in Ceuta on the types of exploitation and violence suffered by women workers on both sides of the border. First, there is simple labour exploitation. Most work without a contract. Being a cross-border worker, the contract would have limited advantages of access to social benefits, allowing access to healthcare but not to unemployment benefits or the pension system. However, the contract allows them (at least in theory) a priority and faster and easier access through the border crossings that they must go through each morning, which is a huge improvement for their daily lives and one of the main demands of this collective. On the other hand, the terms of the contract do not reflect in many cases the real labour situation, such as those women who are hired part-time, as internal workers. In addition, many of them are hired as domestic workers when, in reality, they perform care tasks and care for dependent members of the family, something expressly excluded by the current legislation. To exacerbate this situation, salaries are often inadequate and overtime work is commonly expected. The average salary for those hired is € 400 per month. For domestic workers without a contract, the stipend is more volatile and fluctuates between € 150 and € 400 per month. Workers, who are hired by day, usually receive a salary between € 20 and € 30 per day, understanding that their work is done on a piecework basis, without a maximum of hours: the day ends when they have completed all the tasks that have been imposed. This exploitation is the one that less importance is attributed by women and about which they hardly speak. The fear of losing their jobs and being replaced. The comparative advantage of their salaries with those they could obtain in Morocco, the legal instability and the dependence of their families on their income leads them to accept exploitation conditions, in some cases very severe.

Second, there is a series of specific exploitations, which we could define as personal. This type of exploitation has to do with moral abuse, systematic exercises of power over the personal life of these women, and sexual violence. Most women suffer this type of violence in some way or another, but there are two subgroups of women within the large group of domestic workers who are especially vulnerable to these extreme forms of abuse. The first is the internal workers, whose "vital freedom" is very restricted, having very few free moments throughout the day and a regime of intense seclusion, with very few free days and few or no vacation periods. This is comparable to the experience of most domestic workers, although it is more intense. The second group is more peculiar and although they are a limited number, their cases are extremely serious and show the potential danger that legal defencelessness entails to the ones that the current normative framework submits as non-immigrants and non-immigrants workers. They are women who, in one way or another, have ended up becoming the partner of a native man from Ceuta (Christian or Muslim, without distinction). These women are "wanted" by men older than them, with the aim of satisfying "all their needs, from home to bed," as Maribel Lorente, director of Digmun, explains. The "marriage" does not become official for Spain since they do not pass through any recognised rite nor are registered in the civil registry. Some, after this union, continue working in domestic service outside their own home, while others stop doing so for lack of need and even for prohibition. They invariably go on to take charge of domestic work at their partner's residence in Ceuta, where they go to reside in a non-regular way in many cases. This situation gives rise to the most severe dynamics of labour, physical and sexual exploitation. According to the cases documented by Digmun, there are two particularly serious situations: a) sexist violence, b) the expulsion of the women from their male partners' residence. Helplessness is absolute in these cases.

4   The Limits of Union Participation

The integration of these women in the unions is extremely complicated. As Desdentado Daroca (2016, p. 131) points out: "Domestic work is isolated in the home, it is not organised collectively, nor do domestic workers normally participate in trade union organisations, which cannot carry out their action within the framework of the family home. This does not mean that there is no conflict of interest between employer and employee. But this conflict is not regulated through two essential mechanisms in the workplace: collective bargaining and collective conflict". This characteristic of the labour niche, added to the legal instability of cross-border workers and the enormous competitiveness within the sector, places women in a situation of high vulnerability.

In this article we will not analyse the complex reasons for their participation (or not) in the Moroccan trade union movements. We want to pay particular attention to the unions' limited action in advocating for the rights of cross-border workers on account of others.

The two main unions present in Ceuta are the CCOO (Workers' Commissions) and the UGT (General Union of Workers). Their engagement with cross-border workers has focused on the advocacy for the groups' hiring and regularisation of work. This form of engagement mirrors the action undertaken in Spain, with a few local particularities.

In the first place, both unions have been involved in the advocacy for the rights of domestic workers and have promoted the ratification by Spain of the ILO Convention No. 189, which inspired the reform of the status of domestic workers in the national law promoted through RD 1620/2011. The ratification of the Convention continues to be an important objective at the national level, since it implies a series of recognitions that the current law does not consider. In addition, these unions have taken action against proposals to delay the equalisation of the social security scheme of domestic workers to the general scheme.

Following this line of action, trade unions in Ceuta have repeatedly expressed their support for the regularisation of the situation of cross-border domestic workers. But their claim has not taken into account the characteristics of this group as cross-border migrant women, nor has it resulted in an engagement with this group.

On the other hand, in the local context of Ceuta, these two unions have developed an activity around the figure of cross-border workers that is not exempt from controversy. Since the beginning of the 21st century, unions had fought for cross-border workers to have coverage within the social security system and receive unemployment benefits based on their employment status. With the reform of the immigration law through LO 2/2009, the unions celebrated that this situation had changed. In his doctoral thesis Galan Pareja (2012) shows through his references to trade unions' speeches the double motivation behind their claim: a) the improvement of the conditions of cross-border workers, b) the equalisation of the social security costs that companies had to sustain to hire native and cross-border workers. That is, the companies had now to sustain the costs related to unemployment benefits of cross-border workers. This objective is linked, in a potentially contradictory way, to the defence of the interests of ethno-national workers, who considered the comparative advantage of hiring a cross-border worker for employers to be unfair competition. In fact, the amended immigration law only fulfilled the objective of aligning the employer's costs for hiring cross-border workers and native workers. While the last amendment to the immigration law imposed compulsory social security contributions, the "General Law of Social Security",[4] in its art. 272 (f) includes the transfer of residence or the residency abroad as reasons for the loss of the right to the unemployment subsidy. This situation is in line with the provisions of European legislation, where unemployment benefits are directly linked to the country of residence (European Union, 2017; EU Regulation 883/2004).

---

4 Currently recast by RD 8/2015, of October 30.

The conclusions of the 2017 CCOO report of José Aureliano Martín Segura, responsible for the legal services of CCOO in Ceuta, highlight the contradictory relationship of the objectives between the defence of the national working class and the extension of class solidarity to cross-border workers. Firstly, he states that *"We have a huge mass of workers from the neighbour country, eager to work in our city for – sometimes miserable – wages, but for them it means double or triple the average salary of nationals of their country. This generates a tremendous offer, which is met by the local demand for cheap labour, in many cases the result of the insatiable desires of economic benefits of some unscrupulous businessmen. But also, the result of the delicate situation of the local economy"*. The second basis for his conclusions is that *"the legislation in force and the non-residents status of cross-border workers, or the fact that their situation is not regularised, makes them the object of the most indecent form of exploitation and discrimination"*. These conclusions reflect the discursive formula establishing the subordination of the unions' solidarity towards foreign workers (cross-border workers in this case) to the well-being of national workers, as well as to the situation of the national (local) labour market: *"The unions must respond to both situations. The just demands and needs of the cross-border workers have to be met, but the special difficulties of the native workers and the local economic situation must also be addressed"*.

The de facto situation of cross-border workers has worsened significantly. They have lost the comparative advantage of being hired without the cost of the social security unemployment contribution, a benefit they however still do not have access to. In order to calculate their social security cost, they are still considered as non-resident subjects, which is why the 24% of withholdings on the income of their activity is applied [Article 25, 1) a. of the "Law on Income Tax for Non-Residents", as ratified by the Binding Resolution of the General Directorate of Taxes V1508-05, of June 19, 2005]. And the latest amendments to the "Regulations for the Application of the Immigration Act" reduced the duration of work permits for cross-border workers to one year only renewable for another year consecutively. In addition, these amendments increased the documentation required for the permit procedure, which also implies additional fees costing a total of € 500. The unions have mobilised against this issue, but they have not managed to transform the situation nor have they managed to articulate a network of participation and mutual support with cross-border workers.[5] The distancing between the unions and the workers has become progressive.

---

5   In fact, in Melilla (the twin city of Ceuta), cross-border workers organised to protest against these conditions, as well as to manifest their disappointment towards the union of CCOO Melilla.

The situation of cross-border women engaged in the domestic work sector has therefore been only marginally addressed by trade unions. Embedded within the group of cross-border workers, women have been made invisible in their specificities and have not had adequate support from the unions.

5 The Digmun's Activity. Solving Problems in a Creative Way

The Digmun association of Ceuta was born in 2005. Since then it has been responsible for literacy activities aimed at women who do not have access to public programs (for lack of residence permit or, in most cases, for being domestic workers without contract) as well as minors who are in a situation of "no schooling".[6] At present, the literacy process in Spanish includes three level groups (zero, middle and advanced) in two different time zones with an average of 20 women per group. Thus about 120 women are served by the programs based on a volunteering network. The literacy program faces very different realities in the levels of knowledge, both in the domain of Spanish and in the literacy level of the women enrolled.

In addition to this continuous training, courses on gender and equality are carried out in a transversal and specific manner, as well as celebration days that allow the creation of connections between the different groups of women. Festive meetings organised by the association for these purposes are held several times a year. This strengthens the networks of mutual support built by domestic workers.

Digmun does not maintain formal relations with unions. However, it does maintain informal relationships, through the engagement of union members with organisation's work. For example, Digmun develops its activity in the IES (Secondary School) "Puertas del Campo" of Ceuta, which allows them to use their facilities at no costs. This concession was made thanks to the informal support of a syndicalist, who was member of the staff of the educational facility and was close to some members of the organisation.

The programs developed by Digmun are very different in nature from those developed by the unions. In relation to cross-border work, trade unions in Ceuta and in particular CCOO Ceuta, have developed several awareness programs to encourage the regularisation of employment and the respect for labour rights that correspond to cross-border workers. Regarding the latter, the activities of the Digmun association allow women to acquire skills to avoid

---

6 These out-of-school children are the children of domestic workers and other women who reside in Ceuta without being able to regularise their situation in that city.

labour exploitation. In several cases, the association has helped women to understand the contracts that their employers have given them or to resolve the administrative issues that they face in order to renew their permits as cross-border workers. This means that, although there are public services available for women who have obtained a contract, the networks of trust and knowledge of the association have exceeded their scope of direct action. Many women prefer to go to Digmun because - as a woman assisted with the renewal of her work permits told us - they already know the people who work there. Many women, after having attended the classes, return to consult the association when their working condition has changed. This alteration can occur both towards regulation and towards irregularity; for instance, many ask for guidance when their employers refuse to renew their contract. On the other hand, symbolic tools, beyond language training, are important for women realising cross-border work, as their main concerns have to do with issues indirectly linked to their work. A woman confessed that, for them, *"The worst is the border. The worst, the worst. They hit us, they treat us badly..."*.

Digmun adopts an approach towards the problems and main claims of cross-border female domestic workers in a very different way from the unions. Dedicated to a job where socialisation is a basic pillar, it seeks to empower women's independence through training at the sociolinguistic and socio-professional levels. In the cases in which the women who have gone through the linguistic training of Digmun have managed to regularise their situation, they have been given support so that they could continue with their training to obtain titles of secondary and higher education. An example of this was the case of Isabel.[7] She came from a family with a certain purchasing power in Morocco, where she had studied until she was eighteen. Due to family circumstances, she had to dedicate herself to domestic work for several years. Being literate in Arabic and French, it was easy to learn Spanish and achieve a good level of written accuracy. After the regularisation of her work contract as a domestic employee, she was able to have access to professional training and to perform a technical function in a private health clinic.

In addition to training, Digmun offers support for solving critical situations. Physical abuse, sexist violence and sexual violence are areas in which they provide assistance, making up for the deficiencies of public services and other types of organisations. These interventions do not form the daily nucleus of Digmun's activity. The association only assists women who are in need in cases where no other support is available. Through the creation of a network

---

7   All names are invented. To create more empathy and avoid reification, the authors preferred to use common names in Spain.

of citizen volunteers, they have been able to cover the need for assistance and asylum of many women abused by their partner / employer or expelled from the facility where they had been residing as internal domestic workers for a long period of time. This network has prevented women and their minor children from experiencing extreme indigence in the absence of shelter and of the possibility of seeking help through family networks on either side of the border. Digmun has become a point of reference and confidence where women in situations of extreme vulnerability know they can turn to, even if they have not had a prior direct relationship. Personal acquaintance and trust in this organisation are part of their expertise, mutually supported by the network created by women working in the domestic sphere.

Maria's story is especially illustrative of this type of situation. She started working as a domestic employee for a man more than twenty years older than her, without a contract. Little by little, the relationship between employer and employee became a couple relationship. She moved to his residence with her son, fruit of a previous marriage. He went on to take care of her financial needs, while she took care of all their domestic needs. Subsequently, the man began to physically mistreat Maria. She contacted Digmun to seek refuge. She could not turn to her family, who lived in Morocco, because having maintained a non-marital relationship had broken her family ties. She could not go to the authorities, because, as the union had not been regularised, she was still in a situation of administrative irregularity and was not considered a resident in Ceuta. A member of the Digmun volunteer network welcomed her and her son into his/her home for four years. With no prospect of improving her socio-family situation, after two years she returned to live with the man. A few months later she left the house again after being mistreated. When she went to the association, she asked not only for shelter but also for help to denounce him. The same volunteer welcomed her into her house and another made her a work contract. With her somewhat stabilised situation she reported her ex-partner. From this point, her situation changed. She managed to find stability and obtain a residence permit. She is now a volunteer of Digmun.

Thus, the efforts of Digmun and the citizen network that has been created from this organisation complement the labour-related efforts undertaken by the trade unions in their defence of the rights of cross-border workers. They carry out, even though there is no explicit formulation of this objective by the organisation, de facto advocacy of the main claims of this group and represent a safeguard against the most extreme conditions of exploitation that it suffers.

6   Conclusions

We have presented in this chapter the particular reality of the domestic workers of Ceuta, who suffer several specific types of exclusion linked to their characteristics as women and as cross-border workers.

Given the circumstances of these groups of workers, unions have shown a very limited capacity for action. In our experience and on the basis of what has been explained so far, we can draw two fundamental conclusions.

With regard to the unions' approach, those operating in the territory of Ceuta have not been able to establish mechanisms that allow a stable relationship with the groups of cross-border workers in general, nor with cross-border domestic workers in particular. Lacking structures and mechanisms adapted to the context and local needs of these groups, the unions have not been able to obtain an improvement in working conditions or representation for cross-border workers. This is mainly due to two elements:

a. The unions have historically developed their mediation work in areas of negotiation within national structures. In their interaction in this context, they have progressively adopted the State's tendency to make domestic work invisible based on a bias characteristic of the patriarchal ideology. The engagement of trade unions with domestic work is a very recent phenomenon and is still biased by the impossibility of conceptualizing non-salaried work as part of its field of action.
b. This perspective deficit extends to the lack of capacity to work in areas characterised by irregular work and in which, in cases such as cross-border work, the legislation is partial, fragmentary, and punctually contradictory and exceeds strict margins of labour legislation.

The national perspective has dominated the action of the unions. As a result, it translates into a deficient interaction of the trade unions with cross-border workers. For them, the causes of most of the exploitative labour conditions that they endure are related to their definition in the legislation as workers with a different status.

Beyond the display of solidarity, support and campaigns for regularisation, the position of trade unions in dealing with the situation of cross-border workers has always been subject to the reading and interpretation of the needs of the workers' national labour market.

In the case of Ceuta, illustrated in this chapter, the high rates of local unemployment have marked the attitude of the unions and have posed an unresolved obstacle for a full defence of the interests of these workers. By putting the interests of the national workers before those of the cross-border workers, the unions have left the labour field of domestic work unattended.

With regard to alternative support organisations, we can conclude that in the face of the lack of operation of the unions in this type of context, local humanitarian organisations have a comparative advantage. Organisations like Digmun are ahead of unions in contexts such as Ceuta due to their ability to favour and contribute to the establishment of networks of self-protection and mutual help among migrant workers, to provide assistance of various kinds and to serve as a safeguard against the most serious situations of exclusion. Examples of the preference for local social organisations rather than unions, in situations as different as the context of domestic workers in Ceuta and the context of workers in the fast food sector in New York, highlight the shortcomings of the unions' approach.

If "Bricolage" has been conceptualised as situational tinkering and 'making do' (Visscher, Heusinkveld, & O'Mahoney, 2017), the activities developed by associations such as Digmun are an example of this type of adaptive capacity. The innovations of this kind of organisations can be analysed as examples of trade union bricolage, since they have adapted their strategies to face exclusionary processes of workers beyond the orthodox limits of labour relationship. This is especially relevant for contexts marked by labour precariousness to address unsatisfied social needs though creative ways, similar to those analysed by Mrozowicki & Maciejewska (2016). These strategies can serve to show more effective ways that modify the traditional practices and conceptualisations of the unions, which have proved inefficient for these contexts.

References

Andreo Tudela, J. C. (2013). *Diagnósitco de la situación sociolaboral de las trabajadoras transfronterizas del servicio doméstico. Planteamientos prácticos para su regulación en el contexto de Ceuta*. Ceuta: Instituto de Estudios Ceutíes.

Appadurai, A. (1990). Disjuncture and difference in the global cultural economy, in M. Featherstone (Ed.), *Global Culture. Nationalism, Globalization and Modernity* (Sage, pp. 295–310) London.

Belhorma, S. (2017). El trabajo informal de las mujeres y la pobreza de los hogares en la ciudad de Fez. *Revista Internacional de Estudios Migratorios*, 7(3), 51–73. https://doi.org/2173-1950

BOE. (1985). INSTRUMENTO de Ratificación del Convenio entre el Reino de España y el Reino de Marruecos para evitar la doble imposición en materia de impuestos sobre la renta y sobre el patrimonio y Protocolo anejo, firmado en Madrid el 10 de julio de 1978, así como el Canje de Notas de 13 de diciembre de 1983 y 7 de febrero de 1984 modificando el párrafo 3 del artículo 2.º de dicho Convenio. (Boletín Oficial del

Estado, May 22, 1985.). Retrieved from http://www.hacienda.gob.es/Documentacion/Publico/NormativaDoctrina/Tributaria/CDI/BOE_Marruecos.pdf

BOE. Ley Orgánica 4/2000, de 11 de enero, sobre derechos y libertades de los extranjeros en España y su integración social., Pub. L. No. BOE.es-Documento consolidado BOE-A-2000-544, BOE núm. 10, January 12, 2000. BOE-A-2000-544. Retrieved from https://www.boe.es/buscar/act.php?id=BOE-A-2000-544

BOE. Real Decreto 557/2011, de 20 de abril, por el que se aprueba el Reglamento de la Ley Orgánica 4/2000, sobre derechos y libertades de los extranjeros en España y su integración social, tras su reforma por Ley Orgánica 2/2009., Pub. L. No. BOE-A-2011-7703, BOE.es - Documento consolidado BOE-A-2011-7703. BOE núm. 103, April 30, 2011. Retrieved from https://www.boe.es/buscar/act.php?id=BOE-A-2011-7703&p=20151109&tn=1

BOE. (2016). Intercambio de Cartas interpretativas del Convenio entre el Gobierno del Reino de España y el Gobierno del Reino de Marruecos, para evitar la doble imposición en materia de impuestos sobre la renta y sobre el patrimonio, hecho en Madrid el 10 de julio de 1978. Retrieved from https://www.boe.es/diario_boe/txt.php?id=BOE-A-2016-6756

Brenner, N. (2004). Urban governance and the production of new state spaces in western Europe, 1960–2000. *Review of International Political Economy, 11*(3), 447–488. https://doi.org/10.1080/0969229042000282864

Ciudad Autónoma de Ceuta (2012). *Memoria sobre la situación socioeconómica y laboral de Ceuta 2011.* Retrieved from http://ceuta.es/ceuta/images/documentos/Institucional/Memorias/Memoria2011.pdf

Consejo Económico y Social (2018). *Memoria sobre la situación socioeconómica y laboral. España 2017.* Retrieved from http://www.ces.es/documents/10180/5888552/Memoria_Socioeconomica_CES2017.pdf

Desdentado Daroca, E. (2016). Las reformas de la regulación del trabajo doméstico por cuenta ajena en España. *Investigaciones Feministas, 7*(1), 129–148.

Eizaguirre Anglada, S. (2016). Entidades socialmente creativas en un contexto de gobernanza multinivel. Una comparativa del fomento de la economía solidaria en Barcelona y Bilbao. *Papers. Revista de Sociologia, 101*(1), 31–49. https://doi.org/10.5565/rev/papers.1796

Europa Press (2018, May 22). Miles de manifestantes en Melilla y Ceuta piden más fluidez en la frontera con Marruecos. *Europa Press.* Retrieved from http://www.europapress.es/ceuta-y-melilla/noticia-miles-personas-manifiestan-melilla-ceuta-pedir-mas-fluidez-frontera-marruecos-20180522221432.html

European Union (1985). The Schengen acquis - Agreement on the Accession of the Kingdom of Spain to the Convention implementing the Schengen Agreement of 14 June 1985 between the Governments of the States of the Benelux Economic Union, the Federal Republic of Germany and the Fre. Retrieved from https://eur-lex.europa.eu/legal-content/EN/TXT/?uri=CELEX:42000A0922(04)

European Union. (2017). *FAQs - Unemployment abroad - Your Europe*. Retrieved from https://europa.eu/youreurope/citizens/work/unemployment-and-benefits/unemployment/faq/index_en.htm

Ferrer Gallardo, X. (2008). Acrobacias fronterizas en Ceuta y Melilla . Explorando la gestión de los perímetros terrestres de la Unión Europea en el continente africano. *Doc. Anàl. Geogr., 51*, 129–149.

Fuentes Lara, C. (2017). Las mujeres porteadoras en la frontera hispano-marroquí: El caso de Ceuta. Retrieved from http://hdl.handle.net/10481/48864

Galan Pareja, N. (2012). *Mujeres transfronterizas marroquíes empleadas del hogar en Ceuta*. Universidad de Granada.

Geddes, M. (2006). Partnership and the Limits to Local Governance in England: Institutionalist Analysis and Neoliberalism. *International Journal of Urban and Regional Research, 30*(1), 76–97. https://doi.org/10.1111/j.1468-2427.2006.00645.x

Harvey, D. (2005). *A Brief History of Neoliberalism*. New York: Oxford University Press.

Inda, J. X., & Rosaldo, R. (Eds.) (2002). *The Anthropology of Globalization. A Reader*. Malden, MA: Blackwell.

Jessop, B. (2002). Liberalism, Neoliberalism, and Urban Governance: A State-Theoretical Perspective. *Antipode, 34*(3), 452–472. https://doi.org/10.1111/1467-8330.00250

La Frontera de Ceuta: Vidas al Límite (n.d.) *20 Minutos*. Retrieved November 14, 2018, from https://especiales.20minutos.es/frontera-ceuta-vidas-limite

Martín, E. (2003). *Procesos Migratorios y Ciudadanía Cultural*. Sevilla: Mergablum.

Martín, E. (2006a). De las migraciones del fordismo a las migraciones de la globalización, Europa: 1960–2005. *Africa e Mediterráneo, 54*, 29–35.

Martín-Díaz, E. (2006b). Mercado de trabajo, género e inmigración, in Several Authors, *Mujeres inmigrantes, viajeras incansables* (pp. 55–74). Bilbao: Harresiak Apurtuz.

Martín-Díaz, E. (2008). El impacto del género en las migraciones de la globalización: Mujeres, trabajos y relaciones interculturales. *Scripta Nova*, 12(270–133).

Martín-Diaz, E. (2012). Estrategias migratorias de las mujeres ecuatorianas en Sevilla: Acumulación de capital social en tiempos de crisis. *Migraciones Internacionales*, 6(4), 107–138.

Martin-Diaz, E., & Roca B. (2017). Spanish migrations to Europe: from the fordist model to the flexible economy. *Journal of Mediterranean Studies*, 26(2), 189–207.

Moulaert, F., MacCallum, D., Mehmood, A., & Hamdouch, A. (2013). *The International Handbook on Social Innovation. Collective Action, Social Learning and Transdisciplinary Research*. Cheltenham: Edward Elgar. https://doi.org/10.3935/rsp.v21i3.1225

Mrozowicki, A., & Maciejewska, M. (2016). Bricolage unionism . Unions ' innovative responses to the problems of precarious work in Poland. In M. Bernaciak & M. Kahancová (Eds.), *Innovative Union Practices in Central-Eastern Europe* (pp. 139–159). Brussels: ETUI.

Murray, G. (2017). Union renewal. What can we learn from three decades of research? *Transfer, 23*(1), 9–29. https://doi.org/10.1177/1024258916681723

Parella, S. (2008). Aplicación de los campos sociales transnacionales en los estudios sobre migraciones, in C. Solé, S. Parella & L. Cavalcanti (Coords.), *Nuevos Retos del Transnacionalismo en el Estudio de las Migraciones*. Madrid: Observatorio Permanente de la Inmigración/Ministerio de Trabajo e Inmigración-Gobierno de España.

Sassen, S. (2003). *Contrageografías de la Globalización. Género y Ciudadanía en Circuitos Transfronterizos*. Madrid: Traficantes de sueños.

Schiller, N. G., Bash, L., & Blanc, S. (1995). From immigrant to transmigrant: theorizing transnational migration. *Anthropological Quarterly*, 68, 48–63.

TSJM. (2013). T. S. de J. de M. Procedimiento Ordinario 2535/2012, STSJ M 6414/2013. Retrieved from http://www.poderjudicial.es/search/doAction?action=contentpdf&databasematch=AN&reference=6788736&links=extranjeria&optimize=20130710&publicinterface=true

Villalba Ferreira (Coor.), S. (2015). *Diagnóstico y Buenas Prácticas Hacia la igualdad en el empleo del Hogar : Buenas prácticas para la inserción sociolaboral*. Sevilla.

Visscher, K., Heusinkveld, S., & O'Mahoney, J. (2017). Bricolage and Identity Work. *British Journal of Management*, 00, 1–17. https://doi.org/10.1111/1467-8551.12220

CHAPTER 4

Organising Migrant Porters of the Logistic Sector: The Italian Case of SI Cobas

Giulia Borraccino

1   Introduction

The logistics porters' protests that erupted around 2010 in the north of Italy unexpectedly upset the balance of power in a growing industry. Porters are employed in the final link of a value chain along which the logistics sector is organised. Most of them are migrants employed by cooperatives that are trusted by firms and multi-client logistics companies to manage storage and warehousing services. These protests helped publicise the critical working conditions of this category of workers, which sharply contrasted with the volume of business in such a booming sector.

The unionisation rate among migrant porters was significant, but the level of union membership did not reflect their real power. Logistics porters are under the rules of the cooperative, entities located in a grey area between employment and self-employment. This peculiar status made it possible to overcome sectoral collective agreements and contributed to creating unfavourable working conditions.

In 2010, social movements and union activists founded SI Cobas, a radical union with a Marxist internationalist orientation that arose around the logistics porters. It turned out to be the first union in the sector. Its sudden dramatic diffusion was the result of the crisis of representation of traditional trade unions. The latter were criticised for adopting top-down decision-making and for their conflict-containment style that fed the perception that major trade unions were part of the political establishment. The decision-making process of SI Cobas appeared largely participative, and their collective action style appeared highly conflictual. The status of migrants contributed to attributing a high political significance to the protests of this group of workers. It helped in turn create a proper collective subject, a new class of exploited workers able to create a network of allies reaching a critical mass.

This chapter is based on a collection of literature and documents, as well as on observatory participation in strikes and parades and interviews with trade union and social movement activists performed between 2015 and 2016 in Bologna and Milan. It intends to trace the unique experience of SI Cobas, focusing on the events, the trade unions' choices and strategies fostering the creation of a political actor supported by social movements and local community, and to reflect on the implication of this pattern of mobilisation for the labour movement as a whole.

2   Social Movements, Migrants, and Trade Unions Strategies

The case of the migrant logistics porters is highly representative of new patterns of mobilisation facing new challenges in modern times. In order to frame the issue, one has to take a step backward to the disorders of the 1970s and their strong impact on the labour movements. The social contentions of the 1970s were the field in which the paradigm of "old" and "new" social movements developed. They contributed to marking the switch to the post-industrial era, where new identity-based movements struggled to be recognised as collective identities and social actors. By contrast, trade unions were the "old" movement; they were class-based and arose over material issues such as better salaries and working conditions (Melucci, 1989).

This new wave of protests represents a privileged field of study for social movements and trade unions and was a valuable inspiration for theory-building. Looking in particular at the Italian struggles of the 1970s, Pizzorno (1977) developed a theory on logics of action and the trade union crisis of representation. New actors in the labour movement emerged to contrast with trade unions' strategies of negotiation and self-containment. The logic undertaken by the new collective identities was based on the direct participation of its members. Their protests presented a high level of conflict, and had a very wide scope. In fact, the aim of the conflict was to strengthen the internal cohesion of the group and, consequently, its collective identity. The "logic of organisation" pursued by trade unions point at very specific and negotiable objectives, and is an attitude of structured and consolidated subjects. The capacity of balancing the logic of organizations with the logic of movement is a crucial requirement for consolidating trade unions' influence.

In the current trade unions' crisis of representation, the need for reconciling trade union strategies with internal democracy remains a valid argument for regaining legitimacy in the eyes of the base (Gumbrell-McCormick & Hyman, 2013).

Connolly et al. (2014) stress the role of the migrant workforce as a crucial issue in which one can measure trade unions' capacity to innovate their logic of action in order to try to represent marginal workers. They detect different orientations and strategies pursued by national labour movements. Following and paraphrasing the Hyman model on trade union identity (Hyman, 2001), they build a triangle depicting the trade unions' orientation on migrant workers, combining the dimensions of class, race/ethnicity, and social rights. Trade unions can deal with migrants by: 1) playing on the class solidarity of a specific group of workers, which can be characterised by the predominant presence of migrants; 2) by adopting a citizenship perspective that blends working and social dimensions; and finally 3) by considering migrants as part of a distinct and peculiar fringe of the working class.

In an early study, Marino (2012) attributed the different national experiences of migrant workers' representation to union structure and trade unions' identity. The major Italian trade union *Confederazione Generale Italiana del Lavoro* (CGIL) developed its strategy of migrants organising with two main approaches. The first is the individual protection of migrants, based on free assistance for residency permit procedures through the trade union's system of services. The main Italian Trade Union confederation, in line with a general European trend, developed an important network of services for trade union members and citizens composed of services for tax declarations, employment services, and assistance for resident permit applications. The second is the collective representation through the involvement of migrants into the representative structure of the trade union. Alberti et al. (2013) stress the need for a holistic perspective to account for migrant status and a working dimension, while the existing trend concentrates on a single line of action.

Trade union democracy has actually been shown to foster the inclusion of migrants: bottom-up procedures of decision-making were more effective in involving migrants in the workplace and in the trade union than were centralised decision methods. A top-down approach also implies a further difficulty in focusing on the existing representation gap. The more a trade union is balanced toward a vertical, institutional dimension, the less it will strive to represent migrant workers (Marino, 2015). This perspective is in line with the assumption that trade unions embedded in neo-corporatist countries present major difficulties when dealing with changes in progress (Ebbinghaus & Visser, 1999). Italy cannot be properly defined as a country with a neo-corporative system of industrial relations due to its high component of voluntarism. In fact, Italian trade unions for a long times refused to build proper institutions for social dialogue and collective bargaining. They were led by a concern for losing their scope for action and preferred to alternate between strategies aimed at either getting close to their base by enhancing participation or developing exclusive relationships with political institutions without forging strong bounds (Regalia, 2012). CGIL, for instance, was traditionally close to its base and was particularly supportive of rank-and-file and social movements during the 1970s (Tarrow, 1989). In the 1980s, CGIL decided to switch to a strategy of political exchange and conflict containment, pointing to collective and tripartite bargaining as its main repertoire of action (Regini, 1981). This strategic turn had a consequence for the perception of the base, triggering a crisis of representation that fostered the rise of independent rank-and-file unionism concentrated in some sectors (the *Cobas*).

3 Migrant Unrest and Radicalisation of the Conflict During the Crisis

When trade unions are not effective in (or willing to) represent a fringe of the workforce, self-organisation can emerge. Roca and Martín-Diaz (2017) refer to "interstitial trade unionism" as rising networks of self-organised migrant workers, and view them as an answer to both a representation gap and a representation crisis. Despite the major difficulties this group of workers have to face, migrants are not difficult to organise per se, and their unionisation is attributable to the sectors in which they are concentrated. In fact, migrants are more receptive and more prone to militancy than natives, representing a potential resource for the entire labour movement (Milkman, 2000). This attitude concerns workplace militancy, but it can be applied to the public sphere for more general social claims.

In Italy, in the years immediately after the economic crisis of 2008, Italian migrant communities initiated a series of protests on a national level. The event that triggered the general unrest was the shooting of two African orange pickers in 2010 in Rosarno (Calabria, Southern Italy), initiating a protest in the workforce that had a strong public impact. After that episode, more protests involving migrants spread around the country. The disorders were similar in terms of claims and repertoires of action. In particular, the protestors challenged the neoliberal system of exploitation of the migrant workforce. The discourse the migrant activists carried on embraced a large concept of social justice. Through these protests, they were able to shed a light on the working and living conditions of migrants in the country and became proper actors instead of passive subjects in the public debate. They called into question the mechanism of granting residency permits that was strictly connected to employment status. Such an approach is summarised by the concept of "neoliberal citizenship". They refused to be considered merely as economic resources and denounced the hypocrisy of the right-wing discourse that justified their working conditions by using their illegal status (Olivetti, 2012). Such large social claims helped develop a solidarity that went beyond the workplace or nationality. The narrative of this new collective actor was able to embrace all the subjects suffering from the neoliberal commodification. The movement was endorsed by local communities, social movements, and grassroots unions.

Migrant struggles during this time are inextricably connected with the economic downturn and a more general radicalisation of the conflict. This is due to the exacerbation of working and social conditions and to the crisis of the traditional system of representation. In the Italian case, the mobilisation of logistics porters effectively parallels the concept of "radical and political unionism" defined by Upchurch and Mathers (2011). The authors contest the "social movement unionism" approach in revitalisation studies, which is largely based on the concept of citizenship and claims for enlarging working conflict within the social sphere with the aim of relying on external solidarity. The authors call into question the lack of a critical political discourse that openly challenges the neoliberal system, while a class-based perspective appears to be necessary. Ness (2014) reiterates this view, putting emphasis on new forms of workers' organization spreading around the world starting in 2010. The progressive affirmation of neoliberal reforms and the difficulties traditional unionism has in dealing with that have fostered initiatives based on self-organisation and direct action with a critical view of the capitalistic system.

At the beginning of the twentieth century, the Industrial Workers of the World had grasped the role of migrant workers in reviving a class-based internationalist view. The logistics sector reproduces, on a local and national scale, the global dynamics of exploitation. Nowadays, while the efforts to create international solidarity along the global value chain are hardly effective, logistics porters were able to create their own local network of solidarity.

Research on struggles in the logistics sector have been especially focused in the north of Italy, where the main logistics hubs are located (Cuppini & Frapporti, 2018). Some of these studies define the series of porters' protests as a proper cycle of contention (Curcio, 2016). The concept of cycle of contention is used by Tarrow (1989) to describe the cyclical nature of social movement, mobilising and demobilising according to the structure of opportunities. The cyclical nature of social movements is another central characteristic of these subjects, shaping their logic of action. However, the cyclical nature of migrant porters' protests results in a controversial argument. On the one hand, they actually created a collective subject sharing commonalities with social movements (i.e., the direct action, the high degree of participation, and the radical style of protest). On the other hand, this subject was channelled by a rank-and-file union claiming better working conditions for a precise group of workers. The clear labour content of the protests and the organisation around a structured subject call into question the cyclical nature of this actor. SI Cobas appears as a fitting example of radical political unionism. It was able to effectively merge general social issues with specific labour issues into a critical mass with a clear-cut political consciousness.

4   The Italian Logistics Sector and Cooperatives System

Logistics are industrial services that manage the movement and delivery of goods according to needs set by the producer. In Italy, logistics is one of the few sectors growing during and despite the economic crisis, of 2008 especially due to the significant development of e-commerce.

In the north, where infrastructures are dramatically more developed than in the rest of the country, the presence of the sector is relevant. The so called "Milan Logistic Region" includes the Region of Lombardy and the three extra-regional provinces of Novara, Verona, and Piacenza. They contain most of the logistics companies and hubs of the county. In 2010, the turnover of the logistics market in this area registered almost 12 billion Euros (30% of the Italian logistics revenue) recovering the market loss suffered in 2009.[1] Outside the Milan logistics region, the interport of Bologna is notable as one of the most important intermodal terminals of the country.

The logistics sector is vertically developed along a supply chain. At the top of this chain there are the providers and the multi-client companies such as DHL or TNT, while at the bottom are the sub-contracted entities managing the services related to storage and warehousing. The least favourable working conditions occur at this stage, where the level of automation is very low. The Italian distributional logistics are in fact characterised by a low degree of investment in technology and innovation, while a low-skilled labour force is largely employed in the warehouse (Bologna, 2013). The decline of labour standards in this phase follows two strategic lines: first, the ethnic-based recruitment of porters; second, the outsourcing of such services to cooperatives.

The recruitment of migrants in the Italian logistics sector is a longstanding practice aimed at jeopardising workforce solidarity and undermining the highly unionised core workers' power (Doellgast et al., 2017). In fact, migrants are often unaware of labour laws, and they face economic difficulties. The implementation of "neoliberal citizenship" puts the workers in a marginal position in the labour market and has allowed employers to effectively lower labour standards. The definition of the Italian Statistic Institution ISTAT for

---

[1]   Source: AIDA and Centro Studi Fedespedi elaborated by Creazza et al. (2012).

porters is "Not-qualified personal employee in the movement and shipping of goods." According to the ISTAT annual workforce census, in 2013 26 percent of the total of such class of employee were extra-European, resulting in an important aspect of work with a significant presence of migrants.

The peculiarity of the Italian outsourcing system in logistics are the cooperatives. This system developed at the end of the nineteenth century as a workers' self-employment system reflecting a view of mutualism and participation. The ownership of the cooperative as well as the decision-making are distributed among its associated workers,. The working members of the cooperative are simultaneously employer and employee, assuming a unique status. The incremental development of workers' cooperatives fostered legislative initiatives: in the 1970s, important fiscal incentives were granted to encourage this development model.

The tertiarisation of the economy and the restructuring of the Italian economic system in the 1990s have progressively led the cooperative system to fit a business-oriented model, theoretically based on social promotion and workers' participation, which should be effectively guaranteed through specific procedures. However, the cooperatives were progressively employed in the process of labour segmentation, and the social and mutual vocation aspects were put aside. To the same extent, the procedures of participation were systematically misapplied and the contractor companies often turned out to be the real employer, directly managing the workforce instead its functioning as an entrusted cooperative (Cuppini & Pallavicini, 2015). The status of the working members allowed the sectoral collective agreement to be overcome since the workers were considered on a par with employers. Moreover, many cooperatives managing storage services are constituted ad hoc for a specific job, and they disappear at the end of the contract (Bologna, 2013). This explains the high degree of turnover, which is apparently incompatible with the majority of open-ended hiring. Many empirical studies have documented the situation of exploitation of migrant porters, particularly as reflected in long working hours, low salaries, and constant threats of layoff or working time reduction (Benvegnú et al., 2018; Bologna, 2013; Cuppini & Frapporti, 2018)

The evolution of working cooperatives progressively defines a new heterogeneous sector, "the cooperative sector," where the Italian cooperative associations assume a proper role of employer associations. The "Cooperative Alliance" formed by the three main national cooperative associations currently employs around 1,200,000 people, moving 8 percent of the national GDP.[2] The overall scenario depicts a supposed solidaristic workers' organisation, which actually hides workforce exploitation.

---

2   Source: https://www.alleanzacooperative.it/ visited April 9, 2020.

The presence of traditional trade unions in the Italian logistics sector used to be significant, with a preponderance of the Federation of Transport Workers (Filt) affiliated with the major trade union CGIL. Most of the migrant logistics workers got in contact with and affiliated themselves with the union through the union's system of services for migrants (Cuppini & Pallavicini, 2015). Traditional trade unions were particularly closed to cooperative association because they share common values as well as a similar trajectory. In fact, both historically developed along the two axes of the predominant political cultures in the north of the country: the left wing and the Catholic. The growing relevance of the cooperative sector entailed a progressive influence in the political system and enhanced relationships among political and institutional actors. At the national level, the network of relationships among politics, traditional trade unions, and cooperatives were highly interwoven. This scenario discouraged trade unions from grasping the change in progress in the cooperative sector. For this reason, the level of conflict used to be very low, despite the level of unionisation, and traditional trade unions were not fully aware of, or willing to deal with, the new class of exploited workers that was emerging.

5 Origin and Development of SI Cobas

The acronym Cobas stands for *Comitati di Base* (rank-and-file committees); as their name suggests, they are based on workers' direct participation and refuse to accept the traditional trade unions' vertical structure. They began to spread around Italy in the 1980s, when traditional trade unions switched to a strategy of conflict containment aimed at developing their institutional voice, embracing collective bargaining as their principal means of action. *Sindacato Intercategoriale Cobas* (Inter-branch Rank-and-file Committee—SI Cobas) was founded in 2010, following the separation from the union Slai Cobas, the first inter-branch Cobas union. The forerunner protest of logistics porters was organised by Slai Cobas in 2008 against the food retail company Bennett in Origgio (Varese, Northern Italy), in which warehousing services were outsourced by cooperatives employing mostly migrant workers. A protest arose from a local agreement signed by the traditional trade unions introducing unfavourable conditions with respect to the sectoral collective contract (as a reduction of salary in cases of sick leave).[3] The strikes and pickets lasted five months. During the actions, fright traffic was successfully blocked, obstructing

---

3   In Italy, sectoral bargaining is still the most important level of negotiation. Nevertheless, it is possible to negotiate a company agreement that deviate to the sectoral agreement, even introducing unfavorable conditions.

supermarket provisioning. The level of conflict was particularly high and the police intervened several times, trying to restore service. The participation of the Antiracist Committee of Milan and the Squatted Social Centre "Vittoria"of Milan was fundamental, as was the contribution of workers from other plants and sectors. The conflict resolution was signed by an agreement improving economic conditions and a system of workers' participation in organizing working schedules.

Aldo Milani, one of the Slai Cobas organisers of the protests in Origgio, was particularly inspired by the potentials of migrant logistics porters in reviving class awareness, and made himself the spokesman of a new project of Cobas centred on them. Milani turned out to be an emblematic character in the logistic struggles and the main leader of SI Cobas. Some of the key activists of SI Cobas did not develop their political activity in the workplace, as with Aldo Milani, the union's founder. The decision of getting involved in the organisation of logistics porters was rooted in the high political implications protests had. The growth of the Italian logistics sector during the crisis relied on the exploitation of the migrant workforce, symbolizing to some extent capitalism's exploitation of the Global South. This context had a strong appeal, especially for internationalist Marxists, as the keys actors declared themselves to be. They were aware of the high symbolism surrounding this group of workers, recalling the crucial role the migrant workforce historically had played in the labour movement. The founders of SI Cobas contributed to "arm" porters by organising workplace assemblies. The highly inclusive decision-making process contrasted with the traditional trade unions' methods, based on rare moments of consultation with the base. It contributed to building mutual trust and solidarity.

The news about the protests spread and the first victories of the union helped make SI Cobas popular. The same workers were getting in contact with the union to create a SI Cobas Committee in their workplace. The demands for affiliation and organising constituent assemblies of SI Cobas dramatically increased in a few years. In 2016, SI Cobas had around 10,000 members, most of whom were migrant porters working for cooperatives, but it progressively spread into other fields of the cooperative sector with a significant presence of migrants (for instance, the cleaning sector). SI Cobas established organisational headquarters in several cities in the North of Italy that were run by volunteers, as the union strongly criticised the bureaucratic structure of traditional trade unions. The union organised a sectoral strike of logistics porters in 2014 and a general strike of independent unionism in 2016 (together with the unions USI, CUB, and SGB), against imperialist wars and the government's policies.

The greatest achievement of SI Cobas was contributing to the creation of a proper political subject around the figure of the logistics porter. The radical union was able to penetrate the collective imagination through its narrative and logic of action, activating and mobilising a network of supporters and creating a critical mass.

6 Building a Political Subject: Logic of Action, Repertoires of Contention, and Ideology of Logistics Porters

The construction of the logistics porter as a political subject can be effectively analysed by considering the three logics of organisation described by Connolly et al. (2014). The logics of class, ethnicity, and social rights shape three organisational processes and strategic approaches. In the case of SI Cobas, the union relied jointly and effectively on these three logics during the process of organising migrant porters.

The figure of the porter became a proper "class" of workers that went beyond nationality and workplace, being able to create solidarity based on sharing the same precarious and critical working conditions. The porters have the structural power to sabotage the logistics chain and block the entire distribution process. While the threat of delocalisation affects industrial workers, such strategy cannot be applied in this sector since shipping cannot avoid passing through specific logistic hubs to be distributed. Within this context, the porters represent that powerful working class that seemed to have disappeared with the tertiarisation of the economy.

The logic of class was fostered by solidarity among the different workplaces. "If you touch one you touch all of us" is the identifying slogan of the union, effectively summarising the strategy of Cobas's mutual support. Generally, the porters used to get in contact with unionists from SI Cobas by means of their ethnic-base network and create their own workplace committees (Cobas) to organise a protest. The pickets eventually became their identifying repertoire of action: SI Cobas activists, porters, and workers from different workplaces promoted and supported others' strikes by rallying outside warehouses for better working conditions and blocking freight traffic. The main unions' claims in the majority of the cases was the respect of the sectoral collective agreement, to which cooperatives were not necessarily subject to law.

The participation in these actions was relevant and produced a general blockage of service. SI Cobas and its network used to jointly target the cooperative as well as the contractors, who in several cases were the real employer. In cases of multinational contractors, the protests were complemented by public name-and-shame and boycott campaigns. The economic loss was particularly unsustainable for the firms and it was reported that various cases of conflicts were solved in only a few hours. Picketing often had judicial consequences to the detriment of a large number of activists, who were denounced by public authorities. One of the most important blitz-protests occurred in Carpiano in 2011 (Milan's metropolitan area), a central hub where the multi-shipping company SDA operates; SDA is in charge of shipping for the national postal service (*Poste Italiane*) and Amazon, outsourcing warehousing to external cooperatives. Traffic was blocked by a large group of workers who were successfully joined by most of the workforce. After few days of blockage, the employers agreed to change the internal cooperatives' rules in order to comply with the sectoral agreement. The plant of Carpiano saw further conflicts carried on by SI Cobas that did not resolve as quickly. In 2017, the plant temporary closed due to strikes until a ceasefire agreement was negotiated.

In other cases, the protests were particularly long lasting and characterised by a dramatic level of conflict. A protest notable for its magnitude and impact was the series of strikes in Piacenza starting to 2012 in the hub providing warehousing services for Ikea. The first conflict was triggered by the alternation of working time overload and restrictions unilaterally put in place by the cooperative affecting workers salaries. The first intense wave of protests concluded with the acceptance of most of SI Cobas' claims, but a new conflict emerged in 2014 following a series of layoffs due to demonstrations and strikes, affecting, in particular, SI Cobas activists. This case involved some violent clashes with the police and the crucial participation of local social movement groups.

A further long-lasting and highly conflictual case was the mass protest in Bologna against the cooperative managing the logistics service for Granarolo (an Italian food company). The "Granarolo" case originated in 2013 when the cooperative fired 51 porters due to a wildcat strike for wage increases, SI Cobas organised a national demonstration in June 2013 against the dismissals alongside a series of pickets and blockage of traffic, actions alternating for over 10 months. The police were called to intervene several times. The case was finally solved in July 2014 with an agreement for reallocating the fired workers.

Members of local social movements in Bologna (especially political, housing, and student movements) actively supported the conflict by personally participating in the protests. Their contribution during the street clashes with the police was fundamental, and they were able to transmit their repertoire of action to porters. Direct action was the most important common element linking the porters of SI Cobas and social movements. Protesting together and facing the police created a strong relationship of trust and contributed to strengthening a network of solidarity based on mutual participation in the protests and initiatives. Local movements also promoted a campaign of boycotting the client Granarolo in order to undermine its reputation and keep public attention on the case.

In the case of Granarolo, the company declared itself to be an injured party in the conflict since the protesting workers were employed by the cooperative, while the company brand was complying with its obligations according to the sectoral collective agreement. The campaign of boycotting against Ikea and Granarolo appealed to consumers' civic consciousness. The logic leading these kinds of actions goes beyond belonging to a given class and embraces larger issues of social justice and citizenship.

The general strike followed a similar logic, trying to enclose neoliberal policies and geopolitical equilibrium. SI Cobas organised a general strike in 2016 together with other radical independent unions (USI and CUB), denouncing Italian labour reform[4] and other neoliberal anti-crisis measures. The strikers also wanted to stress the contradictions of European foreign policy, in particular with respect to the repression by Erdogan in Turkey. This strike reiterated a willingness to "represent the anti-systemic force." The aim of representing the logistics porters was part of a bigger plan of representing general social issues together with other subjects fighting against liberalism. The preliminary assemblies were organised in squatted housing, with the participation of independent unionism, various local political movements, and the Kurd community. The March 18, 2016, parades were organised in some major Italian cities. In Milan, the porters initiated the general strikes with symbolic pickets early in the morning in front of factories and warehouses. Later, there was a parade featuring other unions and movements wearing porter uniforms. This represented a strong message of belonging to a proper working class and recalled the industrial workers' struggles of the 1960s. At the same time, the concept of class appeared to be evolving and its borders were not clearly defined, as in the notion of "old" social movement.

Finally, the ethnic dimension also played a fundamental role in the process of organisation. Cuppini and Pallavicini (2015) attribute the push toward mobilisation to the attitude of the migrants "increasing expectations." In fact, the decision to migrate is led by the desire of achieve better life conditions than in their country of origin, and they are therefore less willing to accept the rhetoric on the crisis. The solidarity networks characterising migrant communities and

---

4 The so called "jobs act" was a labour reform approved by the Democratic government led by Matteo Renzi in 2014. It introduced the labour market's flexibility regarding newly hired workers by eliminating the obligation to reintegrate workers in case of unlawful dismissal.

the ethnic network of recruitment in this sector contributed to strengthening the internal solidarity base (Benvegnù et al,, 2018). The sensibility toward the Kurd community had a strong political meaning denouncing the "imperialist's war" and support the act of resistance occurring in the Global South. The Arab Spring further contributed to fomenting the struggles.

In the SI Cobas founders' view, migrant logistics porters were fulfilling the Industrial Workers of the World's legacies and the pickets were symbolically recalling that old strong working class. The radical anti-systemic ideology represented the common thread effectively connecting logics of class, citizenship, and ethnicity, creating the figure of the migrant logistics porters as a collective subject struggling against capitalist forces.

7 Conclusions

The radical union SI Cobas empowered and organised migrant porters of the Italian logistics sector, enlarging a strict labour claim into the social sphere under a political class-based perspective. Such experience represents a fitting and successful example of radical political unionism.

The effectiveness of SI Cobas's action derives from a combination of structural power, solidarity, and organisation. The logistics porters simultaneously had the structural weakness of their status as migrants and the structural power of the characteristics of their sector. Abstention from work in their crucial hub in fact blocks the logistical chain, causing large economic loss and undermining the reputation of the contractor company. The close relations between job tenure and residency permits and traditional trade unions' attitudes used to act as a deterrent to collective action. Traditional trade unions were not prone to react against the cooperative sector. This occurred because of the traditional privileged relationship they had with cooperative associations due to a similarity in ideology. They had problems grasping the emerging of new forms of exploitation, which required to change their logic of action, and increase the level of conflict.

The protagonists and most of the key actors of SI Cobas were migrant porters. However, the push to organise a union was given by Italian activists of social movements inspired by internationalist Marxism working outside the logistics sector. The founders of SI Cobas saw in this category of workers a potential group with which to build a political project, taking up International Workers of the World legacies.

SI Cobas was able to activate the latent structural power of logistics porters by building a collective subject that effectively mixed the dimensions of class, social rights, and status. The logistics porters became emblematic of the migrant workforce's exploitation worldwide, and their struggle became the symbol of the struggles against global capitalism. The victories of migrant porters were perceived as the first victories against capitalism, contributing to the popularity of SI Cobas and to the awareness of porters' struggles around the country. A more general discourse on social justice and the inclusive decision-making nature of the union appealed to activists from local social movements. Whereas building international solidarity is still an idealistic goal at the international scale, SI Cobas re-created, to some extent, international solidarity in a local context.

It is probably inaccurate to define the porters' struggles as a "wave of movement" because of the presence of a specific job-related content in their claims and the lack of a proper cyclical nature typical of social movements. However, SI Cobas's experience demonstrated the increasing cross-contamination of old and new social movements' concepts, contributing to the need for a new paradigm after the crisis. Moreover, it opened new horizons on alternative methods of workers' representation and highlighted the traditional trade unions' difficulties in coping with changes in order to represent new groups of workers.

References

Alberti, G., Holgate, J., & Tapia, M. (2013). Organising migrants as workers or as migrant workers? Intersectionality, trade unions and precarious work. *The International Journal of Human Resource Management*, 24(22), 4132–4148.

Benvegnú, C., Haidinger, B., & Sacchetto, D. (2018). Restructuring Labour Relations and Employment in the European Logistics Sector. In V. Doellgast, N. Lillie & V. Pulignano (Eds.), *Reconstructing Solidarity: Labour Unions, Precarious Work, and the Politics of Institutional Change in Europe* (pp. 83–103). Oxford: Oxford University Press.

Bologna, S. (2013). Lavoro e capitale nella logistica italiana: alcune considerazioni sul Veneto. *40th Anniversario della costituzione di Interporto Padova Spa', University of Padua*, 1–15.

Connolly, H., Marino, S., & Lucio, M. M. (2014). Trade union renewal and the challenges of representation: Strategies towards migrant and ethnic minority workers in the Netherlands, Spain and the United Kingdom. *European Journal of Industrial Relations*, 20(1), 5–20.

Creazza, A., Curi, S., Dallari, F. (2012). Il mercato logistico in Lombardia: trasformazioni in atto e scenari evolutivi. *Liuc Paper*, 251 (19).

Cuppini, N., & Pallavicini, C. (2015). Le lotte nella logistica nella valle del Po. *Sociologia del lavoro* 138, 210–224.

Cuppini, N., & Frapporti (2018). Insubordinazioni del lavoro nella pianura logistica del Po. In C. Benvegnù & F. I. Iannuzzi (Eds.), *Figure del lavoro contemporaneo. Un'inchiesta sui nuovi regimi della produzione* (pp. 82–96). Verona: Ombre Corte.

Curcio, A. (2014). Practicing militant inquiry: Composition, strike and betting in the logistics workers struggles in Italy. *Ephemera*, 14(3), 375–390.

Ebbinghaus, B., & Visser, J. (1999). When institutions matter: Union growth and decline in Western Europe, 1950–1995. *European Sociological Review*, 15(2), 135–158.

Hyman, R. (2001). *Understanding European trade unionism: between market, class and society*. London: Sage.

Marino, S. (2012). Trade union inclusion of migrant and ethnic minority workers: Comparing Italy and the Netherlands. *European Journal of Industrial Relations*, 18(1), 5–20.

Marino, S. (2015). Trade unions, special structures and the inclusion of migrant workers: on the role of union democracy. *Work, employment and society*, 29(5), 826–842.

Melucci, A. (1989), *Nomads of the Present: Social Movements and Individual Needs in contemporary Society*, Philadelphia PA: Temple University Press.

Milkman, R. (2000). Immigrant organizing and the new labor movement in Los Angeles. *Critical Sociology*, 26(1–2), 59–81.

Ness, I. (Ed.) (2014). *New Forms of Worker Organization: The Syndicalist and Autonomist Restoration of Class-Struggle Unionism*. Oakland: PM Press.

Oliveri, F. (2015). Subverting neoliberal citizenship. Migrant struggles for the right to stay in contemporary Italy. *ACME: An International E-Journal for Critical Geographies*, 14(2), 492–503.

Regini, M. (1981). *I dilemmi del sindacato*, Bologna: Il Mulino.

Roca, B., & Martín-Díaz, E. (2017). Solidarity Networks of Spanish Migrants in the UK and Germany: The Emergence of Interstitial Trade Unionism. *Critical Sociology*, 43(7–8), 1197–1212.

Tarrow, S (1989). *Democracy and Disorder*. Oxford: Oxford University Press.

Upchurch, M., & Mathers, A. (2012). Neoliberal globalization and trade unionism: toward radical political unionism?. *Critical Sociology*, 38(2), 265–280.

CHAPTER 5

Migrant Worker Organisations and Overexploitation in the Garment Industry in Argentina

Paula Dinorah Salgado

1   Introduction

This paper describes rank and file garment organisations and the associated dimensions that create and sustain labour overexploitation, mainly composed of migrant workers. The garment industry is a notorious case for this analysis because this form of exploitation is an integral part of its production dynamics. The lack of intervention by legitimate political institutions to eradicate these practices is one side of the dialectical connection that guarantees its continued existence.

At the present moment in Argentina, there is a vast array of social, cultural, sports-related, religious and political organisations connected to the garment industry that involve migrant workers. These organisations operate both for social action and as a place for communal identity.

In this paper, we make a distinction between those organisations that are formed concerning the migrant dimension and those organised around labour. The main goal of this study is to elaborate how the larger organisational processes are carried out under these two collectives: one focused on migration and the other on labour. These collectives have recently experienced an unprecedented jump both in rising memberships and in organisational purpose, which is connected to the recent slowdown of industrial production as well as stricter migration policies. The result has been a consolidation of organisational spaces in which "migration" and "labour" have merged in an unparalleled manner.

Our inquiry is based along two major theoretical lines which create a contextual framework for the case under study. One posits the continuous existence of a large population under precarious working conditions, which is not an exception but a rule, exhibiting a tight link to the migration processes that are usually irregular (Munck, 2011). The other theoretical approach proposes a dialectical bond between labour organisation and capital development. The main focus of these mutual relationships is on the particular influence of the former over the latter (Lebowitz, 2005).

The research question that guides this inquiry is as follows: What are the characteristics of present-day migrant garment worker organisations that take action toward eradicating labour overexploitation?

This question derives from a multi-leveled approach because it integrates several theoretical concerns and supposes the use of different methodological strategies. According to the Hesse-Biber (2010) classification, the inquiry under issue consists of a mixed method that has a sequential exploratory design through which a quantitative approach of data collection provides the context for a qualitative analysis.

Quantitative fieldwork was conducted with population statistics collected by the official statistics body of Buenos Aires.[1] Qualitative fieldwork was done using multiple methods and data sources, such as in-depth interviews of organisation members and workers; shop stewards (*delegados sindicales*) and leaders; participant observation in assemblies and other activities, in addition to documentary and press analysis.

The cases selected for the study share a number of important characteristics which make these comparisons relevant. These organisations have been promoted by militants who are or were members of other organisations that have been active for over a decade. One of them is the Migrant Workers Bloc (*Bloque de Trabajadorxs Migrantes*, BTM), where several organisations converge, creating a new space to achieve shared objectives. Another is the Garment Workers and Employees Union (*Unión de Costurerxs y Empleadxs del Vestido*, UCEV), an alternative trade union formed after the rupture of a recognised rank-and-file organisation within the garment industry. Both organisations are located and cover Buenos Aires.

Consequently, it is interesting to conduct a parallel analysis of their developments because these two organisations had different starting points: the BTM was organised on the basis of migration and the UCEV on labour.

2   Labour in the Garment Industry: Overexploitation and Migration

Historically, the garment industry relies on a significant proportion of manual labour, outsourced to sewing workshops and homebased work (Abramo et al.,

---

[1] "Encuesta Anual de Hogares" (EAH) from *Dirección de Estadísticas y Censos de la Ciudad de Buenos Aires*. Retrieved from http://www.estadisticaciudad.gob.ar/. Details of data processing are described in Salgado & Carpio (2017).

2004; Adúriz, 2009; Belini, 2008; Kosacoff, 2004; Montero, 2011; Pascucci, 2007; Salgado, 2015). Thus, with little initial capital, one can participate in garment production because of low requirements regarding machinery, scale and labour skills. The size of machines allows for concealment within the household environment. In addition, the household, as a productive establishment, facilitates this type of fiscal camouflage. These conditions of clothing production are located at the lowest level within the whole industry. This nature has intensified since the 1970s in direct relation to the increase of labour precariousness.

Over the last few decades, the gap between intellectual and manual labour has widened within the garment industry. This process can be seen by the growing concentration of capital related to big brands and the gradual erosion of the worker's salary and their conditions in sewing workshops (Lieutieur, 2010; Schorr & Ferreira, 2013; Montero, 2011). The economic expansion that began after the 2001 economic crisis[2] strengthened this existing polarity and, in the context of workshop atomisation, new actors emerged: intermediaries who developed a more complex chain of exploitation that further deteriorates the workers' bargaining power.

The growth that began after the end of the currency exchange dilemma in 2001 did not imply a proportional reduction of precarious employment (Chitarroni & Cimillo, 2007; Novick, 2006; Féliz & Pérez, 2007). Following the national trend, textile/garment employment increased by 40% between 2002 and 2008. Nevertheless, the branch could not reach the high levels of employment achieved before the economic slowdown of the nineties (Salgado, 2012). According to estimates made by the National Institute of Industrial Technology[3] (INTI, 2012), between 2003 and 2012, registered employment rose by 57%, whereas non-registered grew by 200%. In addition, based on population statistics, non-registered work represents between 50 and 70% of all employment in the garment industry from 2004 to the present (Salgado & Carpio, 2017; Salgado, 2016 and 2015). Also, for those workers born in neighboring countries, primarily Bolivia, this proportion is 10% higher. Some workers born in Bolivia are employed in unregistered workshops and are recruited through human trafficking networks. Interviews and reports indicate deceitful promises about working and housing conditions in those cases. Their freedom is restricted and their wages remain unpaid till their "debts" are cleared (travelling expenses, travelling documents, food and housing expenses), trapping workers in a

---

2   The pegged currency exchange implemented during the 1990s ended in a macroeconomic collapse in 2001. More information about the economic situation and social struggle within this period is in Svampa (2014).
3   Instituto Nacional de Tecnología Industrial (INTI).

situation of dependency (D'Ovidio, 2007; Lieutier, 2010; Colectivo Simbiosis/ Colectivo Situaciones, 2011). Unregistered migration reinforces this vulnerable situation because workshop owners build a threatening context outside the workshop that ensure workers stay inside due to fear of possible deportation, deportability, and not deportation per se (De Génova, 2002). In addition, there are also more explicit mechanisms, such as the retention of passports and identity documents or physically locking them in the workshop impeding their freedom of movement. In those workshops, people often work over 12 hours a day. Salary payment is discretionary or it is made through "vales".[4] Salaries are paid on a piecework basis and are below the legal minimum wage.[5]

These conditions within the garment industry were publicly brought to light due to a fire in a workshop located on Luis Viale Street[6] on March 30th 2006 where a pregnant woman and five children died. They lived and worked in the workshop and couldn't escape from the fire because the doors had been locked by the manager. In June 2016, these workshop managers were sentenced to 13 years in prison for crimes concerning involuntary servitude as well as being found guilty for the fire which was sentenced as aggravated homicide.[7]

In 2015, nine years after that tragedy, a similar disaster occurred in the Flores neighborhood of Buenos Aires. This time, two children died locked inside a workshop. The lack of intervention, either by the government or by trade unions, caused this terrible repetition who had not developed the necessary precautionary changes between one fire and the other.[8]

---

4   Although the word "vale" means "promissory note", that "vale" consists of a small advance payment that is hardly enough to buy personal items or make phone calls.
5   The wage scale is updated through collective negotiations (*paritaria salarial*). Considering the chronic inflation in Argentina, these adjustments represent an outstanding portion of collective bargaining: 80% of them for the period 2003-2007, according to Atzeni & Ghigliani (2007).
6   The tragedy became known as the Luis Viale Fire (*el incendio de Luis Viale*).
7   The Court also ordered the continuation of the investigation concerning the responsibility of Fischberg and Geiler, "owners of the workshop and machines, in compliance with Federal Police, who received bribes" (CELS, 2017, p. 1, author's translation). On June 1, 2017, both were subpoenaed to testify.
8   After the fire in 2006, the government implemented a few policies oriented mainly toward closing non-registered workshops down, but without policy that properly supports those people left without that (meagre) income. Additionally, there was a policy implemented to accelerate the legalisation of migrants, namely the "Patria Grande" social programme (INTI, 2007). However, none of these policies succeeded in eradicating this type of labour exploitation. In addition, collusion with the police has been found (Courtis & Pacceca, 2006) as well as the lax implementation of the Law regulating home working (*Trabajo a Domicilio*) -12.713- (Arcos & Montero, 2011).

3 Overexploitation: A Conceptual Arrival Point

The concept of labour overexploitation provides an accurate theoretical model for approaching the particular dynamics of labour-capital relations located on one end of the broad spectrum involved within the concept of "precariousness". It allows for an analysis of these dynamics as stable events without defining them as exceptional[9] as well.

The concept was coined by the Brazilian economist Ruy Mauro Marini, an important neo-Marxist dependency theorist.[10] The author defines 'overexploitation' as a "heightened level of the exploitation of a worker's physical force, as opposed to the resulting exploitation related to the increase in their productivity that is revealed through the fact that the labour force is remunerated below its value" (Marini, 1979, p. 158, author's translation). The author identifies three fundamental mechanisms through which overexploitation becomes effective: the expansion of regulated working hours, an increase of intensity of the labour and the remuneration of work below its value. These mechanisms materialise markedly in the garment industry when compared to other the branches of labour as well as to the labour market as a whole. Based on former quantitative analysis (Salgado & Carpio, 2017 and 2015; Salgado, 2014), migration was included as a component variable, particularly from border countries and mainly from Bolivia, due to the fact that the overexploitation of labour has increased around 20 percent for this population (Table 5.1).

Table 5.1 shows data taken from official population statistics from the City of Buenos Aires.[11] Two variables that constitute overexploitation are related and presented on the table below: the elongation of working hours[12] and

---

9   In the beginning of our research we defined growth through the increase of absolute surplus-value as a main characteristic of production in the garment industry (Salgado, 2012). The notion of overexploitation improves this approach by itemizing it and giving an account of the physical deterioration that such a form of labour exploitation implies (Salgado & Carpio, 2017).
10 The appropriateness of this theoretical model and the decisions made concerning the details are presented in Salgado & Carpio (2017).
11 Data shown on Table 5.1 is collected by the official statistics body of the City of Buenos Aires. Because of its nature, it covers just the visible region of the population under study. Consenting to answer the questionnaire implies a particular level of visibility. Possibly, those who work in workshops and are deprived of their liberty are included as 'non-response'. Thus, the presented results correspond to the portion that we define as "visible workers of garment industry" (Salgado & Carpio, 2017).
12 We selected the limits provided by the law governing working conditions, limited to 48 hours per week, according to Article 1 of the Law 11.544.

TABLE 5.1 A distribution of garment industry overexploitation indicators by worker birth place

	TOTAL	CV 2016	Born in the city of Buenos Aires	CV 2016	Born in a border country	CV 2016
Below minimum-wage | Over 49 hours	16,70%	10,30%	5,50%	30,50%	28,80%	12,60%
Below minimum-wage | Up to 48 hours	15,10%	10,80%	13,10%	19,70%	19,30%	15,50%
At minimum-wage | Over 49 hours	3,80%	21,50%	1,40%	60,00%	6,30%	27,10%
At minimum-wage | Up to 48 hours	2,70%	25,60%	1,00%	70,60%	3,50%	36,30%
Above minimum-wage | Over 49 hours	9,50%	13,70%	11,90%	20,70%	8,20%	23,70%
Above minimum-wage | Up to 48 hours	32,00%	7,40%	39,30%	11,40%	21,70%	14,60%
With income, but not specifically declared / No data (N/D) | Over 49 hours	4,20%	20,60%	4,80%	32,40%	3,40%	36,90%
With income, but not specifically declared / No data (N/D) | Up to 48 hours	12,10%	12,10%	18,50%	16,60%	4,80%	30,80%
TOTAL N	96,10% 133.277	4,30%	95,40% 46.153	7,30%	95,90% 51.173	6,90%

SOURCE: PREPARED BY THE AUTHORS BASED ON EAH06, EAH09, EAH12 Y EAH15. DIRECCIÓN GENERAL DE ESTADÍSTICA Y CENSOS (MINISTERIO DE HACIENDA DE GCBA).

remuneration of work below its value.[13] The intensity of labour cannot be calculated through this source.[14] Nevertheless, considering that non-registered workshops wages are generally paid on a piecework basis, a constant level

---

13 We use the floor established by minimum-wage law. In 2004, the National Board of Employment, Productivity and Minimum, Vital and Mobile Salary (*Consejo Nacional del Empleo, La Productividad y el Salario Mínimo, Vital y Móvil*), created on 1991 and inactive for almost 10 years, convened through the National Executive decree 1095. Thereafter, minimum-wage has been adjusted on an annual or bi-annual basis.

14 Population statistics is information gathered directly from workers and not from industrial units. Consequently, linking data from those sources with data given by the industry to quantify 'intensity' is it not feasible.

of high intensity must be considered. A high intensity is associated with this method of payment (Marx, 2011) as well as several control devices as indicated in the following quotation:

> It's a job where you have to work very fast, it's very physically rough; they push you to go faster; they sit and watch you through a little camera to see who's working and who isn't; how long you spend in the bathroom, when you go or when you eat, they controlled all of that (Interview to a former workshop worker and current family workshop worker, author's translation).

The conditions explained thus far are more prevalent for migrant workers coming from border countries: close to 30 percent of them work more than 49 hours a week and their income is below minimum-wage, while only 10% of native residents of the city are under same conditions. The existing set of factors that shapes and sustains overexploitation imply higher levels for migrant workers when compared to those native-born in the city of Buenos Aires. The data shows significant differences between these two groups.

4 The Dialectic of Formality and Informality

Table 5.1 shows how precariousness exists within this branch and at a significantly higher level for migrant workers. Qualitative data gives a strong account of the profound relationship present between the working conditions presented above and migratory status: precarious work - precarious migratory status; whereas, statistical sources that register labour and migratory status cannot be related. The following excerpt from an interview synthesises a common situation within this field:

> My aim was to have stable work and I wanted to be satisfied with the wage. Yes, mostly that and having the 'precaria'[15] (*work visa*) for getting into a registered job because I was always being asked for identity documents (Interview to a workshop worker and member of *PTS*).

---

15 A citizenship document known as "la precaria" in the Spanish language gives a worker provisional migratory regularisation. It enables the worker to access health services, educational institutions and to work under labour laws. However, this should be renewed every three months which causes problems related to labour continuity for formal work (Grabner, 2012).

TABLE 5.2   Classification of prevailing registration characteristics by industry site

	Labor registration	Migratory status	Location registration
Factories	Yes	Yes	Yes
Formal workshops	Yes	Yes	Yes
Semi-formal workshops	Simplified Tax Regime for small contributors	Yes	Yes or improper registration
Family workshops	No	Yes or No	No
Workshops linked to human trafficking networks	No or Simplified Tax Regime for small contributors	No	No or improper registration

SOURCE: PREPARED BY THE AUTHORS BASED ON QUALITATIVE DATA

At this point, it is worth analyzing what 'registered' or 'being on the books' means because of its strong link to overexploitation. Munk (2013) along with Harold Bauder (2006) identify international migration as a regulatory labour market tool "allowing employers to drive down wages and lower labour standards through the introduction of a 'cheap and flexible' migrant labour force" (Munck, 2011, p. 9). Beyond labour registration, other types of registration have a direct influence on this phenomenon: one is related to the production site and affects health and safety standards that bear directly on workers' wellbeing. Other types of registration concern migratory status and influence worker's access to citizenship rights. The lack of citizenship can be used as a part of coercive platform that threatens a worker through stigmatisation, deportation threats, and other means. Table 5.2 classifies the different workplaces related to these concerns. The table shows the characteristics of labour registration, production site registration and migratory status of the foreigners who work there.

Clothing/garment factories are at highest level of formality in the table. There is a wide range of workshops: at the most formal end are those that comply with the Law that regulates home working (*Trabajo a Domicilio*) -12.713-. The law establishes a joint and solidarity liability (JSL) on brands and their workshop owners.[16] The following category corresponds to those workshops

---

16   The Law 12.713 was promulgated in 1941 with the aim of reigning in labour overexploitation by harmonizing working conditions between factories and workshops. However, its enforcement resulted in a huge lack of effective implementation (Jelin et al., 1998). Under these circumstances, home working went increasingly hand in hand with non-registration,

with proper registration for the site and in which employees are registered through the Simplified Tax Regime for small contributors (Monotributo), which represent fraud that is used to mask salaried employment relationships. Lastly, the least formal workplaces may lack the two types of registration. There is a key distinction that is implied between the two: a family workshop may be set up as a household's subsistence strategy; while, other 'households' employ people in involuntary servitude, recruited and relocated through trafficking networks.[17]

Although formality and informality or registered and non-registered seem to be distinct for some scholars of the Sociology of Labour and those who work within media discourses, the distinction within the garment industry is ambiguous. These categories form a homogeneous whole, that show interconnections throughout the different levels of the industry that we have named the "displacement of the precariousness" (Salgado & Carpio, 2017). Munck (2011), as well, notices the analytical weakness implied in the binary use of the terms, formal and informal, because "it posits two hermetically sealed sectors, which cannot simply be distinguished in practice, and mask intermediate or hybrid employment categories. That is not to deny the importance of an unregulated/informal relationship of production and income generation that is not 'marginal' to capitalist development but rather an integral element of its dynamic" (Munck, 2011, p. 7). This relation is described by a factory worker as follows:

> In our factory, where we work for bigger brands, I started noticing vans arriving with exercise tank tops, already assembled and brought into the factory. The transfers were made there and the composition was brought by the brands. This is how brands push factories (...) These big enterprises also use sweatshops (*talleres clandestinos*) (...) Then, the brands intimidate the factory owner and we end up having to give lower prices (...) After all of this, we are the ones negatively affected because we have to increase our production to earn more (Interview to a factory worker, critical shop steward and member of the *Lista Roja*, author's translation).

---

entailing a significant loss related to regulated working and wage conditions. This law contemplates a dual nature for the workshop owner (*tallerista*) as employee of the brands and employer of the workers. In 2008, the Executive proposed to rupture this binding relationship, among other factors, through a reform Project, which finally has not been enacted. Details of this reform attempt are described in Salgado (2016).

17 Those workshops became known as "clandestinos", meaning "black", "illegal". We prefer not to use such adjectives because of the essential bias that it associates with these workers. Also, because of the exclusionary nature implied. These adjectives deny the stable social practices and relationships that this community presents to the larger society.

This interview shows the effects unregistered workshops can have on the production system. This prevailing model, described through the concept of overexploitation, puts pressure on the conditions of registered workers and their workplaces. Therefore, as unemployment, in terms of a reserve army of labour, pressures the currently employed wage-worker, the expansion of precariousness within non-registered work diminishes the demands of registered labour (Salgado & Carpio, 2017; Salgado, 2015).

5   Trade Unions and Organisations in the Garment Industry

Reflecting on labour conditions compels us to analyse the role of trade unions and other organisations that aspire to improve labour conditions and how the lack of organisations create a model that benefits from the advance of capital. With this in mind, we share observations with Lebowitz (2005) that the correlation of forces within the labour-capital relationship mutually determines each other. This means that the forms of working-class organisation determine the advancement of capital. This idea is extensively elaborated by the author on the basis of Marx's work, who argued that "the fixation of its actual degree is only settled by the continuous struggle between capital and labour, the capitalist constantly tending to reduce wages to their physical minimum, and to extend the working day to its physical maximum, while the working man constantly presses in the opposite direction" (Marx, 1865, p. 6).

In light of recent studies, we wondered about the appropriateness of the concept of Trade Union revitalisation. As Atzeni and Ghigliani point out, the reactivation of bargaining and an increase of social mobilisation are not enough to imply a resurgence of unions if change does not involve "new organisational forces, new tactics or new attitudes by organised labour" (Atzeni & Ghigliani, 2007, p. 12). It is necessary to distinguish between revitalisation and renewal. In a former study, we noted that due to the particularities of the Argentine trade union model, Trade Union revitalisation can indicate the strengthening of bureaucratic Trade Unions, as the emergence of grassroots organisations, which question the current system and aim to dispute the power of those structures (Arias & Salgado, 2011). A main feature of the Argentine model, which is substantially different, is the arrangements by the trade union unity regime (*unicidad sindical*).[18] This model lays out the foundation

---

18   The system adopted by Argentine legislation is called "promoted unity" (*unidad promocionada*) or "induced unity" (*unidad inducida*). It implies that just one trade union – the most representative one according to the law- would be ensured with legal protection

for union monopolies and extends the coverage of trade unions to all the workers within the influential area established by the Collective Bargaining Agreement (*convenio colectivo*), whether they are members of the union or not.[19]

The difference we point out becomes clear from analyzing the sources of economic funds for the trade unions: those which developed trade union revitalisation strategies in other countries (where they depend on worker contributions for survival) had membership growth as one of their main goals. Conversely, in Argentina, the economic resources of trade unions with legal recognition do not exclusively derive from a worker's deduction in wages (Haidar, 2016; Ghigliani et al., 2012). Thus, the crisis of representation does not have direct impact on the finances of institutionalised unionism (Arias & Salgado, 2011). However, the growth of non-registered labour has an economic impact because legally protected trade unions (*personería gremial*) within the General Confederation of Labour (CGT)[20] restrict membership to registered workers.

In sum, workers lack solid representation throughout the entire garment industry. This lack is also amplified due to union fragmentation. There are five trade unions involved in the different productive stages within the industry: the garment industry union (*Sindicato Obrero de la Industria del Vestido y Afines, SOIVA*), the fabric cutters union (*Unión de Cortadores de la Indumentaria, UCI*), the union for workshop owners homeworkers (*Sindicato de Trabajadores Talleristas a Domicilio, STTAD*), the association of textile workers (*Asociación Obrera Textil, AOT*) and the union of textile employees and related (*Sindicato Empleados Textiles de la Industria y Afines, SETIA*) (Salgado, 2012). Within this partitioning of the textile and clothing industry, we focus particularly on the SOIVA because this union is for sewing workers and was the main opponent in the constitution process of one the analyzed cases: the UCEV.

In this regard, it is worth emphasizing that the SOIVA, in the trade union statute, restricts representation to workers who are native to the country. As migrant workers could not occupy some representative positions, this means a further lack of representation in this branch that employs a big number of them. Munck (2011) points out that in order to face the current situation

---

        against exclusion from union activities (*personería gremial*) (Article 25 of the Law 23.551 regulating Trade Unions).

19   This reach is expressed through wage increases by collective bargaining (*paritaria salarial*), as in the deduction of percentages of the wage by trade unions for all registered wage-workers (members or not).

20   The General Confederation of Labour (*Confederación General del Trabajo, CGT*), is a third-level union organisation, which links the majority of Trade Unions of private and public sector.

regarding trade unions and other social movements, different possibilities for action are required: "They may incorporate these workers into their organisations and press for the leveling-up of labour standards as against the 'race to the bottom' of neoliberalism or, conversely, they may go along with the mainstream racist and xenophobic discourse and actively lead the exclusionary offensive in the workplace" (Munck, 2011, p. 10). SOIVA is known to follow the second category as is reflected in several studies (Baratini, 2010; Gago, 2014; Lieutieur, 2010; Pascucci, 2011).

In past decades, no systematic mechanism has been developed for improving working conditions, nor for eliminating a particular type of work legally called "subjection to servitude", the most extreme form of overexploitation. This union (SOIVA), in turn, mostly favors employer interests and this alliance has been repeatedly denounced by workers:

> Once she [a member of the organisation] wanted to send a registered letter [to file a lawsuit against her employer] and Ranú [Secretary-General of SOIVA] insulted her by saying: 'You are stupid, don´t you see that we cannot send a registered letter to that company!'. That's how these relationships work (Interview to a factory worker, critical shop steward and member of the UTC, author's translation).

In the same direction, employers of the branch characterised their relationship with the trade union (SOIVA) as positive:

> It could be said that our relationship with the trade union is very good (...) The other day, the union said they needed some pants stitched for a charity event. They called us and within two seconds we said "yes, of course; just say how many you need us to do and we'll do them". [Referring to a mobilisation conducted by the SOIVA] The Secretary-General of SOIVA called and told me "We have to do something, unfortunately I'm sending a bus with some boys (*muchachos*) and a bass drum (*bombo*) to your door; it is just going to take 10 minutes, but I am obligated to do this". It was because they were in a difficult situation within the union confederation (CGT). And, well, they had to do it, we didn't like it at all, but, well,.... (Interview to a Production Manager of garment factory, author's translation).

Repeating Lebowitz's (2005) perspective, the lack of union intervention in eradicating unregistered labour, particularly overexploitation, is one side of the the essential dialectic that ensures its continued existence. As pointed out by Munck (2011) and Fine (2005) from the analysis of cases which transcend political and economic unionism, the overwhelming importance of legal status for migrant workers compels an organisation to get involved with migratory politics because they become questions directly linked to the social matters of labour.

As we will see, the cases studied go beyond other recent experiences within labour organisations. We will use Fine's (2005) perspective on "community unionism" as theoretical support for approaching and characterizing the cases. In the following sections, we will analyse the upstart of recent organisations that are composed of garment workers, which pursue substantial transformations both in their directions and range as well as in their goals.

5.1   Economic and Social Consequences of a New Regime

Recently, major changes have occurred on national political and economic levels due to the rise of a new political force headed by Mauricio Macri, the leader of the "Cambiemos", a multi-party alliance. This right oriented political organisation drove "Kircherismo" from power after twelve years in government in December 2015. The "Cambiemos" alliance designed the Country Programme Framework under neoliberalist tendencies by curtailing government spending and employees, and also through less intervention concerning international commercial relations. This intention was clearly revealed in Macri's presidential campaign who spoke about opening up the market to imports and removing the agro-export sector withholding taxes. Other mechanisms related to this pattern were added, such as the growth of the external indebtedness and the development of mechanisms for promoting financial capital reproduction. Vommaro & Gené (2017) characterised the current macroeconomic context as creating a new logic of political communication through the reduction of subsidies on various fuel, public services and a wide range of social programs. As a result, industrial employment decreased by 3,7% between 2015 and 2016 due to the trade liberalisation (Torres & Nunes Chas, 2017). In the same direction, the index of SMEs industrial production shrank by 7,6% for the garment industry between 2016 and 2017 (Grasso & Perez Almansi, 2017).

The context of a recession alerted workers and was expressed as an increased influx toward union-like community spaces and the development of a new dynamics of organisation, which happens during recessions. Such was the case after the economic crash in 2008.[21] Again in 2016, the economic and political contexts go hand in hand with the reconfiguration of political subjects. In terms of migration policy, the new government created a major

---

21   The recession of 2008 implied a fall in production and also had a severely negative impact on employment within the garment industry: dismissals, suspensions, reduction of overtime, among others (Pascucci, 2011); processes which increase the presence of political organisations.

shift when compared to the former. In 2004, under the previous government, a law on migration (25.871) was enacted to repeal a previous one that was promulgated during the last military dictatorship[22] and sought to refocus the protection of human rights according to international agreements. In that sense, migration was recognised as an essential and inalienable right of individuals and was guaranteed through principles of equality and universality. The 2004 law provides the possibility of judicial appeal for decisions of expulsion by a migration authority, which ensures an effective intervention of a competent judicial authority concerning the issuing of a detention order in cases of migrants in irregular situations. Moreover, it set a new framework for migration from neighboring countries.[23] In January 2017, this migration law was amended by Presidential Decree (DNU 70/2017).[24] In this decree, migration is linked to organised crime and drug trafficking networks, stigmatizing migrants (Canelo et al., 2018). The decree set up a speedy procedure for the arrest and deportation of migrants under criminal prosecution of any kind and for those who have committed administrative offences during migration procedure.

This decree focuses on the administrative and judicial difficulties and proceedings that migration authorities have to go through. As the Center for Legal and Social Studies (*Centro de Estudios Legales y Sociales*, CELS) have pointed out "instead of seeking effective tools for identifying those delays and its causes, the government decided that selected migrant persons would no longer be entitled to access to justice and to necessary legal defense on the migration procedure" (CELS, 2018, p. 2, author's translation).[25] In this connection, it is important to highlight that while this migration law (25.871) was ratified after

---

[22] The law enacted during the last military dictatorship is known as the "Videla law" after the name of the first president of the de facto regime.

[23] About this, Courtis & Pacecca note that according to the nationality criterion outlined in the Agreement on Residency for Nationals of States Members of the Common Market of the South (MERCOSUR) of 2002, that law states that "the opportunity for those people (the vast majority of migrants) who did not comply with any of the criteria established on the 'Videla law' or on bilateral conventions, to be admitted as temporary residents with a two-year work permit, renewable and with multiple entries and departures" (Courtis & Pacecca, 2007, p. 10, author's translation).

[24] Emergency decrees (Decretos de Necesidad y Urgencia, DNU) are enacted by the Executive and require the approval of the legislature. Then, they are established with authority from ratification. The mentioned "DNU" (70/2017) is available on http://servicios.infoleg.gob.ar/infolegInternet/verNorma.do?id=271245

[25] In addition, the argument put forward by the Government that advocates this course of action was based on statistics, in a duplicitous way, holding that 20% of the prison population is composed of foreigners, when it only contains 6%.

several years of debate, the DNU 70/2017 was spearheaded by the Executive, without any deliberation (Canelo et al, 2018; CELS, 2018).

5.2 Collective Organisations: Migration and Labour

Migrant workers in the garment industry have recently formed several organisations in Argentina. These organisations operate at the convergence of migration and labour, but each stress particularly only one of the two dimensions either migration or labour.[26] From one of those perspectives, these organisations approach issues concerning the other one. A brief exposition of their main characteristics and strength is made below. After, we will analyze recent experiences, which have been generated by the recent political and economic changes at the national level whose main milestones are an industry recession and tougher migration policies.

5.2.1 Organisations Primarily Focused on Migration

There are multiple organisations of migrants from bordering countries involving garment industry workers. They have different affiliations: cultural (dance and music ensembles and others), religious, sports (such as neighborhood clubs), social (mutual support associations), politics (radio broadcasts, think tanks and others) and labour (mainly employment cooperatives[27]) (Gavazzo, 2008; Caggiano, 2014; Pascucci, 2011).

These organisations play an important role in the fight against discrimination. In this sense, Gavazzo notes that they "not only helped to create a sense of community (...), but also have constituted the foundation of important demands towards the State and the society of origin and of destination" (Gavazzo, 2018, p. 72; author's translation). This is also evident in their active participation in the elabouration of the 2004 migration law (25.871).[28]

One of the organisations, made up of Bolivian garment workers, is "Simbiosis Cultural", the Cultural Symbiosis Collective. At first, it was composed of young Bolivians and adult children of Bolivians who had arrived to Argentina with their parents or on their own. Several reasons led them to meet up and develop a space for exchanging views and thoughts. In an early publication of

---

[26] This arrangement is also intelligible through their goals and actions, as we will see.

[27] A survey carried out in 2004 by the International Organisation for Migration and the Centre for Latin American Migration Studies (CEMLA) found that organisations with cultural aims represent the largest proportion, secondly the religious and finally sports and social (Caggiano, 2014).

[28] This is a significant indicator of the increasing importance that these organisations have gained over time in having political influence (Gavazzo, 2018).

the organization,[29] Delia, one of its members, said that, "we always need to talk about our problems: what our problems were, for immigrants, young immigrants, immigrant families, labour, identity..." (Colectivo Simbiosis/Colectivo Situaciones, 2011, p. 78; author's translation). First, they developed a space to discuss films (*cine-debate*) at the main square in Flores, one of the neighborhoods in Buenos Aires where a high proportion of Bolivians live. Attendance reached more than 70 people per weekend. Shared enthusiasm and interest led to the constitution of the organisation and on March 8th of the following year, 2008, they organised their first activity under the name, the Cultural Symbiosis Collective. In their mission statement, they propose to "achieve a presence where we can recognise each other and through coexistence and interpersonal relationships establish bonds that give us the strength to expose our identity and to be proud of being Bolivian" (cit. en Olivera, 2009, p. 114; author's translation).

From these spaces, several actions concerning migrant workers of the garment industry were accomplished. Through campaigns that raise awareness about migrant problems (mainly with Bolivians) political and academic documents were produced in coordination with academic circles who conducted action-research.

After the fire in 2015, the Cultural Symbiosis Collective and other organisations united in a broader social group named the "Flores Textile Assembly" (*Asamblea textil de Flores*)". It was composed of social and trade union organisations, sewing workers, neighbors and teachers within the neighborhood. One of the main goals was to reflect on forms of intervention in garment industry workshops as an alternative response to the compulsive raids that "criminalised workers" and "expelled them", as Juan Vázquez, a member of Cultural Symbiosis Collective pointed out (Telam, 2015).

Following in the footsteps of the "Flores Textile Assembly", the "Observatory of Submerged Labour" was formed. Its aim was to gather information and to raise awareness about the dynamics of the work done in sewing workshops. This group seeks to transcend the view of victimisation that is usually associated with these groups and adapt a perspective that focuses on the aspirations of the worker. Along these lines, the manifesto presents the basis of which it was founded:

---

29   "De chuequistas y overlockas" was one of the first books entirely dedicated to showcasing the reality migrants face who work in unregistered garment workshops. The book stems from an action-research co-conducted with another organisation composed by social researchers (Colectivo Situaciones- Colectivo Simbiosis/Colectivo Situaciones, 2011).

> We name submerged labour that world that is separated of "legality" by a border that is mainly regulated by profit and exploitation. Submerged labour is a powerful economic engine due to its reduced production costs as it supplies the market with cheap goods that poor people can afford to pay and draws principally on the efforts, aspirations for the progress of migrants. This submergence relies on the naturalisation of very hard-working conditions and on the tolerance of life-threatening situations as well (Asamblea Textil de Flores, 2015, p. 2, author's translation).

Several campaigns against stigmatisation were launched from this space, such as "taking the popular and migrant economy out of the ghetto" and "opening workshops"[30] (Gago, 2018; Castronovo, 2018). Verónica Gago, a researcher and member of this organisation, stresses to "open and question workshops as a kind of prototype of labour that is replicated in other sectors (particularly agricultural), that challenges many native workers, even registered, because it is framed in an underground context and placed in an increasingly precarious city that benefits from it through a racist and security-based paradigm" (Gago, 2015, p. 3, author's translation). Furthermore, survivors of the "Luis Viale Fire"[31] of 2006 asked for support from the "Flores Textile Assembly" in order to communicate that a lawsuit hearing was about to be issued. A specific group was then formed and conducted a media campaign and were supported with legal counsel as well.[32]

The Cultural Symbiosis Collective has been central in the shaping of the Migrant Workers Bloc (BTM), contributing to their trajectory on action and reflection, which was then translated into the objectives of the BTM.

5.2.2 The Migrant Workers Bloc (Bloque de Trabajadorxs Migrantes, BTM)

> "We are the migrants, together we are breaking boundaries, America is ours", a slogan developed during the social action of March 2017 against the enacting of DNU 70/2017, which was later used in the Migrant Strike (Gavazzo, 2018).

---

30 "Sacar del gueto la economía popular y migrante" and "Abrir el taller", respectively.
31 See footnote 6 above.
32 With this support, the change of caption lawsuit was achieved, tolling of the statute of limitations. That conducts to results exposed on footnote 7 above. The tracking of the trial is set out in https://juicioluisviale.wordpress.com/

The BTM was the result of the convergence process of several organisations worried about the tougher migration policies expressed through the enacting of DNU 70/2017.

In the beginning, the first mobilisation took place at the doors of Parliament. Gavazzo (2018) writes that the BTM brings together some of the oldest organisations as well as several collectives of young Bolivians and the adult children of Bolivians. Other organisations were added[33] to this coordinating body where the aim was to "highlight the risks of that Decree and to raise awareness about the legitimisation of xenophobia (...) and to produce an autonomous voice that supports the right to migrate and to live decent lives in Argentina" (Gavazzo, 2018, p. 140; author's translation).

Among the first steps carried out before becoming the BTM, these organisations called for a Migrant Strike (*Paro Migrante*), which, as Gavazzo (2018) points out, had vast media coverage that was successful in demonstrating their concerns without victimizing the participants. The date and the name of the strike reflect a greater integration of issues concerning labour within these groups. Juan Vázquez, from the Cultural Symbiosis Collective, explained to the press that:

> March 30th is an important date for us. It was when our labour problems as migrants became visible (...). Eleven years have passed since the [Luis Viale] fire and after 10 years the case came up for oral hearing and both of those responsible were convicted. The mobilisation takes place on March 30th with the aim of raising awareness and creating a symbol of our fight on this very significant date (Sur Capitalino, 2017, p. 1; author's translation).

More than 30 migrant organisations concerning the women's movement, trade unions, unemployed movements, left-wing parties and researchers from several universities took part in the strike that was conducted that day. Migrants from different Latin American countries united in force in this unprecedented experience, which has turned out to be a milestone in organizing migrant groups. Gavazzo (2018) notes that various national symbols were used as group identifiers to raise awareness about what the author named as a common and more extended ethnicity (the "Latin-Americanness"[34]) that binds them together within their differences.

---

33   It is remarkable the presence of feminist organisations, which establish a permanent link with women's movement and posed specific gender-related demands.
34   The expansion of the Latin American political subject beyond national borders is revisited in the Final thoughts.

At one of the assemblies after the strike, they resolved to consolidate under the name of the Migrant Workers Bloc (*Bloque de Trabajadorxs Migrantes*, BTM) and remain a stable organisation that follows the discussions started on that day. Organizing and conducting the strike worked as a catalyst combining migratory and labour issues and succeeded in lifting victim stigmatisation from the migrants that is spread by the mass media as well as by some of the older migrant organisations (Gavazzo, 2018). It is important to stress this because it is a main objective of the Cultural Symbiosis Collective. It is relevant because it provides an account for the deconstruction process conducted by that organisation in their reflection-action trajectory. It also exposes an epistemological turn, which formed the basis of the innovative direct action and the weight of an aspect of the identity which had been under-emphasised until then. This new identity focused on labour as well, which was found to be empowering and was projected in the name of the organisation itself, as reflected in their manifesto:

> We are migrants, who are an integral part of society with dignity, we struggle from grassroots, as workers. We are also students, professionals, children, parents; we are neighbors with multiples identities, convinced that there are no boundaries (Bloque de Trabajadorxs Migrantes, 2017, author's translation).

According to Fine's (2005) classification, this organisation could be labelled as a community organisation/no union partner. In this regard, the author stresses that "these organisations are either new, freestanding, community-based efforts to organise around work and wages or new initiatives created by existing community organisations" (Fine, 2005, p.159).

5.2.3 Organisations Primarily Focused on Labour

Several rank-and-file organisations have been formed with the aim of reversing the working conditions that prevail in the garment industry. Grassroots efforts were formed from the most formal workers, those in the factories. Workplace alliances have joined hands with left-wing parties,[35] or as a result of a multi-

---

35 A current member of the PTS (*Partido Socialista de los Trabajadores*, Socialist Workers Party), which is one of the biggest left-wing organisations in Argentina explained their relationship as follows: "The PTS came over and went downstairs to have conversations with the workers, because we usually left work late. (…) I think, they came over after a relative of one of their members was fired and she went and told them what the situation was in the factory. They said: "if you aren't organised, it is difficult to win". Then, they began to hand out flyers [outside of work] (…) [Later, there was an incident where a worker set herself on fire as a result of the extreme pressure she was under at work.] We talked with

dimensional space organised by territory, such as the case of the Sewing Workers Union (*Unión de Trabajadores Costureros, UTC*) that operates within the framework of "La Alameda" Foundation, the case is analyzed below. Other organisations have limited their activities to that of the workplace and were formed in a context of mass dismissal and suspensions.[36]

There is one organisation of garment industry migrant workers that is built on the concept of labour and that must be highlighted because of its singularity and its efforts concerning assembling workers from unregistered workshops, namely: The Sewing Immigrant Bolivian Workers Movement (*Movimiento de Costureros Inmigrantes Bolivianos, MCIBol*). It was created in 2009, and in its two years, undertook the unprecedented objective of syndicate formation that was oriented toward migrant workers in the clothing industry. One of its former leaders shares the story as follows:

> [At the beginning the organisation had] about thirty members. The number declined until we were ten (...) [With regard to *MCIBol's* initiation year] In June 2009, we only lasted about 2 years (...) For me, it was

---

our co-workers and she was someone who gave us this opportunity; now, we have to do something for her, we must help her because of the accident she had, what happened was really bad and the enterprise wanted us to shut up and stay inside... And we sent a press release... We wrote that release with the *PTS*" (Interview to a factory worker, critical shop steward and member of *PTS*, author's translation).

36 A conflict that happened in a registered workshop on Zañartú street that had a lot media visibility is described by a former worker as follows: "Little by little they owed us more and more, and delayed paying us more and more (...) She began to tell us that production was not being made the way it was supposed to. But, everybody was aware of what we were producing. (...) That was the first time. When this happened the second time no one believed her and the third time we started to band together to do something about this. We were registered, on the books, (...) "if we are on the books, this can't be right", we said. She even told us she wasn't going to pay the Annual Complementary Salary (...) She started firing workers in November (...) She noticed we were planning something and on the following week, a co-worker told her who the leaders were and she fired them. I was part of that group. I was fired (...) [Because of this situation, some workers organised a strike and as a result of the negotiations she promised to pay on the following Monday] And on that Monday there was nothing there. Just a doorman, who said it was all closed (...) She fired everybody. After that, we blocked the street. We knew she was inside. She was in there 3 or 4 days. We cut off the building's gas and electricity (...) She walked out under police protection and with her lawyers (...) After that we got a meeting with *La Alameda* and they helped us (...) For 45 days, we camped out by her door until we got the money for the hours we worked, but we didn't get anything for dismissal compensation or anything like that" (Interview to a former workshop worker and current member of a cooperative sewing workshop, author's translation).

magnificent..., all the things we did: we occupied the Embassy, we organised several demonstrations because of Luis Viale fire; we conducted a radio broadcast for nearly a year and a half... and I abandoned almost everything because I had facial paralysis (...) It happened because of the discussions and stress as well (Interview to a former factories and workshops' worker, former leader of *MCIBol*, author's translation).

Another organisation that has been recognised for dealing with informal workshops and managed by Bolivians is the Bolivian Federative Civil Association (*Asociación Civil Federativa Boliviana, ACIFEBOL*[37]). Their objectives differ from those of the other organisations here described because although they present themselves as an advocate for labour rights (Caggiano, 2014), scholars and members of other organisations have described them as an association of workshops owners. Their actions have been linked to interventions, inspections and the closings of workshops but simultaneously protect workshops owners and managers. This organisation is particularly visible because of the grassroots efforts that it mobilises (Lipcovich, 2006), which has been established as a reference within this particular industry.[38] One of the main leaders in the *ACIFEBOL* organisation is Alfredo Ayala. He himself is a workshop owner and has been identified as a promoter of the mafia-like networks that are linked to human trafficking. He is accused of being responsible for generating links with the police and counting on an alliance with the right-wing Buenos Aires government[39] (Colectivo Simbiosis/Colectivo Situaciones, 2011).

---

[37] It was ratified as a Civil Association in 2008.
[38] As was documented in a complaint, a woman who was evicted from a workshop was on her way to finding alternative solutions for that situation, she "called FM Estación Latina, where the phone number of Mr. Ayala was given from the Bolivians Workshop Owners' [*talleristas*] Chamber, who informed her not to report 'paisanos' [other people from Bolivia] because that adversely affects them and that he could not help her" (Proceeding number 1267/99, from 1999; ANNEX IV: extension of the complaint of Ombudsman Office of the city, cit. in D'Ovidio, 2009, p. 153, author's translation).
[39] Gustavo Vera, a member of *La Alameda* describes Alfredo Ayala as follows: "he obstructed a federal justice proceeding during an ordered raid in 2007. He took a firm stand, closed the Street, prevented the federal police from seizing the machinery (as was ordered by a federal judge) and altered the judge's decision (...). He also happily smashed up the home base of *La Alameda*, several times, hit people near police officers, organised mobilisations toward the police station (...). Clearly, no one can act with such impunity, if he is not supported by 'you know who'. You have to look further up the system to the leaders who manage organised crime in Argentina" (Colectivo Simbiosis/Colectivo Situaciones, 2011, p. 47, author's translation).

5.2.4 Garment Workers and Employees Union (Unión de Costurerxs y Empleadxs del Vestido, UCEV)

"The Great Latin American Homeland", is a slogan placed under the name of the list that disputed the leadership of the Clothing Industry Union's (SOIVA) in 2016.

In this section, we will analyze worker organisations that aspired for legal representation (*personería jurídica*) within the customs and traditions of the trade union monopoly outlined above. In 2017, a union was organised as an alternative to SOIVA and was created as an answer to compartmentalisation. This organisation was established also to contest the influence of institutionalised syndicates as well as to showcase the large number of migrant workers that make up the group, which is restricted by the Union's Bylaws: where one determines that only native citizens have access to representation and legally protected positions.[40] This syndicate of rank-and-file workers was penalised by the legally protected trade union (*sindicato con personería gremial*), namely the SOIVA.

Our fieldwork shows three milestones that got in the way of the forming of the UCEV: the separation with the UTC-*La Alameda* which lead to creation of the opposition list (*Lista Roja*) to dispute SOIVA's leadership; the death of Elsa Montero, a worker and activist in the organisation; and, finally, the expulsion of some activists from the trade union (SOIVA) or dismissals from their jobs.

The UTC[41] was formed in 2004, within the former cooperative named "La Alameda-December 20", a group that was formed from the Parque Avellaneda Neighborhood Assembly (*Asamblea barrial*) that emerged as a response to the crisis in 2001. This Assembly drew objectives beyond the immediate needs of the neighborhood and set out a variety of social goals.[42] The location where the Assembly met is in a neighborhood where there is a concentration of unregistered garment production. Therefore, employees of these sewing workshops go to the community kitchen or use the Maternal and Child Care Program. This social space helped raise awareness about the working and living conditions

---

40   Article 16 of SOIVA's Bylaws.
41   The union dynamic developed by the UTC-La Alameda creates a social context for the constitution of the UCEV. Some of the members of the UCEV were activists of the UTC before the rupture.
42   They worked with the local health center, they obtained support from the Social Development Secretary within the Government of Buenos Aires, they set up a community kitchen, among others (Baratini, 2010; Pascucci, 2011).

within those workshops. Quickly, the political organisations oriented to these matters began to take shape. According to Baratini (2010), the first stages of the establishment of the UTC are characterised by complaints in conjunction with the Ombudsman Office, the International Organisation for Migration and the National Attorney General's Office.[43]

The UTC-La Alameda began was spotlighted in the media related with garment industry issues and to its involvement in the Luis Viale fire of 2006. The group continuously became a reference for these events and developed a policy that integrated workers into the union, those who were against SOIVA's leadership. The group aimed to confront all forms of exploitation that coexist within the garment industry. This task was not on SOIVA's agenda because of their policy concerning the confederation (CGT) restricting membership only to registered workers within the union (Arias & Salgado, 2011). During this stage of the formation of UTC-La Alameda, various actions started: a regular bulletin was published and a strategy was created in order to get critical shop stewards (*delegados sindicales*) into the SOIVA. Ever since its first publication, the Bulletin has focused on the inaction of the SOIVA: under the name of the organisation, a slogan reads "the SOIVA must be reclaimed by the garment workers" (Figure 5.1).[44] It is worth stressing that the first bulletin lacks any reference to issues concerning migration which represents much of the workforce within this level of the industry (the illustration omits this as well).[45]

In 2008, as a result of the global economic crash, rank-and-file organisations blossomed. During this time, several actions were prompted towards Employers and the SOIVA. Economic conditions triggered political organisation: the basis overflowed into union leadership that was incapable of articulating worker demands (Baratini, 2010; Pascucci, 2011). In 2009, a demonstration aimed at the SOIVA was organised where workers demanded active intervention.[46] This was the direct referential backdrop of the process in 2016. Moreover, the UTC reinforced its strategy for integrating shop stewards who weren't

---

[43] A joint effort formed, until 2006, when more than 70 complaints were made against the workshops which produced for renowned brands and employed people subjected to servitude.

[44] UTC's bulletins can be seen at https://laalameda.wordpress.com/8-hrs/

[45] Within the first publication, one finds several references to "slave labour" (trabajo esclavo), "sweatshops" (talleres clandestinos) and references of the members' relationship to the formal registered aspect of the industry, namely the factories. Outsourcing is highlighted as well as a global network strategy that includes all forms of exploitation within the garment industry.

[46] In February 2009, the UTC convened to a communal space for "the organisation of the resistance" (Pascucci, 2011, p. 42).

FIGURE 5.1   The First Publication of the Garment Workers Union (Unión de Trabajadores Costureros -*UTC*-)

aligned with the leadership of the *SOIVA*. Their plan of action was based on experiences from the past, which concluded with dismissals and should be highlighted. One member of the *UTC* described it as the following:

> Then we had to go to the *SOIVA* with a public notary, because if you didn't, you would get fired. [We had to] present a legal document with your name on it, write down the names of all those present, just in case, because if they messed with you and made trouble, you could be fired for being an activist… We had to do all that to get a recognised shop steward, if you didn't, they would fire you (Interview to a factory worker, critical shop steward and member of the *UTC*, author's translation).

Because of these strategies, the *UTC* could elect a group of shop stewards in several factories and enlarge their union members who were mostly registered workers.

The *UTC-La Alameda* gradually created alliances with a fraction of the *CGT*, which, as a confederation, includes the *SOIVA*. Another relevant connection is to the then Cardinal Bergoglio, currently Pope Francis.[47] Those alliances helped create visibility to the realities denounced and became evident from the increase of media presence of *UTC-La Alameda* members. Nevertheless, these ties at the leadership level caused a distancing from their members, mainly migrant workers, who represent a significant part of the registered

---

47   Cardinal Bergoglio denounced human trafficking in several occasions and he expressed an appreciation for the work of *La Alameda*. Together, they celebrated several Masses with the aim of raising awareness about numerous social problems including the working and living conditions of garment workshops (La Nación, 2008; Página 12, 2011).

workers and are the huge majority in unregistered production sites. It should be noted that the lack of a special focus on migrant issues causes a distance between migrant workers and the UTC-La Alameda.

Framed within the new national political scene that began in 2016, the UTC-La Alameda in conjunction with other organisations, tried to dispute SOIVA leadership in the elections. Before submitting the list, a fracture was led by the UTC-La Alameda and the rank-and-file workers met in their workplaces about the rupture and decided to continue with the presentation of the opposition list. Thus, the *Lista Roja* (red list) was officially constituted. This fracture brought greater clarity about the differences among workers, their elected union representatives, the union representatives aligned with the SOIVA's leadership and, in an intermediate layer, those organisations recognised as political actors but lack a grassroots basis in workplaces (the UTC-La Alameda). The orientation of the UTC-La Alameda towards alliances at the authority level is the most recurrent explanation in the interviews. It has thus been pointed out by a member of the *Lista Roja*:

> One of the things that was asked for when my colleagues asked me to join the list, is to take *La Alameda* off the list. That's the only reason that my colleagues chose me and I want them to make the decision. If they think I'm doing the wrong things, they vote me out. It is the best of democracy. I saw that La Alameda wasn't following that path, they always wanted to dictate the line of action.... I wasn't comfortable because I knew that one day they will want to make decisions and that's not possible because decisions are made by workers, it's not the representatives that make the decisions. (...) When the *Lista Roja* (red list) was created I was a shop steward and there were more shop stewards from the SOIVA and we planned elections. But what happened is that they [the UTC-La Alameda] got together with the CGT. Then we began to see, that those people who tried to take our group apart supported us at the beginning and then, there were lines drawn by the CGT to take us down. Mr. Ranú, the main leader at the SOIVA, has secretariats within the CGT and ILO. These people turned their backs on our colleagues for political reasons (Interview to a factory worker, critical shop steward and member of the *Lista Roja*, author's translation).

The main objectives of the *Lista Roja* focus on the features of labour overexploitation: low wages; high labour intensity; failure to address the health risks demonstrated in commonly occurring diseases; the need for a well-functioning health care provider (*Obra social*); unregistered work; coercion through illegal manipulation of work time use; discrimination (Illustration 2). One of the members gives account of the above:

> When anyone sees our flyers, they seem shocked because we are asking for basics: diapers, milk, things they should give to us by law, just a break to go to the bathroom (Interview to a factory worker, critical shop steward and provisional Secretary-General of UCEV, author's translation).

This characterisation is the precise outcome of the lack of government and trade union intervention in order to improve working conditions.

This balance was built up in the context of an economic upswing and subsequent stability. It is understandable that the early warning signals of the economic downturn with its promise of a drop in the already precarious working conditions alerted workers. Therefore, they took a qualitative leap forward in terms of organizing. Additionally, the explicit inclusion of discrimination (Figure 5.2) gives account of the appreciation of one of the main features associated with migrant workers. As a result of the vast presence of migrant workers and after several debates, the migration issue was decided to be included

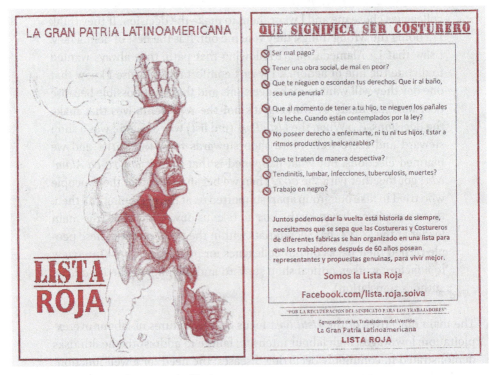

FIGURE 5.2   First flyer of *Lista Roja* (red list)

as a header above the name of the list itself: "La Gran Patria Latinoamericana" (The Great Latin American Homeland). Thus, this special character of labour within the branch is visibly placed. From a local perspective, the homeland is comprised of all Latin-American countries. This axis shift reveals the nature of traditional trade unions as well, framed on the nation-state level.

The presentation of the *Lista Roja* was refuted by the soiva.[48] Facing this situation, hundreds of garment workers tied to the *Lista Roja* mobilised against the Ministry of Labour and Social Welfare Programs. At a legal level, they brought forth a relief mandate to the Justice Department; and as a political strategy, they asked members not to vote in the coming elections. The elections resulted in an overwhelming level of abstention and it is estimated that 80 per cent of union members did not vote. This action reflected their widespread dissatisfaction and demonstrated how the majority of workers wanted alternative representation.

A few weeks later, Elsa Montero, who was one of the driving forces behind the *Lista Roja,* died as a result of the negligent health care (*Obra social*) provided by the trade union. She required a prosthesis as well as the necessary materials for an aortic surgery. The essentials weren't delivered and the surgery, which was necessary to save her life, could not be performed. This alarming development underlines the conditions garment workers suffer due to neglect on the part of the trade union. This was interpreted by *Lista Roja* as a disciplinary and discriminatory action.[49] This unfortunate episode led to escalated tensions with the trade union. Again, a two-track strategy was taken, a legal one as well as social mobilisation. Legally, a formal complaint for negligence concerning the health care provider (*Obra social*) was made, which was framed as a political cause, because of the activism Elsa Montero participated in against the leadership of the soiva. Because of her death, social protest was prompted by rank-and-file activists and a few days later a demonstration at the soiva

---

48   Conducted through several strategies such as the failure to observe the time-limit by law, the statement of an overestimated number of members, collecting endorsements by deceit, so as to restrict representative positions within the trade union to natives fixed by the soiva Bylaws.

49   A member of the Lista Roja reports: "Her medical case report is shameful because, right there it says that the doctors asked the health care provider (*Obra social*) to deliver these valves and that lack caused the loss of a colleague and member (...). Also, it must be noted that there is a lot of discrimination because she was Bolivian. I was a shop steward and I noticed the discrimination all the time in the union. Sometimes the discrimination was because of just a name, because they are unusual names and this discrimination reached a point where it caused a death" (Interview to a factory worker, former shop steward and member of the *Lista Roja*, author's translation).

was organised. Activists called for justice for their colleague in addition to the claims of the *Lista Roja*. Federal police were present at the rally and attacked protesters and the victim's next of kin with pepper spray. The outrage was used by the leadership at SOIVA in order to criminalise their critical positions. Members of the *Lista Roja* were pointed out as responsible, primarily those who were shop stewards. A special meeting was called to expel the shop stewards who participated, which was then decided during that assembly and was effective from December 2016. Other members of the *Lista Roja*, who weren't protected by the law (*fueros sindicales*) were dismissed from their workplaces. This situation has again underscored the collusion between the SOIVA and the employers, and the implementation of disciplinary actions at a hostile new level.

These disciplinary actions along with the defenselessness of the workers relaunched a discussion about the establishment of an alternative Trade Union. Within this framework, consensus was rapidly reached and in March 2017 the Garment Workers and Employees Union (*Unión de Costurerxs y Empleadxs del Vestido*, UCEV) was established within the Central Argentine Worker Union (*Central de Trabajadores de la Argentina Autónoma*, CTA Autónoma).[50] The new Union is very appreciated by its members not only because of its committed role to improve working conditions but also as a way of overcoming union fragmentation within the clothing industry. Moreover, one of main objectives of the UCEV is the integration of migrant workers to representative positions previously blocked by the charter of the SOIVA. In relation to this latter point, the provisional Secretary-General-elect on occasion of the formal constitution of the UCEV pointed out:

> The main thing for the approval of the new Statute is erasing article 16. This article prohibits the participation of all foreign co-workers. I find it more than shameful. We are not even free to sit somewhere without being questioned about birthplace. We are going to change that in the Statute because it is discrimination, whether because of your gender or

---

50   The CTA, Central Argentina Workers Union (*Central de Trabajadores de la Argentina*), is a third-level union organisation that was constituted in 1991 as a result of the fracture with the CGT led by a number of trade unions, most of which are from public sector. While within that sector, it has a relevant presence, it is not enough to challenge the CGT's representation of workers. Within the industry and its services, trade union power is even lower (Retamozo & Morris, 2015). Notwithstanding, the CTA is the only alternative third-level union organisation. In 2010, it split in two: the CTA Autonomous (*Autónoma*) and the CTA of workers (*de los Trabajadores*). The former was on the left side of the previous government. About UCEV's constitution see http://agenciacta.org/spip.php?article23147

the place where you were born or your orientation (Interview to a factory worker, critical shop steward and provisional Secretary-General of UCEV).

Since then, they have launched a massive campaign for a disaffiliation from SOIVA and for incorporation into the UCEV. Based on the typology defined by Fine (2005), the category that best fits this group is "union or unions/not community partners", although we find some differences in reference to the author's definition. For example, Fine states that "these organisations are either new union locals chartered by an international union for the express purpose of organizing in a given community and sector, or new initiatives undertaken as part of a labour union's organizing strategy. They may seek the support and participation of community institutions but it is not a joint effort" (Fine, 2005, p. 159). In this case, the new initiative undertaken was the break with the institutionalised trade union, namely SOIVA. As noted above, the trade union unity regime (*unicidad sindical*) in Argentina introduces another character in this category. Here, the possibility of breaking up the trade union monopoly can happen through the consolidation of an alternative union, but there are limited prospects for reaching legal protection (*personería gremial*). Its political substratum reflects their basis (and not trade union law). Venturing into this critical position is both a great challenge and the only way forward that these organised workers have found.

6 Final Thoughts: Labour and Migration, Community and Unionism

At the beginning of the paper, we emphasised how the close relationship between unregistered migration and precarious labour growth (Munck, 2011) is amplified by stable relations of labour overexploitation. The garment industry is an important case for establishing this analysis because this form of exploitation is a constituent part of its inherent production dynamics. The lack of intervention by the State and political institutions to eradicate this social problem creates an essential dialectic that guarantees the continued existence of overexploitation.

Another fundamental analytical dimension for explaining the permanence of overexploitation can be found by looking at the forms of working class organisations and how labour-capital relationships are determined as well as determining capital advance (Lebowitz, 2005; Marx 1865). In this very sense, Fine (2005) has argued that the limited power of low-wage workers is directly related to the lack of organisations able for largescale intervention on their behalf. Following this approach, we focus particularly on migrant workers because of the constitutive existence of migration within the phenomenon. From the range of relevant organisations, we selected two cases for analysis because they represent innovative initiatives when compared to traditional migrant worker organisations: the Migrant Workers Bloc, BTM (*Bloque de Trabajadorxs Migrantes*) and the Garment Workers and Employees Union, UCEV (*Unión de Costurerxs y Empleadxs del Vestido*). Both of these are comprised of migrant workers in the garment industry (not exclusively in the case of the BTM) and they took a quantitative leap forward in terms of the number of members as well as a qualitative jump regarding the scope of their actions. We found an axial distinction emphasised in this paper: the BTM is organised concerning the migrant dimension and the UCEV is formulated primarily around labour. The weighing of the labour concerns advanced by the BTM opened up doors for an unprecedented experience: the Migrant Strike of 2017 (*Paro Migrante*). Labour identity turned out to be strategic for dissolving the victimisation of being migrants, one of the main objectives of the Cultural Symbiosis Collective since its founding. In a different way, the UCEV is closer to traditional industrial rank-and-file organisational practices. Its identity (included in its name) promotes a multi-national unity. In this regard, they moved beyond the bylaw that is tied to the idea of the nation-state towards a new vision that guarantees the right of legal representation to all of its members, native-born or not, transforming a former privilege into a right.

Several scholars consider that the traditional union model, which is based on the workplace, is being challenged by the community as well as by "other actors" (Wills and Simms, 2004; Martínez Lucio & Perret, 2009). As the authors point out, "migrant and minority ethnic workers are not a 'simply unified' body that require some 'one-off' realignment of union tactics for the achievement of equality. Strategies are normally complex and the question is as much about the purpose and politics of the trade union as anything else – the real politick of inclusion strategies" (Martínez Lucio & Perret, 2009, p. 325).

It is relevant to refer to Fine's (2005) characterisation of community unionism in order to identify the specific features of each case. For the author, this concept "implies that unions and community organisations need not wait, but can organise in ways that will transform the debate in their communities and open the way for organizing" (Fine, 2005, p. 160). There are three main features that differentiate community unionism from craft and industrial unionism. In the first place, the identity of these organisations is closer to ethnic and religious affiliations than to the long-term relationship characteristic of craft or industry unionism. Within this framework, discrimination is at the core and it is from this point that economic aspects can be approached. Secondly, community reflects a prevalent geographical spread in lieu of the workplace. Finally, direct action within the community through campaigns is preferred over public policies. The experiences demonstrated concerning the BTM could fall under this classification. Also, the case with the UCEV shares common characteristics with industrial unionism and brings a change by widening political membership, which for traditional unions has been limited by nationality. By focusing on the migratory condition as the main axis concerning the bylaw of the SOIVA, the UCEV ensures full trade union rights to all of their members.

These experiences express the need to surpass traditional frameworks by defining a broader political subject through building "Latin-Americanness" instead of "citizenship" (which is a restricted view) and by establishing an integrated relationship concerning migration and labour. In both cases, their goals extend beyond the workplace and illustrates a significant potential for further development which focuses on moving forward by incorporating migration and labour as part of their qualitative leap.

Regarding the gender issue, the BTM has had a close relationship with the women's movement since its inception and the UCEV declares an interest on the question but lacks a specific political wing. This could possibly be related to the traditional protest repertoire considered within community unionism and craft and industrial unionism in the Buenos Aires area of Argentina.

Both organisations are recently formed and represent original alternatives that constitute a substantial step forward concerning the inherent dialectic between migration and labour. These organisations do not see these issues as discrete and separate within the political field of action. It is a new scope that amplifies the borders of political subjects and has been able to take a significant step on the way to eradicating labour overexploitation.

References

Abramo, L., Rodriguez Calderón, E., & Rossignotti, G. (2004). *Cadenas productivas, trabajo a domicilio y organisación sindical*. Lima: ILO.

Adúriz, I. (2009). *La Industria Textil en Argentina. Su evolución y sus condiciones de trabajo*. Buenos Aires: FOCO, INPADE.

Almeida Filho, N. (2013). Overexploitation of the Workforce and Concentration of Wealth: Key Issues for Development Policy in Brazilian Peripheral Capitalism. *World Review of Political Economy*, 4(1), 4–24.

Arcos, A. & Montero, C. (2011). Detrás de la industria de la moda. Un estudio sobre talleres clandestinos. Paper presented at *V Encuentro Internacional de Economía Política y DDHH*. Buenos Aires.

Arias, C. C., & Salgado, P. D. (2011). Revitalización sindical en Argentina: el caso del subte. *Revista de Ciencias Sociales* (Cr), 1(131–132). Retrieved May 11, 2018, from https://doi.org/10.15517/rcs.v0i131-132.3901

Asamblea Textil de Flores (2015) "Sacar del gueto a la economía popular y migrante", en *Lobo Suelto*. Retrieved May 11, 2018, from http://anarquiacoronada.blogspot.com/2015/06/no-olvidamos-dos-meses-del-incendio-del.html

Atzeni, M., & Ghigliani, P. (2007). *The resilience of traditional trade union practices in the revitalisation of the Argentine labour movement*. Peter Lang.

Barattini, M. (2010). Trabajo esclavo y organización: El caso de la Unión de Trabajadores Costureros en Argentina. *Estudios Demográficos Y Urbanos*, 25(2 (74)), 461–481. Retrieved May 11, 2018, from http://www.jstor.org/stable/20787559

Belini, C. (2008). Una época de cambios: la industria textil argentina entre dos crisis, 1914–1933. *Estudos Ibero-Americanos*, XXXIV, December, 31–48.

Caggiano, S. (2014). Desigualdades entrelazadas, luchas divergentes: migración e industria textil en Argentina/Entangled inequalities, divergent struggles: migration and the Argentine textile industry. *Revista cidob d'afers internacionals*, 106/107, 151–170.

Canelo, Brenda, Gavazzo, Natalia, & Nejamkis, Lucila. (2018). Nuevas (viejas) políticas migratorias en la Argentina del cambio. *Si Somos Americanos*, 18(1), 150–182. https://dx.doi.org/10.4067/S0719-09482018000100150

Castronovo, A. (2018). ¡Costureros carajo! Trayectorias de lucha y autogestión en las economías populares argentinas. *Íconos: Revista de Ciencias Sociales*, 62, 119–139. https://doi.org/10.17141/iconos.62.2018.3252

Centro de Estudios Legales y Sociales, CELS (2018, January 30). *El dnu contra las personas migrantes: una política selectiva y diferenciada*. Retrieved May 11, 2018, from https://www.cels.org.ar/web/2018/01/dnu-migrantes-una-politica-selectiva-y-diferenciada

Centro de Estudios Legales y Sociales, CELS (2018, June 27). *Los dueños de un taller textil, imputados por la muerte de seis personas en 2006*. Retrieved May 11, 2018, from https://www.cels.org.ar/web/2017/06/los-duenos-de-un-taller-textil-imputados-por-la-muerte-de-seis-personas-en-2006

Chitarroni, H. & E. Cimillo (2007). ¿Resurge el sujeto histórico? Cambios en el colectivo del trabajo asalariado: 1974–2006. *Lavboratorio*, 21.

Colectivo Simbiosis/Colectivo Situaciones (2011). *De chuequistas y overlockas. Una discusión en torno a los talleres textiles*. Buenos Aires: Tinta Limón/Retazos.

Courtis, C., & Pacecca, M. I. (2007). Migración y derechos humanos: una aproximación crítica al nuevo paradigma para el tratamiento de la cuestión migratoria en Argentina. *Revista Jurídica de Buenos Aires*, 134, 183–200.

Courtis, C. & Pacecca, M. (2006). Migración y trabajo precario: ¿un par desarticulable?. *Revista E-misférica. Fronteras. Imaginaciones híbridas /Geografías fracturadas*, 3-2.

D'Oividio, M. (2007) *Quién es quién en la cadena de valor del sector de indumentaria textil*. Buenos Aires: Fundación El Otro and Interrupción.

De Genova, N. (2002). 'Migrant 'illegality' and deportability in everyday life'. *Annual Review of Anthropology*, 31, 419–447. https://doi-org/:10.1146/annurev.anthro.31.040402.085432

Féliz, M., & Pérez, P. (2007). ¿Tiempos de cambio? Contradicciones y conflictos en la política económica de la posconvertibilidad. In R. Boyer & J. C. Neffa, (Eds.), *Salida de crisis y estrategias alternativas de desarrollo. La experiencia argentina*. Buenos Aires: Institut CDC pour la Recherche / Miño y Dávila / CEIL-PIETTE / Trabajo y Sociedad.

Fine, J. (2005). Community unionism and the revival of the American labour movement. *Politics and Society*, 33(1), 153–99. https://doi.org/10.1177/0032329204272553

Bloque de Trabajadorxs Migrantes (2017) *Manifiesto fundacional del Bloque de Trabajadorxs Migrantes*.

Gago, V. (2014). *La razón neoliberal. Economías barrocas y pragmática popular*. Buenos Aires: Tinta Limón.

Gago, V. (2015). Progreso clandestino. *Revista Anfibia*.

Gago, V. (2018). The Strategy of Flight: Problematizing the Figure of Trafficking. *South Atlantic Quarterly*, 117(2), 333–356. https://doi.org/10.1215/00382876-4374867

Gavazzo, N. (2008). Inmigrantes en el Imaginario de la Nación. Una visión desde las organi-zaciones de tres comunidades latinoamericanas en la Argentina del siglo XXI. *Colección*, (18), 2.

Gavazzo, N. (2018). Jóvenes migrantes e hijos de inmigrantes latinoamericanos en Buenos Aires: una generación en movimiento. *Confluenze. Rivista di Studi Iberoamericani*, 10(1), 131–165. https://doi.org/10.6092/issn.2036-0967/8298

Ghigliani, P., Grigera, J. & Schneider, A. (2012). Sindicalismo empresarial: problemas, conceptualización y economía política del sindicato. *RELET-Revista Latinoamericana de Estudios del Trabajo*, 17(27), 140–164.

Grabner, S. (2012). Africans in a Country "Without Blacks": Challenges and Accomplishments of the Integration of Recent African Immigrants in Argentina-Africanos en un País donde "No Hay Negros": Los Logros y Desafíos de la Integración de los Recientes Inmigrantes Africanos en la Argentina. *Independent Study Project (ISP) Collection*. 1398. Retrieved May 11, 2018, from https://digitalcollections.sit.edu/isp_collection/1398

Grasso, G. & Perez Almansi, B. (2017). La industria, un barco sin timón en los tiempos de cambio. *El nuevo modelo económico y sus consecuencias* (Burgos, M., Ed.). Buenos Aires: Ediciones del CCC.

Haidar, J. (2016). La economía gremial, entre la crisis y la recomposición: Luz y Fuerza Capital Federal (1976–2013). *PolHis. Revista Bibliográfica del Programa Interuniversitario de Historia Política*, (16), 68–94.

Hesse-Biber, S. (2010). "Qualitative Approaches to Mixed Methods Practice", *Qualitative Inquiry*, 16(6), 455–468.

INTI (2012). Información Económica Nacional. *Informe del Centro de Investigación y Desarrollo Textil del Instituto Nacional de Tecnología Industrial (INTI)*. Retrieved May 11, 2018, from http://www.inti.gob.ar/textiles/vestirconciencia

INTI (2007). La esclavitud no es fashion. *Revista Saber Cómo*, 51.

Jelin, E., Mercado, M. & Wyczykier, G. (1998). *El trabajo a domicilio en la Argentina*. Santiago de Chile: ILO.

La Nación (2008, July 02). Bergoglio: En el país hay esclavos. Retrieved May 11, 2018, from https://www.lanacion.com.ar/1026529-bergoglio-en-el-pais-hay-esclavos

Kosacoff, B. (Ed.) (2004). *Evaluación de un escenario posible y deseable de reestructuración y fortalecimiento del Complejo Textil argentino*. Buenos Aires, Argentina: CEPAL.

Lebowitz, M. (2005). Más allá del Capital. La economía política de la clase obrera en Marx. España: Akal.

Lieutier, A. (2010). *Esclavos: los trabajadores costureros de la ciudad de Buenos Aires*. Buenos Aires: Retórica Ediciones.

Lipcovich, P. (2006, April 04). Una pelea después de las llamas. *Página 12*. Retrieved May 11, 2018, from http://www.pagina12.com.ar/diario/elpais/1-65172-2006-04-04.html

Marini, R. M. (2000). *Dialética da Dependência*. Petrópolis: Vozes.

Marini, R. M. (1979) *El ciclo del capital en la economía dependiente*. México: ERA.

Martínez Lucio, M., & Perrett, R. (2009). The diversity and politics of trade unions' responses to minority ethnic and migrant workers: The context of the UK. *Economic and Industrial Democracy*, 30(3), 324–347. https://doi.org/10.1177/0143831X09336562

Marx, K. (1865). *Lohn, Preis und Profit*. English edition: Marx K (1969). *Value, Price and Profit*. New York: International Co. Retrieved May 11, 2018, from https://www.marxists.org/archive/marx/works/1865/value-price-profit/index.htm

Marx, K. (2011). *Capital, volume I*. New York: The Modern Library.

Montero, J. (2011). *Neoliberal fashion: The political economy of sweatshops in Europe and Latin America. Durham theses*. Durham: Durham University.

Munck, R. (2011). Beyond North and South: Migration, informalization, and trade union revitalization. *WorkingUSA*, 14(1), 5–18. https://doi.org/10.1111/j.1743-4580.2010.00317.x

Novick, M. (2006). ¿Emerge un nuevo modelo económico y social? El caso argentino 2003–2006. *Revista latinoamericana de Estudios del Trabajo*, 11, 18.

Olivera, C. M. (2009). ¿Bailando por un sueño? Espacios de construcción de identidades. *Temas de Patrimonio Cultural Temas de Patrimonio Cultural. Buenos Aires Boliviana*, 24.

Página 12 (2011, August 08). Con la bendición del arzobispo. Retrieved May 11, 2018, from https://www.pagina12.com.ar/diario/elpais/1-173994-2011-08-08.html

Pascucci, S. (2011). Avances y límites de la acción político-sindical en la industria de la confección de indumentaria. Una caracterización del SOIVA y la UTC-Alameda. *Documentos de Jóvenes Investigadores del Instituto de Investigaciones Gino Germani (FSoc-UBA)*, 26.

Pascucci, S. (2007). *Costureras, monjas y anarquistas: trabajo femenino, Iglesia y lucha de clases en la industria del vestido, Buenos Aires, 1890–1940*. Buenos Aires: Ediciones RyR.

Retamozo, M., & Morris, M. B. (2015). Sindicalismo y política. La Central de Trabajadores de la Argentina en tiempos kirchneristas. *Estudios sociológicos*, 33(97), 63–87.

Salgado, P. D., & Carpio, J. (2017). Superexplotación, Informalidad y Precariedad: Reflexiones a partir del trabajo en la industria de la confección. *Estudios del trabajo*, (54), 55–89.

Salgado, P. D. (2012). El trabajo en la industria de la indumentaria: una aproximación a partir del caso argentino. *Trabajo y sociedad*, (18), 59–68.

Salgado, P. D. (2014). El trabajo en la industria de la confección de indumentaria en Argentina. Aproximaciones a partir de las transformaciones recientes en la cadena de valor. Paper presented at *Congreso de Economía Política Internacional, Universidad de Moreno, Buenos Aires*. Retrieved May 11, 2018, from https://docplayer.es/67100044-Congreso-de-economia-politica-internacional.html

Salgado, P. D. (2015). Deslocalización de la producción y la fuerza de trabajo: Bolivia-Argentina y las tendencias mundiales en la confección de indumentaria. *Si Somos Americanos*, xv, 1. http://dx.doi.org/10.4067/S0719-09482015000100007

Salgado, P. D. (2016). El gobierno argentino frente al trabajo en condiciones de reducción a la servidumbre. Análisis de las declaraciones del Ministro de Trabajo con motivo del intento de reforma de la Ley 12.713 de Trabajo a Domicilio. *Discurso & Sociedad*, 10(1), 58–99.

Schorr, M. & Ferreira, E. (2013). La industria textil y de indumentaria en la Argentina. Informalidad y tensiones estructurales en la posconvertibilidad. *Argentina en la posconvertibilidad: ¿desarrollo o crecimiento industrial? Estudios de economía política* (Schorr, M., Ed.). Buenos Aires: Miño y Dávila.

Sur Capitalino (2017, March 30). Paro Migrante: por un mundo sin muros. Retrieved May 11, 2018, from https://www.surcapitalino.com.ar/detalle_noticias.php?Id=4000

Telam (2015, May 05). Costureros, vecinos y organizaciones conformaron una asamblea permanente por los talleres textiles. Retrieved May 11, 2018, from http://www.telam.com.ar/notas/201505/103832-talleres-clandestinos-asamblea-flores.php

Torres, N. & Nunes Chas, B. (2017). El mercado de trabajo en la gestión de Cambiemos. I. M. Burgos (Ed.), *El nuevo modelo económico y sus consecuencias*. Buenos Aires: Ediciones del CCC.

Vommaro, G., & Gené, M. (2017). Argentina: el año de Cambiemos. *Revista de ciencia política (Santiago)*, 37(2), 231–254. https://dx.doi.org/10.4067/s0718-090x2017000200231

Yechua, D. (2015, June 30). Recuerdos de la muerte. *Agencia De Noticias De La Comunicación, UBA*. Retrieved May 11, 2018, from http://anccom.sociales.uba.ar/2015/06/30/recuerdos-de-la-muerte

CHAPTER 6

Collective Action, Experience and Identity in Global Agrarian Enclaves: The Case of Andalusia, Spain

Alicia Reigada

1 Introduction

Roseberry (1996) maintains that the social history of food can illuminate the cultural history of capitalism. In his analysis of the expansion of coffee consumption in the United States, he drew on Harvey's (1989) theories on the geography of capitalism and the idea of the simulacrum,[1] which, he proposed, acted to obscure the origins of agrifood products, work processes and the social relations involved in their production. Taking a political economy approach, anthropology holds that to understand this phenomenon it is necessary to examine consumption and the associated systems, networks and relations of production, as well as the historical context. Along the same lines, Narotzky reminds us that behind the consumption of every food product and brand are social relations of production and distribution that can be extremely difficult to identify. For her, relations of production and distribution are based on a history of connections between discrete forms of economic, social, cultural and political organisation of different groups of people in distinct geographic locations (Narotzky 2007).

Based on an ethnographic analysis, this chapter deals with a particular dimension of the social relations of agrifood production where we find a conflict of interests between the vested actors that make up global agrifood chains. By articulating the production/distribution and producer/worker conflict in the strawberry production system in Andalusia (Spain) the forms of collective action that emerge from these points of social tension are examined. Specifically, the chapter looks at how the introduction of a system of hiring foreign

---

1 Harvey analyses how, through food, music, entertainment or television, it is possible to experience indirectly different worlds (of goods) in the same space and time in our daily lives; beans from Kenya, celery and avocados from California, Canadian apples, potatoes from North Africa and grapes from Chile can all be found together in the British supermarket. This experience is understood as taking the form of a 'simulacrum' (Harvey 1989 in Roseberry 1996).

workers in their countries of origin gave rise to a series of protests and collective action by agricultural organisations and workers; these later mobilisations driven by self-organisation amongst immigrants and class based unionism.

Based on fieldwork carried out in the strawberry producing area of Huelva, during the 2006 and 2007 campaigns,[2] the analysis relates the socio-historical conditions, the identities and experiences of both producers and male and female workers, and the cultural and moral frameworks in which strategies of collective action are inscribed. During this period, the author spent a year and nine months in Moguer, one of the main strawberry growing areas in Andalusia, where participant observations and 83 interviews with informants from different social groups were carried out

The ethnographic premise of this chapter focuses on the voices, histories and perceptions of some of the people interviewed during the fieldwork. Amongst these are: Javier Moreno, a strawberry grower who migrated to the area as an adolescent with his family, who were day-labourers; Antonio Pérez, another grower who started out on the assembly line in the chemical plant in Huelva; and Francisco López, a grower whose family originally practiced traditional agriculture in an area that converted to strawberry production. In terms of the working class, the study presents interview extracts from: Dolores Gómez, a day-labourer from a village in Seville whose family migrated to work on the strawberry campaigns in the mid-eighties; Ousmane Diop, a young Senegalese labourer who arrived in Huelva in 2006 after travelling to the Canary Islands in a migrant boat; and foreign workers contracted through the Temporary Guest Farm Worker Programme [*Programas de Contratación en Origen*], including Mirela Vicov and Stefana Chiriac from Romania and Ana Podolski, Matzara Petrov and Kati Wozniak from Poland.[3] Additionally, the chapter includes extracts from interviews with María Carrasco and Luis Fernández, union representatives and members of the Temporary Workers Board [*Mesa del Temporero*].

Following Narotzky and Smith (2010), by analysing class relations and the conflicts that result from social reproduction under capitalism, the study attempts to explain people's experiences in relation to the material conditions and sociohistorical forces beyond their everyday lives. This approach moves away from an objectivist understanding of social class to an historical

---

2   This research, which was funded by the Regional Government of Andalusia, is being continued through a project titled "Quality governance in global agrifood chains: A comparative analysis of Spanish agri-exporting territories" (2018-2020), funded by the Spanish National Plan for Research and Development.
3   Pseudonyms are used throughout the text.

and constructivist perspective that defines class as an active process that is formed in human relations and embodied in a real context (Thompson 1966).[4] From this standpoint, class struggle is not interpreted as a spontaneous and mechanical response to relations of exploitation, but as a process constituted in material conditions, moral values and shared political, economic and cultural experiences. In these processes men and women "feel and articulate the identity of their interests between themselves, and as against other men whose interests are different from (and usually opposed to) theirs" (Thompson 1966:9). Similarly, and in accordance with Wells (1996), it is necessary to connect the positions and trajectories of agricultural producers and workers in order to understand how social classes are formed through conflict, and how it shapes social relations in agrifood production.

2 Socio-Historical Context and the Work-Life Trajectories of Producers and Workers

2.1 *Strawberry Growers: From Fishermen, Manual Workers and Day-Labourers to Landowners*

As in other areas of Andalusia, Huelva saw a dramatic change in the organisation of agricultural production toward a new intensive model in the 1950s and 60s. However, it is the underlying social structure of strawberry production in this area -the way that the land was acquired, the class origins of producers and workers, and the economic orientation of production- that distinguishes it from the old bourgeois estate owner model. In a relatively short period of time, people who had previously subsisted by multi-jobbing became full-time, modern agricultural cultivators exporting produce. This reconversion of fishermen, factory workers, peasants and day-labourers to producers and landowners was driven by a number of factors. The government, under Franco, favoured a land redistribution policy that encouraged smallholdings (Márquez 1986; Martín-Díaz 1995) and the almost immediate success of the model encouraged the illegal and disorganised occupation of common land. Today, smallholdings still predominate in the area, in spite of a certain tendency towards land concentration and the presence of multinationals such as Driscoll's.[5] Along with land

---

4 See Carrier and Kalb (2015) for a current analysis of the pertinence of the concept of social class that has a special emphasis on the perspective of Thompson and other anthropological contributions.

5 Based on the fieldwork, smallholdings are under 7ha, medium sized holdings are between 8 and 25ha and large holdings are over 25h.

access and farm size, the importance of the family farm in the initial development of the model constitutes an essential element in the construction of the local cultural identity. Feelings of pride at being self-made stand in contrast to the position that the large landowner occupies in the collective imaginary. Whilst the big production companies are viewed as being disconnected to the land, those who work the land with their own hands are highly valued. And, as opposed to the objective of capital accumulation, in general, the aim of the smallholders in Huelva is upward social mobility while reproducing the family farm and domestic model.

The life history of Javier Moreno is representative of this trajectory and collective identity. As he walked through his farm he recalled his arrival in the strawberry growing area of Huelva as one of many migrant workers and day labouring families that made the annual journey from other parts of Andalusia: "I'm from Alcalá del Valle, a village in the mountains of Cádiz, a village of migrants, people who have always migrated." This sense of identity is displayed symbolically in the central square of Javier's hometown. Called *La Plaza del Emigrante* [The Migrants' Plaza] it has a statue of a travelling peasant and the following eulogy: "to all the migrants who leave their homes to work. From here many went and still today many go."[6] Following five years as a seasonal worker, and having married the daughter of his employer, he moved permanently to the strawberry growing area and began to run his own greenhouse in the year 2000. When Javier describes the workforce that is necessary for the planting phase of the season, he includes himself within the team of workers: "During the planting nine people work. (...) I have these five [foreign labourers from Ecuador, Morocco and Mali], I bring three Romanians [female workers] and with me that's nine." In the following extract he emphasises his own work preparing the hills that the strawberries are planted in: sowing, covering the crop with plastic, monitoring the plants to make sure they don't go yellow and that the flowers don't curl ("if they curl the fruit will be no good"), and harvesting. Andrés Romero, a grower from Almeria who identified with the saying "The land belongs to those that work it" [*La tierra es de quien la trabaja* is an historic slogan from the Mexican peasant resistance], insisted on the necessity of this personal dedication to working the land:[7]

---

6 See the webpage of the Town Council of Alcalá del Valle: http://www.alcaladelvalle.es/
7 In Almeria the average farm size is approximately 2 hectares and, although the development of agriculture in Almeria shares many similarities to that of the strawberry growing region, the identification with the figure of the farmer is stronger than in Huelva. The quote is taken from the collective project: Social sustainability of the new agricultural enclaves: Spain and Mexico (2012-2014). See Reigada, Soler Montiel, Pérez Neira and Delgado Cabeza (forthcoming).

> I hate the term entrepreneur. (...) A farmer is someone who only has a few hectares, he might have quite a lot because he inherited them, but a farmer is someone who works the land. But a guy who doesn't even go to his farm once a month, is he a farmer? (...) They are businessmen, instead of investing in a restaurant, or a garage, or whatever, in shares, well look, they invest here. But a farmer, a farmer is always on the land working. It's true what they say, "the land belongs to those that work it".

This social and symbolic world is connected to two historic forms of collective action. The Andalusian peasant anarchist movement between the later half of the 19th century and just before the beginning of the Spanish civil war[8] (Díaz del Moral 1969) and the day-labourer unionism that emerged during the transition from dictatorship to democracy in the late 1970s (Ocaña 2006). These movements defined the ownership of land by old nobles and the great bourgeois families as intolerable and fought for agricultural reform. However, the incorporation of these collective memories into the present model of intensive agriculture and the experiences of smallholders also brings to light certain contradictions. Within the framework of the transition from traditional agriculture to productivist agriculture, the social value attributed to the work of the farmer is articulated within the symbolic meaning acquired by a change in class position and new material conditions. The dimension and meaning of these changes explains why, depending on the context, producers emphasize their identity as farmers *or* entrepreneurs. Javier Moreno, not long after stressing his daily work in the fields, states: "I used to be a day-labourer, today I am a businessman, and there are many like me. (...) we contract many foreigners, we produce many kilos of strawberries, we feed many households." Antonio Pérez, while recounting the stage of his life when he started in intensive farming, expresses a similar sentiment about the transformation from peasantry to agricultural enterprises:

> I was studying, but at 17 I didn't like it much, so I left. I went to work in the companies on the industrial complex that they were setting up. I worked there until I went to do my military service, when I was 20. And, when I came back my girlfriend had a parcel of land that had belonged to her parents, and I, well, I was starting out, the strawberries weren't like today, but there were lots of people starting with the strawberries, not

---

8   As well as the most common form of action such as strikes to demand better wages, the abolition of piecework and the distribution of land, there were also violent protest actions such as arson and robberies (Solana 2000).

as peasants [like before] but as companies [...]. When I started we were already using the plastic [plasticulture] and all that.

The growers' identity incorporates, as such, other cultural meanings that are related to agricultural industrialization processes and a conversion from farming based on the work of the domestic group to the hiring of waged labour. In contrast to the traditional peasant agriculture, now seen as archaic, the entrepreneurial spirit of the family farmer is socially valued, as is increased productivity, the professionalisation of the sector, a tendency toward land concentration, the expansion of holdings, and exporting. However, these changes have taken place within the framework of global agrifood chains, which are extremely hierarchic and which situate farmers in a very fragile position (Ploeg 2009). Class origins, dedication to work and professionalisation are all inscribed within a cultural framework that interprets private ownership of land and land inheritance as legitimate systems, because they have been acquired through work and effort. From this interpretative framework we can understand the nature of these farmers' grievances toward the Common Agricultural Policy (CAP), and their demand that it should support "professional and productive farmers", instead of protecting large holdings run by absentee landowners.

Furthermore, as the economic success of the model in the 1980s and 90s lead to many female and young members of the domestic group abandoning labouring (substituted by waged labour), class aspirations are not limited to the ownership of land, they also incorporate a new position as agricultural employers that manage large numbers of waged labourers. Hence, in Huelva we can also see the changes that Camarero, Sampedro and Vicente-Mazariegos (2002) observed in the socio-cultural identities of Almerian horticulturalists: a transformation from a model that was based on the family to an industrial agricultural model.

2.2 *From the Regional Migration of Andalusian Day-Labourers to International Migrations*

Andalusian day-labourers' identity, cultural and moral values are defined by family oriented farming, a tradition of migrating to find work, Andalusian regional identity, a strong connection to the land, and their position as temporary waged workers. These five fundamental pillars underscore their individual and collective objectives, behaviour and social struggle (Palenzuela 1996; Talego 1996). Historically, their sense of identity was forged within the large estate owner model, the dominant system from the middle of the 19th century that defined the transformation of rural Andalusia. Concentration of land ownership, social polarization, labour migrations, modernization and mechanization, and labour control became associated with conflict, strikes and worker repression.

Land questions, however, not only affect the material conditions of life and work, but also symbolic values in the way they become markers of identity around which collective sentiment coalesces and takes shape (Moreno 1988; Talego 2010). Hence, out of these historical origins we find the emergence of Andalusian class trade unionism, the formation of the day-labourer as a political subject, and the beginnings of the most significant forms of collective action, such as the formation of The Fieldworkers Union of Andalusia (SOC) [*Sindicato de Obreros del Campo de Andalucía*] in 1976 (Ocaña 2006; Roca 2014). Although the trade union movement emerged in the context of the large estate owner model, it only set in under the new model of intensive agriculture when SOC established itself as the champion of the rights of Andalusian day-labourer families and later as a voice for the foreign temporary workers.

The families that continue to cultivate strawberries in the present day remember the very hard living and working conditions of the 1970s and 1980s. In particular, how they had to fight against the lack of habitable housing, child-minding and spaces in local schools, unregulated labour, low wages, and the absence of a collective labour agreement within the strawberry cultivation sector. Additionally, a lifestyle based on temporary work and mobility added to the hardship, which is still illustrated in narratives of labour migration in the present day:

> Around the end of June or beginning of July [the end of season in Huelva] I go to Utrera, and after my husband goes to Navarra [in the North of Spain], and does the fruit harvest there alone. I stay at home, with my boy, the one who still lives here, then after my grandchildren go, and the summer is better. When September comes, the end of September, beginning of October, we're back here again. (Dolores Gómez, day-labourer from Palmar de Troya, Seville)

In the 1990s, many of the Andalusian day-labourer families abandoned work in strawberry cultivation, leading to the arrival of the first wave of immigrant workers, which were predominantly Moroccan (Gordo 2002). However, by the end of the 1990s, they were joined by a second wave of immigrants from Mauritania and countries in sub-Saharan Africa, such as Senegal, Mali, Nigeria and the Ivory Coast. Whereas previously, the common forces of identity and social relations were a direct association with the land, Andalusian identity, and the common life trajectories of the workers from the provincias of Cadiz and Seville, now the landscape became more heterogenous and complex. In this new setting, relations and forms of collective identification were formed on the basis of national and ethnic identity and gender, as well as the shared life trajectories, kinship relations and friendships that make up migratory networks. Amongst these new day-labourers, immigration, the family dimension, and their condition as waged labour acquired characteristics and meanings that were distinct from the Andalusian day-labourers, although equally relevant.

The immigrant's experience is often defined by long, hazardous journeys, such as crossing the Straits of Gibraltar, encountering many obstacles to regularising their position in Spain, as well as social and institutional racism and exclusion. In contrast to the emigration and migration of the Andalusian families, the African workforce is young and predominantly male, but similarly motivated by a need to provide for their domestic groups. However, their objective wasn't to come to Spain to work the agricultural season and return to their home countries but rather to establish themselves in Andalusia and bring their families as soon as they could. As waged labour, they occupied a precarious position characterised by poor working conditions, irregular work (often in spite of having the correct work permits), greater instability, extreme levels of geographic and labour mobility, and many difficulties finding decent accomodation.

The vulnerability of their work conditions was reflected in the daily sight of large groups of men from North and sub-Saharan Africa gathered on street corners and in town squares waiting for offers of work from growers, while the poverty of their living conditions was evident in the emergence of large shanty settlements. Ousmane Diop, a 24 year old Senegalese man, arrived in the Canary Islands in 2006 on a migrant boat and from there he travelled to Huelva while under a 'pending deportation' order. There, he lived with hundreds of other African migrants in a shanty settlement in a pine grove close to the strawberry farms, where they used discarded plastic from the fields, wood, cardboard and old rope to construct shacks. When interviewed that season he had hardly managed to work more than a few days at a time.

A key turning point in the organisation of the workforce, in particular the substitution of workers, occurred at the outset of the 21st century when the Spanish government introduced the Temporary Guest Farm Workers Programme, which started by recruiting workers from eastern Europe and soon after from Morocco. Based on a contract signed in the country of origin, the programme offers a short-term work permit that is covered by the local collective bargaining agreement and includes transport and accomodation, but is restricted to a specific geographic area and requires workers to return to their home countries once the contract has finalised.[9]

---

9   The principles and objectives of the Temporary Guest Farm Worker Programme in Spain are similar to other countries' programmes, although there are some important local differences. See Griffith (2006), Preibisch and Binford (2007) and Sánchez and Lara (2015).

From a base of 6,500 contracts in the 2001/2002 growing season, the number of contracts issued under this programme grew exponentially over the following years to around 40,000 in 2007/2008. Initially, most workers were recruited from Poland and Romania but in the 2006/2007 campaign there was a switch to Moroccan workers and recruitment from Eastern European countries reduced.[10] Similarly to other intensive farming sectors that are sustained on a nexus of labour feminization, flexibility and precarity (Lara 1998; Preibish & Encalada 2010),[11] the programme drove a progressive reorganisation and feminisation of the immigrant workforce (Author 2012; Hellio 2017) by redefining the ideal type of worker as older adult women from poor rural areas with young dependents:

> Why women and not men? Well it's very simple. First the women have more stamina than the men. Women have more capacity to suffer than men. Women are more submissive than men. Women are more selective than men, more inquisitive. You're just better than us! (Francisco López, grower)
>
> Why do the Romanian women work better? Because they're used to working in the fields, being in the snow, cleaning their houses, keeping their vegetable garden and their pigs, working. My Romanians work in factories for 12 or 13 hours to earn five euros. They're women who know how to work and that's what we need in this country, women who know how to work. (Javier Moreno, grower)

For Javier Moreno, from his position as a strawberry grower, 'good' women workers are those that are subjected to extreme relations of exploitation, hard work in the fields or the factory and in the home, and a labour system that demands mothers without their families, as well as restricted geographic and labour mobility. A Romanian woman worker describes this type of relation from her perspective:

---

[10] Following the economic crisis in 2008 the Spanish government limited the number of contracts issued under the Temporary Guest Farm Worker Programme to give priority to the national workforce and the foreign immigrant workers settled in Spain. At the time of writing the number of contracts being issued is increasing.

[11] The variability of the selection criteria used in the different forms of agriculture requires us to examine the specific mechanisms of feminisation and segmentation that operate in the local labour markets. See also Barrientos, Kabeer and Hossain (2004), Deere (2005), Figueroa (2015).

It's very difficult for a mother like me. 'Like all of us' [adds a colleague]. Yes, like all of us. We all have children in Romania, we have families and it's very difficult. I work here, my husband is in Romania, when he comes here to work, I go back to Romania. He works in Cordoba, I work here on the strawberries. The Spanish government doesn't want to work with families. (...) We want to work with our husbands, it's the employer who doesn't want it.

Mirela Vicov's narrative highlights how immigration, as a strategy to gain a means to a livelihood, has costs for the organisation of the family and domestic group[12] and the position of women as waged workers in a sexually segmented labour market. In other words, it speaks to the material conditions, social relations and the feelings and desires that frame the day-to-day experiences of the temporary female day-labourers. As Narotzky and Smith (2010) observe, these conditions and experiences are intimately connected to the conflicts that come about from social reproduction under capitalism. Hence, it is important to explore how these conflicts are expressed in the context of intensive strawberry production.

3 Meanings of Justice, Dignity and Rights in the Collective Actions of Different Social Actors

3.1 *"They Need to Stop Devaluing Our Work": Strawberry Growers and the Production/Distribution Conflict*

During the harvest, the period of most intense work, Javier Moreno spends a large part of the day either on his 7-hectare farm, at the warehouse or at the agricultural cooperative. As I accompany him to his farm, the tracks and the roads that connect his farm to the cooperatives and local villages are busy with the movement of fruit, goods, machinery and people that is typical during the peak agricultural season. As we access a plot, very close to the housing units for the temporary workers, Javier points to the structure of the greenhouse to explain the advantages of the large tunnel, which encloses a number of strawberry hills, compared to the small tunnels that only enclose an individual hill. On the right, a crew of male and female immigrant workers are

---

[12] Within the concept of "good mothers", Morokvasic (2007) observes how, in comparison to men, women bear much more of the burden and social costs of emigration. The author's idea of "incomplete families", associated with the migrations of women from Yugoslavia in similar work programmes, also helps to illustrate this idea.

collecting strawberries, it's midday and the sun is beating down on the plastic tunnels. The workers salute us without stopping from picking the mature fruit and placing it in the boxes that they push on trolleys. The height of the plants means that they spend a large part of the day bent double, never kneeling as it slows down the work. Javier started to run his own greenhouse in the early 2000s just when profit margins were most severely hit by increased production costs and a reduction in prices (Delgado y Aragón 2006). This explains why, in spite of making the change from being a day-labourer to a businessman, Javier emphasises the risks and difficulties of running a successful strawberry farm:

> Of all my friends my age, 32 years old, I'm the least well off, because although you see a farm, I have 30 people working for me, I have equipment. I'm an unfortunate wretch. I have a friend who doesn't even have a high school diploma, they're plasters, they have a crew and they're raking it in. Friends who do flooring, plumbers, they have companies that are going well because there's been a boom in construction. They're not as stressed as me. (...) A lot of money comes in with the strawberries but the costs are very high. On a hectare of land you need to spend easily about €12,000 and in a bad or not so good year you might only earn about €6,000. All businesses are a risk, if I knew that next year I'm not going to earn anything then I wouldn't sow anything, but who knows that? Nobody. There have been some very good years for strawberry growers, 15 years ago there was money in strawberries. Why? Because wages were lower, everything was cheaper and a kilo of strawberries was worth the same as today. Wages have gone up, rubber has gone up, bromide has gone up, plastic has gone up, and the price for a kilo of strawberries is still the same or even cheaper! That's what's happened. (...) Farming at the moment is like gambling. You have to do everything really well to make anything out of it.

Javier Moreno is a member of the Coordination of Farmers and Livestock Organisations (COAG) [*Coordinadora de Organizaciones de Agricultores y Ganaderos*], the first professional agricultural organisation in Spain, which set up during the transition to democracy in the late 1970s. A member of *La Via Campesina* and a promoter of a family farming model, COAG's historical references come from the peasant movements that emerged in the 1960s and 70s in Spain. Known as *the price wars*, the mobilisations at this time were characterised by slogans such as "those who work the land want to live from the land".[13]

---

13 https://www.coagandalucia.com/index.php/quienes-somos

To fully understand the place from which the agricultural organisations speak in the strawberry sector, it is necessary to remember that they represent farmers whose status as agricultural employers is articulated from their position as dependents of big capital. The social relations of production -and the exploitation of the workforce- are inscribed in a structure whereby the producers occupy a subordinate position to the multinationals and large supermarket chains in a highly competitive market (Bonnano & Busch 2015; McMichael 2009). This situation has lead to a generalized feeling of grievance that is expressed through the demands and actions of agricultural organisations.

In the strawberry sector, three organisations are most influential at State and local level: COAG, UPA and ASAJA.[14] These organisations, which were fundamental in uniting the sector, have two main objectives: firstly, to support farmers by offering them services and secondly to safeguard their interests and rights. This was the principal reason behind the establishment in 1983 of the lobbyist organisation FresHuelva (*Asociación Onubense de Productores y Exportadores de Fresa* [Association of Strawberry Producers and Exporters, Huelva]). In spite of a weakening of the services they offer to growers, these associations continue to be active through advocacy and protest their grievances with the large supermarket chains and public administration.

Amongst the principal demands of the agricultural organisations is a fair CAP that doesn't exclude the fruit and vegetable sector from the grant system and that stops favouring large landowners. They also lobby for the establishment of a support plan for emergency financial situations that can arise from sudden falls in demand or prices, which can ocurr through unexpected climatic effects, outbreaks of infectious disease (e.g. the 2011 E. coli scandal in Europe), political crisis (e.g. the 2011 Russian embargo) and economic uncertainty (e.g. Brexit). Additionally, complaints in relation to preferential deals with third countries, such as Morocco, have particular importance, with much blame attributed to public institutions, such as the European Union, who they consider to be responsible for the advantages enjoyed by neighbouring countries. The agricultural organisations believe that these countries are permitted to export too great a volume of product into Europe while benefiting from lower production costs and less stringent quality control standards. While this competitive environment is viewed as unfair, their attitudes also relate to the fact that the majority of the large fruit and vegetable companies are linked to the Moroccan royal family and because some producers from Huelva have relocated to Morocco. Paradoxically, this feeling of comparative grievance is what

---

14   Unión de Pequeños Agricultores y Ganaderos (UPA) [Union of Small Cultivators and Farmers] and Asociación Agraria-Jóvenes Agricultores (ASAJA) [Association of Young Farmers].

French strawberry producers have been expressing for decades with respect to Huelva's strawberry producers. Of all these grievances, the demand for a 'fair price' by producers has come to occupy a central position in the concerns of the sector and a key element in a revitalisation of their identity as farmers.

Large supermarket chains have played a decisive role in farm enterprises' plummeting profitability, a global trend that doesn't look like changing within the current neoliberal agrifood model that has transformed and undermined the expectations and living conditions of peasants and small farmers (Edelman 2015). In Andalusia, while some farmers' organisations demand a fair price but are also against market regulation, other growers and agricultural associations are pro regulation and want the government to stop the abuses by the large supermarket chains that has resulted in a huge discrepancy between the prices paid to farmers and retail prices. Javier Moreno explains:

> Our problem is with the market, it's a free market and everyone does whatever they like. That's where the government needs to get involved, and at least do a bit of research on the free market, and enforce reasonable prices.
>
> (...) do you not see that it's free [the market]? They set the prices at whatever they like. And that's what we talk about a lot, that the government should intervene in some way. The market has to earn what the market has to earn, but not 300%. That's where it's just crazy [...]. I think that it should be the government, the state should take measures and establish a pricing structure, a scale, and regulate the price we sell at in relation to the retail sale price. (Antonio Pérez, grower)

Faced with an agricultural policy that they view as giving free rein to speculation, they demand political mechanisms to stop the price collapse. This idea of a fair price and regulation as a means to achieve it reveals a contradiction between the dependence that the producers have on market value and the way that social value is employed to establish a fair and equitable price (the reproduction of the domestic unit and a devaluing of day-labourers work) (Martínez 2014). Following Polanyi's line of thinking, Martínez (2014) observed that the producers' conceptualization of a fair price was one based on a regulated or controlled market and not a free one; demands that make sense within a regulated economic framework inherited from the Keynesian state, which was designed to control market excesses.

When the tolderable becomes intolerable, the growers fight to defend their interests and rights and to have a 'dignified' sector has taken the form of protest marches, tractor rallies, roadblocks, attempts to stop the import of Moroccan produce, as well as handing out free fruit and vegetables at supermarket entrances. The definition of their objectives and demands in terms of rights, dignity and a differentiation between the just and unjust shows the importance of retaining the moral economy that orients collective action in the context of crisis (Edelman 2005; Hossain & Kalita 2014; Narotzky & Besnier 2014).[15]

The distinction that these producers draw between the just and unjust reflects how moral values impregnate economic behaviour. They place great value on work, effort and the recognition of a job well done. They feel that their overriding goal, which is to provide for their families, is a legitimate and dignified one, in contrast to the abusive behaviour of the large supermarket chains who they claim to be "playing with the livelihoods of a million families". In this sense, their principal demand is that the supermarkets "stop devaluing our work by agreeing low pricing pacts that only do one thing: destroy our income" (Miguel López, General Secretary of COAG, during a protest march in 2001 entitled "the supermarket chains are destroying us"). For the farmers, the unfair fruit prices offered by the supermarkets represents a manipulation of the market that devalues their work and misappropriates money from the value chain. In this context, speculation is considered to be a morally illegitimate practice that requires protest (Author 2018: 234–235).

This localising factor helps to understand the growers' grievances that supermarket chains, such as Carrefour, Lidl or Mercadona, misappropriate the value that the growers add to the product: "There are times when they say, 'no, the added-value of the fruit…'. But, hang on, the only one who adds value to the fruit is the farmer" (Jose María Baroso, Secretary of COAG-Huelva). In 2006, an awareness campaign entitled "Who gets what *you* pay for?" was launched by a coalition of agricultural organisations and consumer groups.[16] The campaign's purpose was to raise awareness about the huge difference between the prices paid to farmers and retail prices and, amongst other actions, the organisers handed out information leaflets at the entrances to supermarkets (Antentas y

---

15 The concept of moral economy has great analytical capacity. E.P. Thompson (1971, 1991) used it to explain the social protests of the English plebs in the 18th century after the dominant classes crossed the culturally established line between the acceptable and the intolerable. Along with Scott's (1976) analysis of the moral economy of peasant rebellions in Southeast Asia, this concept has proved very useful for exploring current protests, such as those of the transnational peasant movement (Edelman 2005), the mobilizations that resulted from the 2007-2008 food crisis (Hossain & Kalita 2014) or the crisis of social reproduction linked to the 2008 financial crisis (Narotzky & Besnier 2014).

16 Including COAG, the Union of Spanish Consumers [*Unión de Consumidores de España* (UCE)] and the Spanish Confederation of Homeworkers, Consumers and Users [*Confederación Española de Amas de Casa, Consumidores y Usuarios* (CEACCU)]

Vivas, 2007). In 2017, the Andalusian Interprofessional Strawberry Association (Interfresa) took a legal action against the supermarket chain ALDI for publishing promotional brochures that advertised strawberries from Huelva for sale at below-cost prices. All of these actions are inscribed within a moral framework that articulates the values of fairness and legitimacy with the value of loyalty: "there just isn't any loyalty, they are discrediting the image of our products across the whole sector".[17] UPA's public denunciation of Aldi also integrates the symbolic and social value attributed to the farmer's effort:

> Aldi sucks the life out of the farmers. (...) On top of that, Aldi seems to laugh at our efforts with their slogan, "What's worth a lot, costs very little". In fact, it costs us a lot to produce food.[18]

Although the differentiation with traditional farmers lead to an identification with the figure of the agricultural entrepreneur, currently the importance of the positioning against the large supermarket chains means that the framework of these protests and grievances has reactivated their identity as farmers. In this sense, even though they abandoned their livelihoods as fishermen, subsistence farmers and their positions as wage earners, the majority of the strawberry growers haven't left behind their condition as agricultural workers. Nevertheless, we have to be cautious in the way that we interpret the moral economy (Scott, 1976; Hossain and Kalita, 2014), as it could represent a political strategy that provides producers with an ideological justification for their demands and protests. Furthermore, the importance placed on the tensions between the growers and the large supermarket chains could also act as a rationale for poor working conditions. For this reason it is necessary to assess other conflicts and perspectives in the agrifood chain, such as those found between producers and their workforces, which adds another layer to the analysis.

3.2 "He Didn't Respect Us": Male and Female Immigrant Workers and the Producer/Worker Conflict

Ana Podolski, a young Polish woman that studied business administration, left her country for the first time aged 19 in search of better work opportunities in Germany. Two years later, after being selected to work on the Temporary Farm Guest Worker Programme, she began to combine six-month stints working on the strawberry campaigns in Huelva with 2-month stints on the lettuce harvest in Germany, from where she went back to her family in Poland, before

---

17   Diario *Huelva Información* (01/02/2017)
18   *eComercio Agrario* (31/01/2017)

returning for the next programme. Now married to a local man, pregnant and settled in the town of Moguer, Ana recalls the first years she worked on the strawberry campaign:[19]

> It's, well, working the strawberries isn't that easy, it's really hard, and depends on the boss that you get. (...) My boss wasn't good, none of the women who came with me went back to work with him [the following year], he didn't respect us like the other strawberry growers that the women always went back to. If something happened, if you had to ask for the doctor, you had to sort it out yourself, whatever way you could, and when you've just arrived you can't speak the language, you don't know what you can and can't do. They tell you that you are on trial for two weeks, but really all the time you're working he's watching you. He could fire you at any moment, for anything at all. Later, when you start to learn and you know how to ask for something or he sees that you could complain, then he started to pay more attention to you, but at the start its a total sham. In time, you learn to speak Spanish, and you know that if you have a problem you can go to the cooperative. We help each other a lot, especially the ones who have been doing it longer and know what to do.

Indignant, Ana complained that on her farm the boss not only controlled the immigrant women during work hours but also during their leisure time. He would question workers and visit the accommodation units, and local bars and discos to see "who had gone out and who hadn't and what they were doing." If he discovered that some women had been out, he would punish them by not giving them work for two days, meaning they lost two days wages. Ana Podolski's narrative illustrates how the temporary workers place the direct, personalised and antagonistic relationship with employers in the foreground of the conflict, while the multinationals and large supermarket chains are perceived as distant agents to their day-to-day problems. As the boss and owner of the farm, the waged workers hold the grower responsible for the injustices they suffer. Hence, we see a perspectival change in the narratives of the different social agents from concerns related to the rights of farmers and the abuses suffered in the production/distribution relation to concerns related to the rights of workers and the abuses perpetrated by employers in the producer/worker relation.

Historically, there have been periods when this producer/working class conflict has been more intense and received greater social visibility through

---

19   In the first rounds of the Temporary Farm Guest Worker Programme the selection criteria didn't specify that women should be older adults and have dependent children.

strategies of collective protest and action. Notably, this has included the Andalusian day-labourer movement in the 1980s and 90s, the male immigrant worker mobilisations at the beginning of the century, and, more recently, the actions of the female immigrant workers on the Guest Farm Worker Programme. As such, changes in the composition of the workforce have corresponded to the emergence of new forms of resistance conditioned by the socioeconomic and political context, the migrant worker system (Burawoy 1976), and the circumstances and experiences of the different immigrant collectives and their organisational capacity.

The Temporary Guest Farm Worker Programme was introduced during a period of great social and work conflict. The mobilisations at the beginning of the 21st century represented a new phase in producer/worker conflict (Author 2017:247–248). Organised by Ecuadorian, Moroccan and sub-Saharan Africans, these protests constituted a response to poor living and working conditions and the rejection of applications for the regularisation of work. Lead by about 850 immigrants (mostly from the Maghreb) a series of protests took place in the province of Huelva during the 2001 agricultural campaign and ended in hunger strikes and sit-ins (Gualda 2004). In Lepe [a strawberry growing town], the regularization of 'undocumented' immigrants following a sit-in and nineteen days on hunger strike was considered a great triumph for the movement. In the city of Huelva, five sit-ins lead to an agreement between employers (Freshuelva) and the The Platform Against the Immigration Act (Huelva) [*Plataforma contra la Ley de Extranjería de Huelva*] to regularize the situation of immigrants with the necessary pre-contracts. This was administered by the central government through an extraordinary regularization process that started in June 2011, although one hundred and thirty five immigrants remained ineligible (CGT, 2003). However, the processes of ethnic and gender substitution of the workforce meant the displacement of older temporary immigrant workers who held work permits that limited their activity to agriculture in Huelva on the basis of the pre-contracts that came out of the 2001 protests (Gualda 2004). This situation resulted in new mobilisations in demand of better working conditions, one of the most important of which was the March for Dignity from various strawberry cultivating towns that culminated in a rally in the capital of Huelva.

In 2002, Huelva became the base of action once more when 500 immigrants from Mauritania, Ivory Coast, Senegal, Mali, Nigeria, Morocco, and Algeria mobilised to organise a sit-in at the University Pablo de Olavide (Seville).[20] These protests took place in a national context characterized by diverse forms

---

20   Distinct visions of this sit in can be found in CGT (2003) and Martin-Díaz and Castaño (2004).

of self-organisation and mobilization of immigrants, which included sit-ins and hunger strikes in Almeria, Madrid and Barcelona and the March for Lorca's Life [*La Marcha por la Vida de Lorca*] in Murcia. The protests in the strawberry producing area and those in other parts of the country broke out at similar times and share the same socioeconomic, political-legal and sociocultural background. Most notably, this was defined by extreme employment instability and precarity and the deterioration of labour, social and cultural rights, as well as a hardening of immigration policies and laws, growing criminalisation of undocumented immigrants, exclusion, racism, ethnic segregation, and difficulty accessing housing.

They also share commonalities in the type of response to this regime of living and working. Based on self-organisation and focused on concrete demands and proposals, these groups have a significant capacity to mobilise direct actions that can exert significant political pressure and create widespread social visibility. Their actions are also based on cooperation with unions, social and non-government organisations, such as the Platform Against the Immigration Act (Huelva) [*Plataforma contra la Ley de Extranjería de Huelva*], which is made up of various non-profit organisations, the political party United Left [*Izquierda Unida*], General Confederation of Work (CGT) [*Confederación General del Trabajo*], USTEA Trade Union [*Unión de Sindicatos de Trabajadoras y Trabajadores en Andalucía*] and Unitary Trade Union [*Sindicato Unitario*]. These organisations share a common belief in the interstitial trade unionism proposed by Roca and Martín-Díaz (2017), the extreme precarity of employment, direct action as a prioritised tactic, the horizontal nature of networks, and complex relations with the trade union movement.

If, as Aguirre Rojas (2010) states, the moral economy mobilises and renews itself when the masses act collectively, convincingly, challengingly and publicly, then this was the case with the responses of immigrant workers when they felt that producers and public administrators crossed a culturally established red line between the acceptable and intolerable (Thompson 1971, 1991). The shared experiences of Ecuadorians, Moroccans, Algerians, Mauritanians, Nigerians and Malese within the same system of immigrant work helps us to understand their feelings, sense of identity, and the manner that they articulate their interests in opposition to those of producers and the State. The specificity of their interests corresponds to the particularities of their condition as temporary immigrant workers.[21] It is from this position that their insistence on a dignified labour agreement as a basic right of any human being relates

---

21 In his analysis of the relation between structure, thought and action, Durrenberger (2002) holds that people construct meaning from their place in social structures and based on

to their demand for the abolishment of Spain's Immigration Act and the regularisation of their status as workers. This corresponds to a moral economy in which the struggle for justice, dignity and rights moves away from the call for agricultural reform and transcends the sphere of labour conditions to integrate demands such as "papers for everyone", "we are not illegals, we are people", "stop deportations", "decent housing" and "zero tolerance against racism."

The close of this cycle of mobilisations and the consolidation of the Temporary Farm Guest Worker Programme gave way to a new scenario defined by, on the one hand, the growth of shanty settlements and camps made up of thousands of unemployed African immigrants and, on the other hand, the work and living conditions imposed by the new system of recruitment. Non-government organisations such as Huelva Welcomes [*Huelva Acoge*], ACCEM and the Red Cross have assumed the role of providing assistance and services to the camps that set-up during each campaign (APDH-Huelva 2015). The Andalusian Regional Government's emergency plan has contributed to this situation by delegating most of the services to NGOs with no comprehensive or holistic solutions to a structural problem. The Temporary Workers Board would subsequently proposed a continuation of the demands and protests that arose in the previous cycle of mobilizations and to orient trade union activity and social work to the new socio-labour scenario.

The Board of Migration [*Mesa de Migraciones*] is the public body where the labour needs for each agricultural campaign are negotiated. Its members include the large trade unions such as The Workers' Commission (CC.OO) [*Comisiones Obreras*] and the General Workers' Union (UGT) [*Unión General de Trabajadores*], the growers' associations and the government. Agreements reached in this body made way for the introduction of the Temporary Guest Farm Worker Programme, which the participating members consider to be the ideal model for the organisation of labour migrations and to ensure adequate transport, housing and employment. However, the Temporary Workers Board was created as an alternative to the official Board of Migration and is made up of the smaller trade unions (SAT-SOC[22] and SU) and social organisation such as the Social Rights Office of Seville (ODS) [*Oficina de Derechos Sociales de Sevilla*] and the Human Rights Association of Huelva (APDH) [*Asociación Pro Derechos Humanos de Huelva*]. The Temporary Workers Board holds that the

---

their day-to-day experiences of class. He understands that this is what shapes forms of thought.

22   In 2007, SOC activists created the Andalusian Workers' Union (SAT) [*Sindicato Andaluz de Trabajadores*] with the aim of expanding and establishing the union's presence in other labour sectors.

current model is a mechanism for the control and limitation of rights and the demobilisation of workers:[23]

> One way to be done with the mobilisations in Huelva, where they were looking for papers and rights, was the guest worker programme. What's more, they bring women, with family responsibilities, and people who don't know their rights, they come to earn money, and most of all they bring availability [as in being constantly available to work] (María Carrasco, trade unionist, responsible for gender equality, SAT-SOC)

Some of the more notable actions carried out by the Temporary Workers Board, include: the provision of information through face-to-face communication and pamphlets that detail labour rights and the conditions of the collective bargaining agreement; making complaints and demands through legal actions, protest campaigns and social actions; as well as providing social and legal advice and organising members. It also promotes self-organisation amongst immigrants and cooperates with organisations such as La Vía Campesina and pro-immigrant groups like the *Confèrération Paysanne* and *Colectif de Défense des Travailleurs* étrangers *Saisonniers dans l'agriculture* (CODETRAS). However, unlike in Almeria, where the presence and leadership of foreign immigrants in trade unions such as SAT-SOC stands out, in Huelva, to date, no immigrants are on the Temporary Workers Board or act as union representatives. Another limitation is the tendency, amongst some parts of the unionist movement, to homogenize the working class under an ahistorical interpretation of the capital-labour contradiction that does not take into account that "the working class has two sexes" (Hirata and Kergoat 1997), is ethnically stratified and inserted in diverse labour regimes:

> There's no difference, they're day-labourers, they're the same conditions and the same circumstances, there are few differences. The difference is having your parent's house 5,000km away or having it in the next town, but apart from that... (Luis Fernández, union representative, SU and member of the Temporary Workers Board)

In spite of this, the makeup of the Board, its organisational model and its main areas of action conform to Roca and Díaz-Parra's (2013) definition of SAT as a

---

23 Different academic studies have concluded that temporary agricultural worker programmes are based on forms of 'captive labour' (Basok 2003) and 'not free' labour (Décosse 2017).

paradigmatic case of renewal of trade unionism based on social movement (direct action, objectives that go beyond labour conditions, and close relationships with social movements). It also corresponds to Pedreño, Gadea and de Castro's (2014) proposal that the improvement of labour and wage conditions in the agrifood industry are related as much to intense labour conflict as collective negotiations. As is evident from the case in Huelva, the strategies employed by business owners during such conflicts seek to counteract social and union actions, contain labour demands and regulation, and limit the negotiating power of workers. This commonly includes tactics such as only offering temporary contracts, rotation of workers, applying pressure to undermine take up of union membership, and recruitment strategies that weaken the direct relationship between business owner and worker (Pedreño, Gadea y de Castro 2014).

Compared to the image that the producers have of the female immigrant workers as a docile workforce, the empirical analysis reveals a different picture, in particular when we examine the actions of the new temporary women workers and the position of the Temporary Workers Board. The case of a complaint by a group of four female Romanian workers, who asked for help from APDH to report their employer for non-payment of wages, helps to illustrate this point. Through APDH they got in contact with SAT-SOC to report the case and make a formal claim for the money owed. However, as they were unable to reach agreement for the arbitration of their complaint, they decided instead to speak to their lawyer. The outcome of the meeting illustrates some of the difficulties that the temporary workers on the guest worker programme face when trying to exercise their rights. During an interview with her four colleagues, Stefana Chiriac, the only one of the Romanian women who was fluent in Spanish, acted as a translator and recalled, somewhat agitatedly, what had happened. She explained that they did not know that the labour agreement relevant to their sector requires the payment of overtime and full days once three hours of work is exceeded. Responding to a question, she asked what *La Vida Laboral* [employment, income and tax history] was and how she could get a copy of her own record. She also complained that for the workers it is difficult to take a day off to do the necessary paperwork. As they had only just started with the employer and it was peak season they were worried that complaining or engaging in an official processes would mean losing work or not being recalled for the following season.

Another case is that of Matraza Petrov, a polish worker contracted to work in storage, handling and packaging. She got in touch with the Temporary Workers Board, along with two colleagues, to make a complaint about not being paid for extra hours, a practice that had been going on for years but which had never been reported by autochthonous workers. During the previous campaign, when Matraza worked collecting strawberries in the fields, she was an organiser of one of the few protests that have taken place since the introduction of the guest worker programme. On the 1st of May, almost one hundred female workers from Eastern Europe initiated a work stoppage on their farm and demanded to be paid for extra hours.

The actions of women workers not only reflect an attitude of protest, but also the feeling of indignation provoked by the treatment they receive from farmers, in which the unequal position of class, ethnicity and gender play an important role. After complaining for half an hour to an agricultural organisation that her employer doesn't respect the labour agreement, Crina Pop berated that "in Spain they think that Romanian women can't speak, but Romanian women understand well enough. They think Romanian women are stupid, that they don't know." A similar sentiment was expressed by Kati Wozniak, a Polish Woman, when she asked rhetorically:

> What is the owner going to do with 90 women? Is he going to fire us all? Well who's going to work then? (...) Also, the gate to the farm is always closed. We have to crawl under it, like mice. He wouldn't let us leave. But I think we're all adults, I came here to work, I do my hours and the rest of the day is mine, I can do what I want with it, right?

Ana Podolski's narrative, with which I opened this section, is similar to these other women and shows the way that women workers distinguish between 'good' and 'bad' employers on the basis of a value system that judges attitudes of respect, support and control within and exterior to the spatial and time boundaries of work. By stating that her employer wasn't 'good' because he didn't respect the workers or support them when they needed to go to the doctor and was always monitoring them, Ana brings to light how support networks amongst the women immigrants counteract these circumstances: "We help each other a lot, especially the ones who have been doing it longer and know what to do." In addition to the shared experience of working in the fields and in the accommodation units, within the framework of the guest worker programme, nationality, gender and kinship play an important role in the formation of these networks. Often, these mutual support spaces contain forms of adaptation and resistance that have little visibility. At other times, they give rise to explicit practices of confrontation and protest, such as those pointed out. In this sense, the analysis supports Mills' (2005) findings which show how the capacity of women workers to respond and organize problematises the essentialist notions of passive femininity and conformity that is often associated with women. As she observes, the question is not whether these women can organise themselves or not, but rather: what are the conditions that permit mobilisation in spite of the obstacles?.[24] In other words, the structures of possibility that favour the emergence of these spaces (Martín-Díaz & Roca in this volume).

4 Conclusions

An analytical approach to the social relations involved in strawberry production that focuses on the contradictions and tensions between distribution and production and agricultural employers and workers demonstrates the importance of the conflicts that are engendered in social reproduction under capitalism. The analysis has illustrated how class origin and the expansion of agriculture through a smallholding model, the new positions of former day-labourers as employers, and the subordination of the local producer to the large supermarket chains are all key elements of the production/distribution conflict in strawberry cultivation in Huelva. The text reveals the importance of growers' demands for a fair Common Agricultural Policy and fair prices and the cultural and moral values that orient their struggle for justice, dignity and the rights of farmers.

Examining the tension in the employer/working class relation also brings to light the importance that migration acquires as a strategy with which to achieve the means to a decent livelihood and the costs that this has for the organisation of the domestic group, the position of the male and female agricultural workers, the national immigration laws, labour laws and agreements and the composition of the workforce. Situating the experiences of the male African day-labourers and the female day-labourers from Eastern Europe in this context permits us to understand the characteristics and values that guide their struggle for better living and working conditions. Their actions range from self-organisation to the formation of alliances with social organisations and trade unions and the development of networks of immigrants, and actions such as sit-ins, protest marches, strikes, work stoppages and other labour demands. They call for dignified treatment, labour agreements and work conditions, as well as the abolishment of Spain's Immigrant Act, "papers for all" and "proper housing."

---

24 Mills (2005) analyses the subjectivity of the activists and the strategies they employ to organise unions in intensive work industries (electronics, textiles, foodstuffs) in Bangkok. A sector in which protests and strikes lead by women workers are frequent.

The ethnographic approach has helped to show that both male and female immigrant workers are important points of reference for collective mobilisation and the challenges that trade unionism must face. Apart from readjusting trade union activity to address the needs that are borne out of increased instability, precarity and mobility of labour, the research found a capacity to recognise and respond to the heterogeneity of the current working class and the demands and organisational models that the different collectives propose.

References

Aguirre Rojas, C. A. (2010). *Economía moral de la multitud*. México D.F: IIS/UNAM.

Antentas, J. M & Vivas, E. (2007). Las resistencias a las cadenas de la gran distribución comercial. In E. Vivas & X. Montagut (Eds.), *Supermercados, no gracias. Grandes cadenas de distribución: impactos y alternativas* (pp. 135–148). Barcelona: Icaria.

Asociación Pro Derechos Humanos-Huelva. (2015). APDHA-Huelva exige actuaciones a las administraciones públicas tras nuevo incendio en un asentamiento de Palos. Asociación Pro Derechos Humanos de Andalucía.

Basok, T. (2003). *Tortillas and Tomatoes. Transmigrant Mexican Harvesters in Canada.* Ontario: McGill Queen University Press.

Bonanno, A. & Busch, L. (Eds.) (2015). *Handbook of the International Political Economy of Agriculture and Food*. Cheltenham, UK/Northampton, MA, USA: Edward Elgar Publishing.

Bonanno, A. & Josefa S. Cavalcanti. (2012). Globalization, Food Quality and Labor: The Case of Grape Production in North-Eastern Brazil. *International Journal of Sociology of Agriculture and Food*, 19 (1), 37–55.

Burawoy, M. (1976). The functions and the reproduction of a migrant labor: Comparative Material from Southern Africa and the United States. *The American Journal of Sociology*, 81(5), 1050–87.

Camarero, L., Sanpedro, R. & Vicente-Mazariegos, J.L. (2002). Los horticultores: una identidad en transición (1988). *AREAS. Revista de Ciencias Sociales*, 22, 43–69.

Carrier, J. & Kalb, D. (Eds.) (2015). *Anthropologies of class: Power, practice, and inequality*. Cambridge: Cambridge University Press.

CGT. (2003). La fresa amarga. Movilizaciones de inmigrantes en Huelva. Encierro en la UPO de Sevilla. *Materiales de Reflexión*, 2, 1–19.

Díaz del Moral, J. (1969). *Historia de las agitaciones campesinas andaluzas*. Madrid: Alianza editorial.

Décosse F. (2017). Persistent unfree labour in French intensive agriculture: A historical overview of the "OFII" temporary farmworkers program. In A. Corrado, C. de Castro & D. Perrotta (Eds), *Migration and Agriculture: Mobility and Change in the Mediterranean Area* (pp. 140–148). London: Routledge.

Deere, C.D. (2005). *The feminization of agriculture? Economic restructuring in rural Latin America*. Geneva: United Nations Research-Institute For Social Development (UNRISD).

Delgado, M. & Aragón, M.A. (2006). Los campos andaluces en la globalización. Almería y Huelva, fábrica de hortalizas. In M. Etxezarreta (Ed.), *La agricultura española en la era de la globalización* (pp. 423–474). Madrid: Ministerio de Agricultura y Pesca.

Durrenberger, P. (2002). Structure, Thought, and Action: Stewards in Chicago Union Locals. *American Anthropologist*, 104 (1), 93–105.

Edelman, M. (2005). Bringing the moral economy back... to the study of the 21st- century transnational peasant movements. *American Anthropologist*, 107(3), 331–345.

Figueroa, T. (2015). Gendered Sharecropping: Waged and Unwaged Mexican Immigrant Labor in the California Strawberry Fields. *Signs: Journal of Women in Culture and Society*, 40(4), 917–938.

Gordo, M. (2002). *La inmigración en el paraíso. Integración en la comarca de Doñana*. Sevilla: Junta de Andalucía / Instituto de Desarrollo Local.

Griffith, D. (2006). *American Guestworkers: Jamaicans and Mexicans in the U.S. Labor Market*. University Park: The Pennsylvania State University Press.

Gualda, E. 2(004). Del magrebí a la europea del este: sustitución de la mano de obra agrícola en la provincia de Huelva. In B. López & M. Berriane (Eds.), *Atlas de la Inmigración Marroquí en España: Atlas 2004* (pp. 250–251). Madrid: Ministerio de Trabajo y Asuntos Sociales.

Harvey, D. (1989). *The Condition of Postmodernity*. Oxford: Blackwell.

Hellio, E. (2017). 'They know that you'll leave, like a dog moving onto the next bin'. Undocumented male and seasonal contracted female workers in agricultural labour market of Huelva, Spain. In A. Corrado, C. de Castro & D. Perrotta (Eds.), *Migration and Agriculture: Mobility and Change in the Mediterranean Area* (pp. 140–158). London: Routledge.

Hirata, H. & Kergoat, D. (1997). La clase obrera tiene dos sexos. In H. Hirata & D. Kergoat, *La división sexual del trabajo. Permanencia y cambio* (pp. 77–86). Argentina: Asociación Trabajo y Sociedad/CEM.

Hossain, N. & Kalita, D. (2014). Moral economy in a global era: the politics of provisions during contemporary food price spikes. *The Journal of Peasant Studies*, 41(5), 815–831.

Lara Flores, S.M. (1998). *Nuevas experiencias productivas y nuevas formas de organización flexible del trabajo en la agricultura mexicana*. México: Juan Pablo Editores.

Márquez, J.A. (1986). *La nueva agricultura onubense*. Sevilla: Instituto de Desarrollo Regional de la Universidad de Sevilla.

Martín-Díaz, E. (1995). El cultivo del fresón en la zona de Palos y Moguer: Cambios socioeconómicos y sectores sociales implicados. *AESTUARIA. Revista de Investigación*, 3, 31–55.

Martín-Díaz, E. & Castaño, A. (2004). El encierro de inmigrantes en la Universidad Pablo de Olavide. In B. López & M. Berriane (Eds.), *Atlas de la Inmigración Marroquí en España: Atlas 2004* (pp.251–252). Madrid: Ministerio de Trabajo y Asuntos Sociales.

Martínez, B. (2014). About moral economy: fair price, quality and sustainability in Galician farming exploitations. Paper presented at the *Value and values in agro-food processes* workshop, EHESS, Marseille, 10–12th June.

McMichael, P. (2009). A food regime analysis of the «world food crisis». *Agriculture and Human Values*, 26, 281–295.

Mills, M.B. (2005). From Nimble Fingers to Raised Fists: Women and Labor Activism in Globalizing Thailand. *Signs: Journal of Women in Culture and Society*, 31(1), 117–144.

Moreno, I. (1988). La cuestión de la tierra y la identidad andaluza. In E. Sevilla & K. Heisel (Eds.), *Anarquismo y movimiento jornalero en Andalucía* (pp.99–106). Córdoba: Ayuntamiento de Córdoba.

Morokvasic, M. (2007). Migration, Gender, Empowerment. In Ilse Lenz et al. (Eds.), *Genders Orders Unbound. Globalisation, Restructuring and Reciprocity* (pp. 69–97). Opladen: Barbara Budrich Publishers.

Narotzky, S. (2007). El lado oscuro del consumo. *Cuadernos de Antropología Social*, 26, 21–39.

Narotzky, S. & Smith, G. (2010). *Luchas inmediatas. Gente, poder y espacio en la España Rural*. Valencia: Universitat de València.

Narotzky, S. & Besnier, N. (2014). Crisis, Value, and Hope: Rethinking the Economy. An Introduction to Supplement 9. *Current Anthropology*, 55(S9), 4–16.

Ocaña, L. (2006). *Los orígenes del SOC. De las comisiones jornaleras al I Congreso del Sindicato de Obreros del Campo de Andalucía (1975–1977)*. Sevilla: Atrapasueños.

Palenzuela, P. (1996). *Buscarse la vida. Economía jornalera en las marismas de Sevilla*. Ayuntamiento de Sevilla: Sevilla.

Pedreño, A., Gadea, E. & de Castro, C. (2014). Labor, gender and political conflicts in the global agri-food system: the case of agri-export model in Murcia, Spain. In A. Bonanno & Cavalcanti, J. S. (Eds.), *Labor Relations in Global Food* (pp. 193–214). Bingley, UK: Emerald Publishing.

Ploeg, J. D. van der. (2008). *The New Peasantries. Struggles for Autonomy and Sustainability in an Era of Empire and Globalization*. London and Sterling, VA: Earthscan.

Preibisch, K. & Binford, L. (2007). Interrogating Racialized Global Labour Supply: An Exploration of the Racial/National Replacement of Foreign Agricultural Workers in Canada. *Canadian Review of Sociology and Anthropology*, 44(1), 5–36

Preibish, K. & Encalada, E. (2010). The Other Side of el Otro Lado: Mexican Migrant Women and Labor Flexibility in Canadian Agriculture. *Signs: Journal of Women in Culture and Society*, 35 (2), 289–316.

Roca, B. (2014). Izquierda radical, sindicalismo y acción colectiva en Andalucía (1976–2012). *Cuadernos de Relaciones Laborales*, 32(2),135–163.

Roca, B. & Díaz-Parra, I. (2013). De la tierra a los supermercados: El Sindicato Andaluz de Trabajadores como ejemplo de particularismo militante y revitalización sindical. *Anuario del Conflicto Social, 2012*, 855–876.

Roca, B. & Martín-Díaz, E. (2017). Solidarity Networks of Spanish Migrants in the UK and Germany: The Emergence of Interstitial Trade Unionism. *Critical Sociology*, 43(7–8), 1197–1212.

Roseberry, W. (1996). The Rise of Yuppie Coffees and the Reimagination of Class in the United States. *American Anthropologist*, 98 (4), 762–775.

Sánchez, M.J. & Sara Lara. (Eds.) (2015). *Los programas de trabajadores agrícolas temporales ¿una solución a los retos de las migraciones en la globalización?* México DF: UNAM-Instituto de Investigaciones Sociales.

Scott, J. C. (1976). *The moral economy of the peasant: Rebellion and subsistence in Southeast Asia*. Yale University Press: New Haven.

Solana J.L. (2000). Las clases sociales en Andalucía. Un recorrido socio-histórico. *Gazeta de Antropología*, 16, 1–17.

Talego, F. (1996). *Cultura jornalera, poder popular y liderazgo mesiánico. Antropología política de Marinaleda*. Sevilla: Fundación Blas Infante.

Talego, F. (2010). La memoria y la tierra en el imaginario de los jornaleros andaluces. In *Patrimonio Cultural en la Ruralidad Andaluza*. Sevilla: Junta de Andalucia.

Terrón, A. (2004). Migraciones y relaciones con países terceros. España. *Documentos CIDOB*. Barcelona: Fundació CIDOB.

Thompson, E.P. (1966). *The making of the English working class*. New York: Vintage.

Thompson, E.P. (1971). The moral economy of the English crowd in the eighteenth century. *Past & Present*, 50:76–136.

Thompson, E.P. (1991). *Customs in common*. London: Penguin.

Trinidad, M. L. (2005). Inmigrantes y mercado de trabajo: la apuesta por la contratación en origen. In M. Lª. García & J. Martín (Eds.), *Una forma nueva de ordenar la inmigración en España. Estudio de la Ley Orgánica 14/2003 y su reglamento de desarrollo* (pp.150–173). Valladolid: Editorial Lex Nova.

Verdier, M. (2006). *Reflexiones en torno a la situación actual del sector fresero de Huelva*. Huelva: Freshuelva (unpublished).

Wells, M. (1996). *Strawberry fields. Politics, class, and work in California agriculture*. Ithaca: Cornell University Press.

CHAPTER 7

Transforming Labour Law or Recurring to Grass-Root Mobilisation? The Struggles over the Empowerment of Tomato-Picking Migrant Workers in Southern Italy

Giuseppe D'Onofrio and Jon Las Heras

1 Introduction

Critical Political Economy literature identifies the formation and development of Global Value Chains (GVCs) with the outsourcing and offshoring of the labour process, i.e. strong centripetal forces that displace the labour process from established industrial relations frameworks towards companies and territories with comparatively lower working standards (Moody, 1997; Silver, 2003; Charnock & Starosta, 2016). The disempowering effects that the introduction of 'lean production' methods has had upon well-organised industrial workers (Stewart et al., 2009; Mulholland & Stewart, 2014), translates into the difficulties to (self)organize and (self)support those workers located along the lower TIERs of the supply chains (Doellgast & Greer, 2007). Simultaneously, employers located at the inferior levels of the GVCs are forced to cut wages and working-standards, to relocate or to face shut-down if they seek to preserve a certain rate of profit under increasing competitive pressures from the firms located in superior levels of the GVCs (cf. Starosta, 2010; Iñigo-Carrera, 2016). Such *homogenising stratification* erects strong barriers among workers, especially for peripheral workers who cannot bargain with their 'real' employers – i.e. the firm governing the GVC –, and they cannot but only fight for a lower share of the value-added than if the whole GVC was integrated vertically as during Fordist times (Flecker, 2009; Wills, 2009).

Complementarily, *global labour mobility* supports the development of global capitalism in some important aspects. In industrial sectors with lower capital accumulation and greater geographical-fixity, migrant workers have come to constitute a key segment of the labour force insofar as those low-wage jobs cannot be relocated easily (Sassen, 1998; Struna, 2009). For example, in Southern European countries migrants have underpinned the restructuring of the agricultural industry and ensured agri-food capitals to maintain, if not

© GIUSEPPE D'ONOFRIO AND JON LAS HERAS, 2021 | DOI:10.1163/9789004464964_009

even increase, their profit rates within a more competitive context (Colloca & Corrado, 2013). In that sense, outsourcing and migration (i.e. mobility of capital and labor) have become two mirroring aspects of global restructuring, and thus, two fundamental ways used by capital to increase its profits (Smith, 2016).

This chapter studies the structure and mechanisms regulating the working of the *global tomato value chain* in the province of Foggia (Southern Italy) from an International Political Economy of Labour (IPEL) perspective. Following the contributions of Harrod and O'Brien (2002), Silver (2003), Davies and Ryner (2006) and Selwyn (2014) among others, Las Heras (2018a) and Roca and Las Heras (2020) have recently advanced an analytical framework that enables us to study the production and transformation of class relations from the strategic position of the (alienated) worker. These authors build upon Gramsci's methodology of the subaltern in order to transcend both traditional 'top-down' and 'bottom-up' analyses that simplify the production of class power and its complex nature. In posing a strategic approach to the various forms in which class relations are mediated, IPE scholars, sociologists and industrial relations scholars can trace better the fragmentation and restructuring of the working class as a result of their contradictory engagement with (global) capital and other (global) working class fractions.

Fundamentally, the struggles among capitals are nothing but the *visible expression* of the intra-class and cross-class struggles underlying working class formation, and thus, the study of the former should only be a starting point to accurately apprehend the latter. Therefore, and as we will do next, understanding the power and economic relations between leadings firms and supplier companies along the global tomato value chain is a necessary *moment* for the subsequent production of a more complete study that can allow us to put over the table the emancipatory possibilities of workers in a particular context (see also Cleaver, 2000[1979]).

Italy is the third tomato producer in the world, and the province of Foggia is the first supplier of fresh tomatoes among southern Italian processing companies that produce and export for private labels of food retail chains. The power of retail chains to set prices, standards and conditions of exchange have resulted in a race to the bottom mainly affecting farm workers (Burch, Lawrence, 2005; Brown, Sander, 2007; Barrientos & Kritzinger, 2003). Within the farms, a significantly racialised labour force carries out its work informally, that is, without any kind of legal, monetary and health security. The number of irregular workers who work outside the supervision of the Italian state revolves around the shocking cipher of 400,000 workers; however, being a regular migrant worker does neither imply to have better conditions. Therefore, in the Italian tomato industry, the employment-relations (regular or irregular) are consistently related to working very long hours and for very low wages.

When explaining the need for greater coordination between trade unions and migrant workers Penninx and Roosblad (2000) identify two major dilemmas: (1) whether unions should resist, cooperate or actively intervene in the recruitment of migrant workers; and (2) how many resources should be devoted to incorporate such workers within unions' struggles. In that sense, the global mobility of labour poses national trade unions with the challenge of whether they should treat migrant workers in the same way as native workers are treated or, even, whether if they should provide them with larger resources since they depart from a much more precarious situation (for a literature review see Marino, 2015; Marino et al. 2015). The dilemmas in between strictly devoting to one's membership, i.e. corporatism, or fighting to build stronger broad-class alliances comes to the fore (Hyman, 1975; Hobsbawm, 1984). As it will be shown in the second-half of the chapter, despite having resorted to institutional and organising strategies at national and local level, Italian unions are still far from having empowered migrant workers effectively and, hence, we argue that they reproduce, to an extent, the dynamics in and through which neoliberal global capitalism has been entrenched across Western Europe.

In terms of the research methods applied, our study builds upon a qualitative analysis of archive-documentation, secondary literature and semi-structured interviews; and it has been undertaken in three major steps. First, along the collection of secondary and primary documentation, fifteen interviews were carried out in Naples, Salerno and Foggia, with experts on the sector that gave us information about the various companies constituting the GVC: the producers, the intermediate traders and the processing companies. After such 'top-down' study of tomato value chain, the working conditions of the farmhands have been analysed through semi-structured interviews with workers and union delegates. Twenty-five interviews were organised with workers living in the informal settlements (or *ghettos*) at the Foggia district. Such fieldwork was carried out with the support of five migrant workers, during the summers of 2017 and 2018 (during the harvesting season), in a very difficult context characterised by a lack of social and work rights, and by strong housing segregation and poverty. Finally, trade union strategies and labour regulation issues have been analysed through ten interviews to trade union officials, employers' organisations and labour inspectors in the regions of Foggia and Rome.

The rest of the chapter is structured as follows: first we will present the case of migrant workers' exclusion in Southern Italy and the dire living and working conditions of tomato-picking workers in Foggia, another sad example of spreading precarious trends across Europe. After, we will briefly review the literature on union strategies towards the organisation of migrant workers and union renewal tactics. Then we will focus on the struggles of both FLAI-CGIL and USB in their active assistance to displaced and marginalised workers in the province of Foggia. Finally, we will discuss the limits and possibilities of the strategies that these two unions have adopted and advance what it can be learnt from them.

2   After the Mediterranean There Is Also a Sea of Poverty and Exclusion

After the Second World War, Italy started to turn into an immigration country. One of the first sectors of the Italian labour market affected by the presence of migrant workers was agriculture. The emergence of migrations in Italy coincides, in fact, with the restructuring of agriculture production and with the transformation of agri-food chains. Within Italian agriculture, migrations started in Sicily during the seventies with migrants arriving from Tunisia and other Maghreb countries. Then in the eighties, migrants started to arrive from Sub Saharan Africa and later, during the nineties, from Eastern Europe (Pugliese, 2006). Only since the early 2000s did the agriculture sector begin to employ an increasing number of migrant workers. Their presence in the sector has been steadily growing especially in the last two decades (Pisacane, 2017).

Following official statistics, in 2015, foreign workers in the agriculture sector were 405,000: 52% of them (211,000) were EU citizens (mainly Romanian, Polish, and Bulgarians) and 48% (194,000) were non-EU citizens (mainly Indians, Moroccans, and Albanians) (Crea, 2017). However, this data is underestimated because a structural component of the Italian agriculture sector is the large use of *irregular work*. The estimates indicate the presence of 400,000 irregular workers in Italian agriculture (Agromafie & Caporalato, 2016). This practice mainly affects migrant workers employed in the harvesting of tomatoes, fruit, grapes, and olives, and it especially takes place in the southern Italy countryside (Inea, 2009).

The exploitation of labour, especially migrant labour, has been one of the primary factors in the restructuring of the Italian agricultural sector in the context of neoliberal globalisation. As noted by Corrado et al. (2016, p. 10), "the over-exploitation of migrant labour appears to be one of the strategies employed by southern European farmers in resisting the liberalisation of international markets and the retailer driven transformation of supply chains".

The deterioration of working conditions of farmhands can be considered as the result of power and economic asymmetrical relations between leading firms and small farms along the GVC. Within these smaller firms, which carry out their activities during the periods of 'great harvests', the pricing policy imposed by buyers is reflected on a great demand for unskilled, flexible, precarious and cheap labour. In southern Italy, this demand is covered by migrant workers from Africa and Eastern Europe, and it is linked to the 'seasonal circuits' (MSF, 2005; Struna, 2009) of the agricultural labour force. The system of hiring day labourers is managed by informal intermediaries called *Caporali*, and the farm work is carried out in sweatshop working conditions: bad health and safety conditions, with a lack of labour and social rights (MSF, 2018; Perrotta & Sacchetto, 2012; Perrotta, 2013; 2014; Palmisano & Sagnet, 2015). The majority of these workers live in extremely precarious conditions, at makeshift slums or ghettos built by the workers themselves in the countryside.

The work in the agricultural sector is increasingly viewed by migrants no longer as temporary employment but as long-term employment, even if seasonal and cyclical (Rigo & Dines 2017). Until a few years ago, several studies showed how most of agricultural migrant workers were illegal both in terms of residence permits and employment status. In the present, in almost every Italian region, the majority of workers in the agriculture industry come from other European Union states, mainly from Romania, Poland, and Bulgaria (Inea, 2014). Meanwhile, extra-European migrant workers are increasingly coming from India, Morocco, and Albania (Fondazione Fai-Cisl, 2017). Migrant workers from Africa come from the sub-Saharan Africa, and are mostly employed in the south: most of them are asylum-seekers and some of them have subsidiary or humanitarian protection (Barbieri et al. 2015).

Even though a part of migrant farmworkers in the Italian agriculture sector has a residence permit and an employment contract, these conditions are often not enough to protect them from abuse and exploitation. As an NGO has recently denounced: "to have an employment contract is no guarantee of equal and right employment relation" for many workers (Barbieri et al., 2015, p. 283). In Italy the working conditions of farmhands are extremely rigid especially in the South, in the provinces of Campania, Puglia, Calabria, and Basilicata. In these geographies, extremely low wages and intense exploitation are commonplace (Zanfrini, 2014). Not surprisingly, in terms of working and living conditions, the most vulnerable workers are extra-European migrants, especially Sub-Saharan Africans. Minimum wages, both with and without contracts, are lower than those set by national and provincial collective contracts of employment. The salary does never exceed 40 euros for a day of hard work, and it will vary depending on the type of product harvested and on the migrant's nationality: 30 to 35 euros for Eastern European workers and 20 to 25 euros for African workers (Corrado and Perrotta, 2012).

3 Foggia's Global Tomato Value Chain

As it was mentioned before, Italy is the world's third largest producer of industrial tomatoes after the U.S. and China, and the largest producer in Europe. Tomato production is the 'national champion' of the Italian agro-food system. The turnover is 3 billion euros on a yearly basis, and *sixty percent* of the production is absorbed by foreign markets such as Germany, UK, France, USA, Japan, Russia, and only forty percent by the domestic market (Anicav, 2018).

The main areas of fresh tomato production are Puglia (17.146.500 quintals in 2017) and Emilia Romagna (18.479.800 quintals in 2017). These two regions produced the largest proportion of industrial tomatoes in Europe and together account for about 70% of Italy's production (AgriIstat, 2018). In the Puglia region, the production is concentrated in the province of Foggia (also called Capitanata): 94% of all the region's production and 30.7% of all of Italy's production comes from this province. In the Emilia Romagna region, it accounts for about 35% of Italy's production. The production is mainly located in the provinces of Piacenza, Ferrara, and Parma that represent, respectively, 43%, 25% and 16% of all of the region's production (AgriIstat, 2018).

Retailers, especially European, purchase tomato products from Italian suppliers. These suppliers are processing companies that transform fresh tomatoes into products such as peeled tomatoes, pulp, sauce, and concentrate. The processing companies are located both in Northern and Southern Italy. They buy tomatoes from organisations of agricultural producers (OPs). The OPs are supplied from several farms both large and small. The farmers of Capitanata satisfy the requests for supply of processing companies located in the southern district. These processing companies are specialised in the supply of *private label products* to large international buyers. These big buyers seek to maximise their market share by obtaining products by suppliers at the lowest possible costs.

The territory of the Foggia is characterised by the presence of labourers of different ethnicities and nationalities who follow a plurality of migratory models. In addition to migrant workers, EU as well as non-EU, who permanently live more or less in the province, there are the migrant labourers who follow diverse cycles of the seasonal agricultural harvest in the countryside of Southern Italy, and migrants who live in an European Union country who move to Capitanata for a short period of time during the tomato harvesting period (Perrotta, 2013, 2014b). Low-wage migrant labourers have settled in the many informal settlements of the province. More specifically, in the Capitanata area, they mainly live in informal camps - farmhouses, abandoned buildings, and shacks - located almost all in the countryside and quite far from the city center.

These are places without any utilities - water, electricity, heating, etc. - where legal and illegal migrants decide to settle even for very long periods of time. These places represent the main labour reserves from which intermediaries and employers tap into during the tomato harvest season. The residential segregation is produced by the mixture of a multiplicity of factors such as legislation on migration and labour, the impossibility of accessing the private market of rentals, the informality of labour relations (many of these labourers work without a contract or a faulty contract), low salaries and the seasonality of employment.

With respect to the employment-relations proper, in the province of Foggia, ninety percent of those employed in agriculture, both natives and migrants, do not have a regular salary framework.[1] Irregular work concerns the entire workforce, but it registers high percentages especially among migrant workers. Labour exploitation mainly affects working hours and wages. The provincial collective labour agreement in the province of Foggia provides a work schedule of six hours and thirty minutes a day with a daily pay of €54,58. In the countryside of Capitanata, only Italian workers are able to get this pay. Migrant workers, both EU and non-EU, take what is commonly called *"paga di piazza"* (public pay), which ranges from a minimum of three euros and a maximum of four euros per hour.

> I work ten hours a day. A working day is €35 for ten hours of work. There are those who pay €3.50 per hour and those who pay €4. It depends on the boss. The problem is that €35 a day is nothing. You can work like this for eight years, but in the end, you are nobody to the state because you have always worked without a contract. The team consists of twenty-five/thirty people. In one day, we could fill even seven trucks, all by hand. The countryside is all around here, half an hour/an hour away from the ghetto. The owners of the farms are all Italians. They don't care about making a legal contract or about us. You just have to do your job.[2]

In the case of piecework, pay is by *cassone* (chest) and it is attested at €3,5 per chest. The two methods result in the same pay for in order to fill 15 chests it would take a labourer more than ten hours, therefore, the pay almost always comes to being €30-€40 a day. Only a few, especially those who have greater physical strength, working on a piecework basis with a pay per chest, manage to earn more, but are forced to work for more than twelve consecutive hours:

---

1 Interview with Daniele Iacovelli (August 2018).
2 Interview with Omar, informal settlement of via Borgo Mezzanone (August 2017).

> I always work by chest because I earn more. In a day, I can even fill fifteen chests. I work this way because when the harvest season arrives, I have to take advantage and earn all that I can because the harvest does not last more than two months. During the tomato season, I work almost every day. Sometimes I rest because the work is quite heavy and it hurts my back.[3]

African labourers are by far the most oppressed because many of them have no regular residence permit and are in turn blackmailed to accept lower wages. The regulation of labour relations in the tomato sector takes place mainly in an informal manner and through the appeal of agricultural companies to those that are commonly referred to as *"caporali"* (informal labour contractors/recruiters of day labourers). The *caporale* is an informal intermediary, often a labourer or former labourer belonging to the different migrant communities present in the territory, who recruits workers on behalf of a third party company and keeps for himself, through different methods, a part of the salary paid by the business for every single labourer. The majority of the recruiters operating in the Italian countryside belong to the various foreign communities present in the territory. They mainly recruit labourers who belong to their own national or ethnic group.

In order to understand the role of informal labour contractors in the tomato sector we have to take into account that agricultural farms are now included within transnational agri-food chains led by big buyers. These companies need to resist the pressure that is carried out by companies at the head of the transnational supply chains, keeping labour costs as low as possible. Factors such as production instability and harvest seasonality also require the availability of a very flexible workforce. The informal labour contractors satisfy the needs of flexibility desired by companies, helping the latter to manage the highs and lows in labour demand through the provision of temporary and low-cost labour. The control of the labour force by recruiters is organised on different levels and covers a series of activities ranging from the transportation of the labourer to the workplace, up to the payment of wages at the end of the season, passing through a series of services provided by the recruiter directly on the worksite, earning economic compensation as a result.

> We workers are paid at the end of the harvest season. When we finish, the recruiter comes and says: 'you worked twenty days, you thirty, you

---

3 Interview with Amadou, informal settlement of Borgo Mezzanone (September 2017).

twenty-five, etc.', and then he pays us. But there are also those who do not pay. I am still waiting for money from my boss.[4]

At dawn, labourers are overloaded into vans without insurance and any type of safety measure and are then accompanied to crammed fields; they are obliged to pay the recruiter €5 a day for the ride to the countryside.[5] They also often buy water and food from him; in some cases, especially when the pay is carried out by piece, the labourers are also forced to pay part of their earnings to the recruiter.

The availability of flexible and low-cost labour is for companies located in the lower rings of the chain - those involved with low added value activities - a true buffer against the risks deriving from the instability of production and against the competitive pressure carried out on them from other companies in the chain. The demand for flexibility and competitiveness from companies situated in the intermediate segments and at the top of the chain is passed onto the labourers of the supplying companies, therefore, creating and reinforcing the practices of informal regulation of labour relations (illegal employment, use of labour contractors, etc.) and further worsening working conditions (wages, working hours, rhythms, etc.). The possibility for these companies to continue to extract a share of the surplus from the production activity can only be achieved by the exploitation of the more informal and invisible segments of the labour force present on the territory, such as migrant labourers.

4   Unions and Migrant Workers

The empowerment of migrant workers has been an old and serious problem for trade unions. The *strategic* division that capitalists intelligently foster in between 'insiders' (or native workers) and 'outsiders' (or migrant workers), and which the insiders may tend to embrace and reproduce as it may secure their short-term interests, has often been an instrument for companies to: pay migrant workers lower salaries than what would otherwise be a 'fair wage' in the territory; and to put a downward pressure upon better-off 'native' workers salaries' as the average value of the labour power decreases with the enlargement of a set of lower paid workers (e.g. Hobsbawm, 1984; Preibisch, 2010). The creation of 'identitarian', 'nationalistic' or, simply, 'corporatist' divisions among the workforce can thus be related to the disempowerment of the whole

---

4   Interview with Mbaye, informal settlement of San Severo (September 2018).
5   Interview with Badgi, informal settlement of via Manfredonia (July 2018).

workforce as radical discourses and integral forms of class organisation wither away, and because individualistic and beggar-thy-neighbour dynamics multiply (Panitch, 1981; Las Heras, 2018b).

The problem is nevertheless more salient when migrant workers are 'illegal' or, more subtly, when migrant workers lack any *formal status* in a territory in which demanding and implementing labour and social rights is intrinsically related to the notion of 'citizenship'. The division among insiders-outsiders becomes more problematic when acquiring legality is the crucial struggle to later proceed *within* the normal state of affairs, i.e. the 'industrial legality' in-itself (Gramsci, 1977). In the period until illegal workers attain their legal status, employers may use to their favour such gap to further pressure-down insiders' wages, while a nationalistic rhetoric that blames the migrant workforce instead of the capitalist class gains force. Moreover, the movement of a precarious labour-force in between countries with different standards induces migrant workers not to struggle for better conditions as their frame-of-reference is that of their original country (Binford, 2009). Therefore, the deeper the structural barriers in between workers the more encompassing and transformative the class strategies must be in order to subvert the state of affairs.

In such difficult scenario, this study discerns two set of strategies which could potentially complement each other in the empowerment of migrant workers (Marino, 2012; Marino et al., 2015). On the one hand, trade unions may seek to modify state's *mediation* in the labour market and, hence, look for the state's intervention in the recognition and defence of 'the whole' working class' rights, including migrants', within a specific territory. On the other hand, in conditions in which the former strategy is not successful (Rye & Andrzejewska, 2010; Selwyn, 2013), trade unions may also seek to directly organise and mobilise workers, in a sort of strategic by-pass of labour laws and paternalistic behaviour towards unorganised workers (Rogaly, 2008), to achieve an *immediate* improvement of the living and working conditions. What is at stake is that since migrants struggles lie well-beyound normalised patterns of collective bargaining, "trade unions today must act as a civil society actor ... rather than as a strictly labour-related interest body"(Marino et al., 2015, p. 10).

In Italy the relations between trade unions and migrant workers have represented a special case comparing to other European countries (Marino & Rinaldini, 2017). In between the 1980s and 1990s actions of the main the Italian trade unions (CGIL-CISL-UIL) toward migrant workers have been based on inclusion and cooperation. Starting with an approach oriented to provide services and solutions for practical problems, trade unions aimed to involve migrant workers in unions' membership enabling their participation and inclusion within unions' organisation (Marino & Rinaldini, 2015). However, since the 2000s their attitude to empower migrant workers has been increasingly undermined by economic crises (Pradella & Cillo, 2015) and by the less influence of Italian trade unions in socio-economic decision-making processes at state level (Marino, 2012). As a result, the current relation between trade union and migrant workers in Italy has lost its original trait based on inclusion and cooperation (Marino & Rinaldini, 2015). Our chapter aims to show how, in a context of European trade unions decline in organising migrant workers, the action of the main Italian trade union in the agri-food industry confirms: (1) the loss of capacity to organise and protect migrant workers from work exploitation; and (2) that the prevalence of conservative positions among major trade unions sows the seeds for new forms of class resistance and organisation to emerge, either in the form of left-wing grass-root projects or right-wing nationalism.

5 CGIL: The Contractors Law and the Caravans

Italian trade unions have not been successfully responding to the shifts in the organisation of production and labour relations in agri-food sector. Their action is still linked to a strategy that aims to counter labour exploitation, and therefore claim more rights and better working conditions, by putting pressure mainly upon 'direct employers'. The actions of the main Italian trade unions against the exploitation of migrant farmhands have taken place in line with this pattern of union's response oriented to exercise legal pressure on the "formal"/"direct" employers, i.e. the farmers.

The most important trade union in the Italian agricultural sector is FLAI-CGIL.[6] In the last few years its response toward labour exploitation has been implemented both at national and local levels. At *national level* the union has put the issue of labour exploitation of farmhands in Italian countryside on the policy agenda of the Italian Department of Agriculture and achieved the inclusion of new requirements in labour law (199/2016). The law is the outcome of several sector strikes, demonstrations and national campaigns organised in the last few decades both by migrant farmhands and Italian trade unions in order to denounce work exploitation and informal work in agricultural sector (Valentini, 2018). It contains several measures against informal work and labour exploitation in the agricultural sector. The most important measure affects the

---

6 FLAI (Agroindustry workers federation) is a Trade Union of Italian General Confederation of Labour (CGIL) that organises farm workers and agri-food workers. The number of its affiliates is 250,090 at 31/12/2017.

fight against labour exploitation punishing informal labour contractors and employers by imprisonment of between one and six years.[7] Furthermore, the law provides the government to take judicial control over the firm where the workers have been exploited illegally, and establish the proceedings for their regularisation in terms of wages, contracts and social security contributions. The law also set up the 'High Quality Farm Work Network": job centers, employment agencies, workers' organisations, and employers may join the network on a voluntary basis in order to manage at local level the demand and supply of (migrant) labour within agricultural areas.

At *local* or *workplace level* proper, where labour exploitation takes place, FLAI's response has been organised in different ways, depending on the type of production and on the number of union's members available in the territory. In the province of Foggia, FLAI's response has been organised around three actions: First, support migrant workers through assistance points wherein free services as check on social security position, wages and work contracts were offered. Second, support to migrant workers through 'street unions squads'. During the summer harvesting season, for three months, the squads go out early in the morning every day. In Capitanata each squad consists of three trade unionists. On three caravans, trade unionists travel around the countryside to meet farm workers and give them information about their working rights – wages, working time, health, contracts, social security, unemployment benefits and especially information about the possibility to denounce informal labour and exploitation to the labour inspectorate. Their major aim is to meet workers, make direct contact with them and, when possible, encourage them to come to the union's office. As reported by a street unionist:

> If we find evidence of labour exploitation taking place we cannot stop the labour process. We rather prefer to meet the workers later in order to protect them from the employer and labour contractors. For example, last year, a Moroccan worker got beat when he denounced his employer during a labour inspector control. So, it is obvious, that it's definitely safer if we meet them later in a different place far from employers and labour contractors.[8]

---

7 See Legge 29 ottobre 2016, n. 199 Disposizioni in materia di contrasto ai fenomeni del lavoro nero, dello sfruttamento del lavoro in agricoltura e di riallineamento retributivo nel settore agricolo. (16G00213) (GU Serie Generale n.257 del 03-11-2016).
8 Interview with Tony, street unionist, Foggia (August 2018).

The third action consists in supporting migrant workers to build a 'grass-root union representation' system. More specifically, the FLAI-CGIL is training migrant trade unionists in order to have delegates in the main informal settlements of the Capitanata, by giving them the skills to support other migrant workers in their claims. The action is still on-going and it seeks to train at least sixteen trade unionists in the province of Foggia who will be able to give information to the farmhands about their working rights. These trade unionists shall have the responsibility of pushing workers to denounce exploitation, informal labour contractors and informal employers to have right wage and better working conditions.

FLAI's efforts to develop these two mentioned strategies, at the national and local levels, have barely up until today produced positive results. For example, despite unions' membership has increased among migrant workers – today almost the 30% of FLAI-CGIL union's membership in the province of Foggia are foreign workers[9]– the number of legal-complaints for labour exploitation is still low. In 2017, within the entire province, only forty workers reported to the labour inspectorate and the general working conditions of migrant farmhands remains miserable.[10] Moreover, the 'High Quality Farm Work Network' set up by the law (199/2016) has been a failure because very few employers have joined it[11] and, most problematically, because the law provides no disposition for any extra budgetary expenditure to secure its real implementation at workplace level.

Similar to the patterns found across the lower TIERs of the automotive GVCs in Spain (cf. Las Heras, 2019), the enforcement of labour law cannot be left to the voluntary implementation of employers nor to the periodic supervision of labour inspectors that will more often than not interpret the law softly. Instead, it is rather up to the capacity of unionised workers to *actively* defend and implement their rights at the workplace. A *formalist* or *institutionalist* perspective may obviate that class power relations are constituted integrally, by formal and informal relations (Marino, 2012; Fairbrother, 2015) and, most importantly, that it is the capital-labour relationship which constitutes labour's exploitation, i.e. that regardless the provisions established by labour law, it is the *concrete* relationship in between tomato producers and migrant workers what determines

---

9   Following latest available data in 2015 the FLAI-CGIL union's members in Puglia Region were 35,020: 7,298 in Foggia, ,.973 in Andria, 6,657 in Bari, 7,692 in Brindisi, 5,370 in Lecce, 5,030 in Taranto (Archivio Tesseramento CGIL).
10 Interview with Daniele Iacovelli FLAI-CGIL (August 2018).
11 Interview with Daniele Iacovelli FLAI-CGIL (August 2018).

the actual conditions in which the labour process is organised and its produce distributed in South Italy (Braverman, 1974; Spencer, 2000).

Strategically, we find that FLAI's efforts to inform and mobilise migrant workers against their 'direct employers' is hindered by some infrastructural constraints. We understand that in not transcending the representative structure that the union preserves, it maintains a union structure functional to support the interests of core workers who are already organised, rather than of incorporating workers located in the periphery of labour market. The adoption of various 'organising' strategies of migrant workers after a critical reading of the limits to social dialogue and institutionalised forms of collective bargaining (Marino et al., 2015, p. 11–12) has not really taken place in our case-study. Significantly, in the province of Foggia the number of FLAI union officials is only six, a ridiculous number for the amount of workers living from the agricultural industry and the approximately 20,000 irregular migrant workers who have few power resources. Whether if it can be argued that FLAI has adopted a multi-level strategy in the empowerment of migrant workers in Foggia, through the caravans and information points that we have mentioned, is quite problematic because most of the migrant workers have had none or very little connection with this actions[12] and, hence, have suffered from the limited infrastructural resources that have been devoted to them.

In addition to these infrastructural constraints, we can spot a weakness in FLAI's culture to produce the necessary cognitive knowledge (Levesque & Murray, 2013) to learn from and incorporate migrant workers' claims, especially in the capacity to voice the interests of the most mobile seasonal workers. FLAI's strategy has been rather predominantly oriented to put pressure exclusively on the direct employer and prohibit irregular work. The law punishes informal labour contractors and direct employers not contemplating in the least the role played by leading firms in determining the prices and, so, the working conditions and labour processes within the supplying firms of the GVC. FLAI's strategy has been thought and adopted vertically, and have not sought to build alliances with other workers and trade unions operating across the agri-food sector to update, learn from and unify their claims. As it will be shown in the next section, FLAI's demands remain distant from the more urgent needs that migrant workers have both at the workplace and in their living areas/ghettos. In trying to voice them better, however, a grass-root union has taken some space and deployed its efforts to build the associational ties that FLAI has missed to produce.

---

12 Interview with Samba, immigrant farmhand (August 2017).

6   Radical Unions Creating the Space for Migrants' Empowerment

As noted by Appay (1998), in the context of GVCs, acting upon the smaller 'direct employers' can be an ineffective or even counterproductive strategy because their profits, which derive from unstable contracts with larger firms that buy their products, are too limited for a substantial raise of wages and the improvement of working conditions. Workers face the challenge of finding different strategies in order to put pressure on real employer and counteract the deterioration of labour relations within supply firms (Wills, 2009).

In the Italian agri-food sector it is the work of USB (Unione Sindacale di Base) which we may say to be heading towards this direction. USB is an independent union that was born in 2010 as an alternative to historical and traditional Italian trade unions, including FLAI-CGIL. This union is far less representative in terms of union's delegates and has far fewer resources than the main Italian confederations. The action of this union aims to regain social and union's rights through the strategies of organising and unionising the workers along the entire agri-food chain, 'from field to table'. This trade union asserts the role of migrant farmhands in Italian agriculture and the amount of economic value produced by them within agri-food sector. The union denounces to be the oligopolistic power and pricing policy of the firms at the head of agri-food chains the cause for labour over-exploitation in the agricultural sector (USB, 2018).

The strategy of this union is based on building an integral alliance between local workers and farmers, and national consumers so that they can pressure 'from the beginning until the end' of the GVC the dominant firms at the top of agri-food chains. Their major claim is to defend the production of healthy food through securing a decent life for all the workers. The workings of the union have led to the birth, in September 2016 in Venosa,[13] of the 'USB National coordination group' for agri-food sector with delegates for any territorial agricultural area. Two years later, a trade unionist member of this group, Soumaila Sacko, got murdered in Calabria in June 2018. In response, USB organised a regional strike in Calabria and a national demonstration in Rome. In august 2018, other 12 migrant farmhands died in Foggia when the migrant driver who was taking them home, and who had also been working all the day long, went-off the road. USB and other Italian Unions organised a huge strike in Foggia in order to claim their rights and better working conditions for all farmhands.

---

13   Venosa is located in the province of Potenza in Basilicata Region. Also in this region immigrant farmhands and farmers supply fresh tomatoes to southern Italian processing companies.

In September 2018, after several demonstrations, USB has presented in Foggia a platform for the respect of the agricultural workers' union and social rights. The platform aims to introduce an ethical code within agri-food supply chains able to ensure respect for the workers' union and social rights and for the rights of farmers and consumers (USB, 2018b). The most important points of the platform are: equal work and equal pay (decent work and fair pay), compliance with employers' social security contributions, the regularisation of migrants and refugees (the repeal of Bossi-Fini law and the access to the *residence permit for social protection* according to the art. 18 (286/1998) and the delinking of residence permit from labour contract),[14] solutions to the structural housing problem (with the direct involvement of local authorities, employers and workers to provide affordable housing for all migrant workers), a public management of work recruitment, and the conditionality of the aids for firms (European subsidies subject to the compliance with minimum standards of workers' rights) (USB, 2018b).

According to USB, only by rethinking the whole agri-food system and the consequent policies that regulate the agricultural world, it could rebuild the proper balance between producers, consumers and workers (USB, 2018). Last September of 2018, in Foggia, the union opened a great international campaign that aims to involve all stakeholders along the global tomato value chain: siding farmers and labourers, as well as consumers and authorities at the European, national and local levels (USB, 2018). The outcome of this action will depend on how much this union will be capable of pressuring leading firms and governmental authorities to affect the production, logistic and marketing strategies of the former, i.e. from the relations in between firms within agri-food supply chains up until their merchandise to the consumers, and the infrastructural resources of the latter to provide political solutions to the dire living conditions of the workers at the local level. In the day this chapter is been written, the fight for producing an integral solution is still on-going.

7   Discussion: The Limits and Possibilities of Bridging Italian Unions with Migrant Struggles

Based on the findings presented in the previous two sections we would like to conclude the chapter by advancing four arguments. First, against the progressive

---

14   The residence permit for social protection is issued to the community and non EU-person who has been in situations of violence or serious sexual and/or labour exploitation related to certain serious crimes.

deterioration of living standards of 'illegal' tomato-picking migrant workers the agricultural federation of the major socialist Italian trade union *Confederazione Generale Italiana del Lavoro* (CGIL), i.e. FLAI-CGIL, has directed most of its organisational resources into the negotiation and validation of a national-level labour law that criminalises labour contractors for hiring 'illegal' workers. Although the law is more than welcome, as it encourages 'direct employers' to legalise irregular employment relations if they want to avoid prison, the strategy is flawed because the law provides no dispositions for any extra budgetary expenditure to secure its real implementation at workplace level. Trade unions then must adopt the supervisory role of the state but without having as many infrastructural resources and political power to enforce it.

Nevertheless, and as it has also been showed, FLAI-CGIL has complemented such national strategy through an increasing engagement at the local-level: informing migrant workers on legal and working issues, unionising migrant workers, and denouncing criminal contractors. Although 30% of the FLAI-CGIL membership is of foreign origin, we argue that the union has not been effective in the mobilisation of migrant workers since, among other things, has not deployed as many resources to such purpose as they would be necessary, e.g. the union has only made use of three union officials to organise and supervise around 20,000 migrant workers who are geographically dispersed. In that sense, we follow recent arguments against institutional trade union strategies that downplay the importance of engaging the rank-and-file in the empowerment of the working class in the age of post-crisis austerity (Bailey et al., 2017; 2018; Las Heras & Ribera-Almandoz, 2017), and also for the actual implementation of labour law and collective agreements along GVCs (Las Heras, 2019).

Second, a more radical and grass-root union, the USB, has by-passed FLAI-CGIL's strategy and engaged with the contractor-worker relationship 'from below'. Instead of criminalising the employer and ignoring their crucial position in possibly new forms of collective bargaining in the territory, USB has made repeated efforts to gather primary information of the entrenched structure of the tomato-picking industry. USB has repeatedly organised meetings and networked with marginalised and highly-precarious migrant workers, as well as with other civil society organisations at the local level. Visiting the ghettos and organising the workers in their living space has been a major task undertaken by the USB. The result has been a more nuanced understanding of the real conditions and needs of these workers who, among other things, demand a legal-status and citizenship that the labour-law falls to secure. However, we can also argue that such strategy has failed to substantially improve workers' conditions because USB is a small union and lacks the infrastructural resources that bigger unions have. In this sense, to directly engage with the employers and the workers is not in opposition to FLAI-CGIL's strategy, but we can understand it as rather complementary (Marino, 2012; Marino et al., 2015). A complementary strategy that derives from an *emerging* working class fraction (Las Heras, 2018a; Roca & Las Heras, 2020) that overcomes path-dependencies and struggles for a more democratic and participatory organisation of workers' interest (Marino, 2015), a logic that stresses that trade unions need to be built as much 'from below' as from 'from above'.

Third, and as a corollary of the above two, we argue that institutionalist reductionism may *mistakenly* portray a legalistic strategy as a *real* all-encompassing class strategy. Instead, the Foggia experience shows that FLAI-CGIL has: (1) incorporated or voiced the demands of those who they pretend to represent quite limitedly; and (2) that in so doing it has predominantly reproduced its already-existing organisational structure that separates 'insiders' who already have institutionalised patterns of collective bargaining from the 'outsiders' who lack them (see e.g. Hyman, 1975, p. 44–60). Or put it differently, traditional trade unions in Italy have not yet redirected significant resources to defend and unionise those workers who are more in need, and they have neither made the effort to educate their 'core' membership that such strategy ought to be prioritised under current historical conditions. It follows that major Italian trade unions have not advanced the interests of all workers under a unitarian strategy, but that they have rather reproduced to an extent the strong class-fractioning processes prevailing global capitalism that, no matter how contradictorily, homogenise and downgrade workers position vis-à-vis capital (e.g. Starosta, 2010; Charnock & Starosta, 2016).

Fourth, the strategic division in between 'insiders' and 'outsiders' locates migrant workers on a secondary plane within the overall strategy of union renewal. This may have much more important repercussions for Italian workers in the short-run than what we may even think of. In the companies located in the lower links of the global tomato value chain, the labor force is strongly racialised. This labor force is locally and socially built according to the substandard working conditions, that is, comparably inferior to those that are generally accepted because they are immigrants, foreigners, precarious workers in conditions of housing marginalisation. The increasing pauperisation and fragmentation of farmhands does not only erode the ideological power of trade unions to gather and mobilise workers along left-solidarity transformative projects since their particular material interests differ (see Las Heras, 2018b), but most importantly, it gives the space for a fascist management of migration and integration policies, based on criminalisation of immigrant workers and on an increasingly declining of their social rights, hence, contributing to the reproduction of this social construction around an immigrant workforce that can be everlastingly exploited. However, when migrants try to work regularly, the government tries to stop the process (Giuffrida, 2018). When, in turn, migrants are forced to live and work in precarious conditions the government tries to criminalise their 'illegal' situation to reduce their rights further: the latest law (Decreto Sicurezza) adopted by the Italian government goes in this direction (Camilli, 2018). All of this provides fertile soil for the growth of authoritarian and violent sentiments among core-workers' who can blame peripheral workers for lowering their working standards. That is, if migrant workers do not become active partisans alongside native workers, it may result in the normalisation of a *profound* contradiction: that of simultaneously being a member of a socialist-left-oriented union and voting for a right-wing government.

References

Osservatorio Placido Rizzotto (2016). *Agromafie e Caporalato. Terzo Rapporto*. Roma: Author.

Bailey, D., Clua-Losada, M. Huke, N., & Ribera-Almandoz, O. (2018). Challenging the age of austerity: Disruptive agency after the global economic crisis. *Comparative European Politics,* 16(1), 9–31.

Bailey, D., Clua-Losada, M., Huke, N., & Ribera-Almandoz, O. (2017). *Beyond Defeat and Austerity: Disrupting Neoliberal Europe*. London: Routledge.

Barbieri A., Bari G. A., & Pesca M. (2015). Terraingiusta: indagine sulle condizioni di vita e di lavoro dei braccianti stranieri in agricoltura. In Centro Studi e Richerche IDOS (Ed.), *Dossier Statistico Immigrazione 2015* (pp. 281–286). Roma: Edizioni Idos.

Barrientos, S., & Kritzinger, A. (2003). *The poverty of work and social cohesion in global export: the case of South African fruit*. In D. Chidester, P. Dexter & J. Wilmot (Eds.), *What Holds Us Together: Social cohesion in South Africa*. Cape Town: HSRC Press.

Binford, L. (2009). From Fields of Power to Fields of Sweat: the dual process of constructing temporary migrant labour in Mexico and Canada. *Third World Quarterly*, 30(3), 503–517.

Brown, O. & Sander, C. (2007). *Supermarket buying power: Global supply chains and smallholder farmers*. Winipeg: International Institute for Sustainable Development.

Burch, D. & Lawrence, G. (2005). Supermarket own brands, supply chains and the transformation of the agri food system. *International Journal of Sociology of Agriculture and Food*, 13(1), 1–18.

Camilli, A. (2018, Septembre 24). Cosa prevede il decreto Salvini su immigrazione e sicurezza. *Internazionale*. Retrieved from https://www.internazionale.it/blocnotes/annalisa-camilli/2018/09/24/decreto-salvini-immigrazione-e-sicurezza

Charnock, G. & Starosta, G. (2016). Introduction: The New International Division of Labour and the Critique of Political Economy Today. In G. Charnock & G. Starosta (Eds.), *The New International Division of Labour* (pp. 1–22). London: Palgrave Macmillan.

Cleaver, H. (2000 [1979]). *Reading Capital Politically*. New York: AK Press.

Colloca C. & Corrado, A. (Eds.) (2013). *La Globalizzazione delle campagne. Migranti e società rurali nel Sud Italia*. Milano: Franco Angeli.

Corrado A., De Castro C., & Perrotta D. (Eds.) (2016). *Migration and agriculture. Mobility and change in the Mediterranean area*. London: Routledge.

Corrado A. & Perrotta D. (2012). Migranti che contano. Percorsi di mobilità e di confinamenti nell'agricoltura del Sud Italia. *Mondi Migranti*, 3, 103–128.

CREA (2017). *Annuario dell'agricoltura italiana 2015*. Roma: Author.

Davies, M. & Ryner, M. (Eds.). (2006). *Poverty and the Production of World Politics*. Basingstoke: Palgrave Macmillan.

Doellgast, V. & Greer, I. (2007). Vertical disintegration and the disorganization of German industrial relations. *British Journal of Industrial Relations*, 45(1), 55–76.

Fairbrother, P. (2015) Rethinking trade unionism: Union renewal as transition. *Economic and Labour Relations Review*, 26(4), 561–576.

Flecker, J. (2009). Outsourcing, spatial relocation and the fragmentation of employment. *Competition & Change*, 13(3), 251–266.

Fondazione Fai-Cisl Studi e Ricerche. (2017). *Lavoratori immigrati in agricoltura, Quaderni.1*. Roma: Author.

Gramsci, A. (1977). The Turin Workers' Councils. In R. Blackburn (Ed.), *Revolution and Class Struggle: A Reader in Marxist Politics*. Glasgow: Fontana

Giuffrida, A. (2018, October 2). Pro-refugee Italian mayor arrested for 'aiding illegal migration'. *The Guardian*. Retrieved from https://www.theguardian.com/world/2018/oct/02/pro-refugee-italian-mayor-arrested-suspicion-aiding-illegal-migration-domenico-lucano-riace

Harrod, J. & O'Brien, R. (Eds.) (2002) *Global Unions? Theory and Strategies of Organized Labour in the Global Political Economy*. London: Routledge.

Hobsbawm, EJ. (1984). *Workers: Worlds of Labor*. New York: Pantheon.

Hyman, R. (1975). *Industrial Relations: A Marxist Introduction*. London: MacMillan

INEA (2009). *Gli immigrati nell'agricoltura italiana*. Roma: Author.

INEA (2014). *Indagine sull'impiego degli immigrati in agricoltura in Italia*. Roma: Author.

Iñigo-Carrera, J. (2016). The general rate of profit and its realisation in the differentiation of industrial capitals. In G. Charnock & G. Starosta (Eds.), *The New International Division of Labour* (pp. 25–33). London: Palgrave Macmillan.

Las Heras, J. (2018). International Political Economy of Labour and Gramsci's methodology of the subaltern. *The British Journal of Politics and International Relations* 21(2): 226–244. DOI:10.1177/1369148118815403

Las Heras, J. (2018b). Unions as "managers of precariousness" The entrenchment of micro-corporatism in the Spanish automotive industry and its drawbacks. *Employee Relations, 40*(6), 1054–1071.

Las Heras, J. (2019). To sign or not to sign? Union strategies towards provincial metal sector agreements in the Catalan and Basque automotive industries. *European Journal of Industrial Relations*, 25(2), 181–200.

Las Heras, J & Ribera-Almandoz, O. (2017). When corporatism fails: Trade union strategies and grassroots resistance to the Spanish economic crisis. *Journal of Labor and Society* 20: 449–466.

Lévesque, C. & Murray G. (2013) Renewing union narrative resources: How union capabilities make a difference. *British Journal of Industrial Relations, 51*(4), 777–796.

Marino, S. (2012). Trade Union Inclusion of Migrant and Etnich Minority Workers: Comparing Italy and the Netherlands. *European Journal of Industrial Relations,* 18 (1), pp. 5–20.

Marino, S. & Rinaldin,i M. (2015). Il rapporto tra sindacati e immigrati in Italia in una prospettiva di lungo periodo. *La rivista delle Politiche Sociali,* 2–3, 87–112.

Moody, K. (1997). *Workers in a lean world: Unions in the international economy.* London: Verso Books.

MSF (Medici senza frontiere) (2005). *I frutti dell'ipocrisia. Storie di chi l'agricoltura la fa. Di nascosto.* Roma: Sinnos.

MSF (Medici Senza Frontiere) (2018). *Fuori Campo. Insediamenti informali, marginalità sociale, ostacoli all' accesso alle cure e ai beni essenziali per migranti e rifugiati.* Roma: Author.

Mulholland, K. & Stewart, P. (2014). Workers in Food Distribution: Global Commodity Chains and Lean Logistics, *New Political Economy,* 19(4), 534–558

Palmisano L. & Sagnet I. (2015). *Ghetto Italia. I braccianti stranieri tra caporalato e sfruttamento.* Roma: Fandango.

Panitch, L. (1981). Trade unions and the capitalist state. *New Left Review,* 125(1), 21–43.

Penninx R. & Roosblad J. (2000). *Trade Unions, Immigration, and Immigrants in Europe, 1960–93.* Oxford: Berghahn Books.

Perrotta D. (2013). Traiettorie migratorie nei territori del pomodoro. Rumeni e burkinabé in Puglia e Basilicata. In C. Colloca & A. Corrado (Eds.), *La Globalizzazione delle campagne. Migranti e società rurali nel Sud Italia* (pp. 118–140). Milano: Franco Angeli.

Perrotta D. (2014). Vecchi e nuovi mediatori. Storia, geografia ed etnografia del caporalato in agricultura. *Meridiana,* 79, 193–220.

Perrotta D. (2014b). Il lavoro migrante stagionale nelle campagne italiane. In M. Colucci & S. Gallo (Eds.), *L'arte di spostarsi. Rapporto 2014 sulle migrazioni interne in Italia* (pp. 21–38). Roma: Donzelli.

Perrotta D. & Sacchetto D. (2012). Il ghetto e lo sciopero: braccianti stranieri nell'Italia Meridionale. In V. Borghi & M. Zamponi (Eds.), *Terra e Lavoro nel capitalismo contemporaneo, Sociologia del Lavoro 128* (pp. 152–166). Milano: Franco Angeli.

Pisacane L. (2017). Lavoratori immigrati nell'agricoltura italiana: numeri e sfide verso una prospettiva di integrazione. In C. Bonifazi (Eds.), *Migrazioni e integrazioni nell'Italia di oggi* (pp. 157–168). Roma: CNR-IRPPS.

Pradella L. & Cillo R. (2015). Immigrant Labour in Europe in Times of Crisis and Austerity: An international Political Economy Analysis, *Competition and change*, 19 (2), pp. 145–160.

Preibisch, K. (2010). Pick-Your-Own Labor: Migrant Workers and Flexibility in Canadian Agriculture. *International Migration Review*, 44(2), 404–441.

Pugliese E. (2006). *L'Italia fra migrazioni internazionali e migrazioni interne*. Bologna: il Mulino.

Rigo E., Dines N. (2017). Lo sfruttamento umanitario del lavoro. Ipotesi di riflessione e ricerca a partire dal caso delle campagne del Mezzogiorno. In S. Chignola, & D. Sacchetto (Eds.), *Le reti del valore. Migrazioni, produzione e governo della crisi* (pp. 90–107). Roma: DeriveApprodi.

Rinaldini M. & Marino S. (2017). Trade unions and migrant workers in Italy: Between labour and social rights. In S. Marino, J. Roosblad, & R. Penninx (Eds.), *Trade Unions and Migrant Workers. New contexts and Challenges in Europe* (pp.266–286). Chentelham, Northampton, Geneva: Edward Elgar Publishing.

Roca, B., & Las Heras, J. (in press). Trade Unions as Retaining Walls against Political Change: A Gramscian Approach to Remunicipalisation Policies in the Spanish City of Cádiz. *Capital & Class*. https://doi.org/10.1177/0309816818815242

Rogaly, B. (2008). Migrant Workers in the ILO's Global Alliance Against Forced Labour Report: a critical appraisal, *Third World Quarterly*, 29(7), 1431–1447

Rye, JF. & Andrzejewska, J. (2010). The structural disempowerment of Eastern European migrant farm workers in Norwegian agriculture. *Journal of rural studies*, 26(1), 41–51.

Sassen S. (1998), *The Mobility of Labor and Capital: A Study in International Investment and Labor Flows*, Cambridge: Cambridge University Press.

Selwyn, B. (2014). *The Global Development Crisis*. Cambridge: John Wiley & Sons.

Selwyn, B. (2013). Social upgrading and labour in global production networks: A critique and an alternative conception. *Competition & Change*, 17(1), 75–90.

Silver, B. (2003). *Forces of Labor: Workers' Movements and Globalization since 1870*. Cambridge: Cambridge University Press.

Smith, J. (2016). *Imperialism in the Twenty-First Century. Globalization, Super-Exploitation, and Capitalism's Final Crisis*. New Tork: NYU Press and Monthly Review Press.

Spencer, D. (2000). Braverman and the contribution of labour process analysis to the critique of capitalist production-twenty-five years on. *Work, Employment and Society*, 14(2), 223–243.

Starosta, G. (2010). Global commodity chains and the Marxian law of value. *Antipode*, 42(2), 433–465.

Struna, J. (2009). Toward a theory of global proletarian fractions. *Perspectives on Global Development and Technology*, 8, 230–260.

USB (2018). *Agricoltura Eticoltura. Per un sistema agroalimentare basato sul rispetto della dignità e dei diritti sindacali dei lavoratori, sui doveri dei produttori e sui diritti di tutti i cittadini a produzioni sane*, Foggia, 22 Settembre 2018.

USB (2018b). *Agriculture/Ethiculture, A Platform for the respect of the agricultural workers' union and social rights*, Foggia, 22 September 2018.

Valentini A. (2018). Dalla denuncia alla proposta, dal sindacato di strada alla legge n.199/2016. In Osservatorio Placido Rizzotto (Eds.), *Agromafie e Caporalato. Quarto Rapporto* (pp. 26–28). Roma: Ediesse.

Zanfrini L. (2014). Tra terra e cibo. Il lavoro immigrato nella filiera alimentare. In Caritas e Migrantes (Eds.), *XXIV Rapporto Immigrazione* (pp. 329–358). Roma: Caritas.

CHAPTER 8

Putting the Pieces Together: Post-Fordist Migrations, Community Unionism, Solidarity Networks and Bricolage

Beltrán Roca and Emma Martín-Díaz

As stated in the introductory chapter, migrations during the Fordist period were substantially different from their counterparts under flexible capitalism, and there are both continuities and discontinuities between these two periods. This is particularly the case for intra-European migrations. As we have suggested elsewhere, although the organisation of labour markets is substantially different in both models, generating diverse labour and social integration strategies and policies, an articulation of national economies based on territorial imbalances persists as a structural factor—the centre-periphery relationship persists. Simone Castellani and Beltran Roca state that the free circulation of workers has its roots in a series of bilateral agreements made during the period from the Treaty of Rome (1957) to the Treaty of Amsterdam (1997). The literature on contemporary intra-EU mobility based on the data collected mainly before the economic crisis of 2008 highlighted that most people who moved within the EU shared a common socio-demographic profile defined as 'cosmopolitan' as opposed to the 'proletarian' intra-Western Europe migration of the 1950s and 1970s on a south-north axis. Nevertheless, the systemic dynamics of the dependence of the secondary economies on the economies of the centre that have historically taken place within the EU are clearly demonstrated in the effects of the economic recession that began in 2008. As the authors show, from 2008 to 2013, most of the peripheral countries (above all from Southern and Eastern Europe) displayed a negative or near zero GDP growth and high levels of youth unemployment. The central countries (Northwestern Europe) showed an opposite tendency.

Relating to the same model of migration, but focused on the case of Spanish nurses in the German care Industry, Mark Bergfeld has chosen a different approach, the commodification of care. Following Hochschild (2000), among other researchers, his approach adopts the concept of 'global care chain'. Here again, the unbalanced relationship between central and peripheral countries is highlighted because the mobility of healthcare professionals and care workers within the European Union disproportionately benefits wealthier EU member states. However, following Yeates (2005), the author is aware that this concept does not account for the service nature and gender concerns of care work. In this context, he argues that the corporatisation of care could be a useful tool for understanding labour relations in the nursing industry.

Global care chains are also the theoretical approach of Emma Martín-Díaz and Juan Pablo Aris-Escarcena. Here, the authors focused on Moroccan domestic workers who crossed the border from the Spanish city of Ceuta. They characterised this migration as a swinging model based on the possibility of accessing Ceuta without a visa. However, this free circulation was determined by the impossibility of regularizing the workers' situation, mainly because of the absence of legal contracts. This is a very specific case that cannot be understood without taking into account the location of the city of Ceuta as a Spanish enclave surrounded by Moroccan territory and the close relationships established between the city and its neighboring cities.

Alicia Reigada, Giuseppe D'Onofrio and Jon Las Heras, in their respective chapters, deal with the concept of global value chains. Both are focused on global agrifood chains. In chapter six, the Reigada analyses people's experiences in relation to the material conditions and socio-historical forces beyond their everyday lives by analysing class relations and the conflicts that result from social reproduction under capitalism. Following Thompson (1966), her approach moves away from an objectivist understanding of social class to an historical and constructivist perspective that defines class as an active process that is formed in human relations and embodied in a real context. With these tools, the author concludes that the contradictions and tensions between distribution and production and agricultural employers and workers demonstrate the importance of the conflicts that are engendered in social reproduction under capitalism.

Like Alicia Reigada, Giuseppe D'Onofrio and Jon Las Heras analyse the agrifood chain from a critical political economy perspective. The authors see global labour mobility as a complement to the development of global capitalism. They study the structure and mechanisms regulating global tomato values. Following the work of Roca and Las Heras (2020), these authors build upon Gramsci's methodology of the subaltern in order to transcend both traditional 'top-down' and 'bottom-up' analyses that simplify the production of class power and its complex nature, The authors state that the struggles among capitals are nothing but the visible expression of the intra-class and cross-class struggles underlying working class formation, and that understanding the power and economic relations among leadings firms and supplier companies along the global tomato value chain is a necessary moment for the subsequent production of a more complete study that can allow us to put the emancipatory possibilities of workers in a determinate context.

As Martín-Díaz and Roca (2017) have pointed out, post-Fordist migrations take place in a context of underlying conflict between nation states and transnational organisations. In this context Schiller, Bash and Blanc (1995) proposed the concept of transnational social fields that include and combine, in different ways and in different moments social, actors, networks, organisations and subjects that transcend the national containers that defined migrations during the Fordist period.

Castellani and Roca deal with the concept of transnationalism by stating that Spanish and Italian emigrants in Germany are involved in transnational social spaces involving people, goods, services, artefacts, and currency, but ideas and practices also circulate. The authors state that migrants' political practices are oriented toward origin and destination localities and countries and involve both migrant and non-migrant actors and organisations. They establish that migrants' labour activism and collective actions have to be understood as a form of political transnational practice.

Although this concept is not present in Bergfeld's contribution, the author mentions Clare Ungerson's (2003) claim that solidarity and community are multi-directional, and he illustrates this idea with the example of the Grupo de Acción Sindical (GAS), which, he states, 'draws on forms of activism and trade unionism imported from Spain, as well as using communication techniques and messages to undermine the dominance of business in the sector.'

Transnationalism is a key concept in Martín-Díaz and Aris-Escarcenas' chapter, although the authors criticise the notion that the centrality acquired by the study of migrants' agency led on many occasions to an excessively optimistic analysis that overestimated the ability of subjects, networks and relationships to make migratory projects and design strategies, concealing social structures that have determined the specific forms adopted by post-Fordist migratory models.

Paula Dinorah Salgado only mentions transnational practices in the section devoting to organizations primarily focused on migration. According to the author:

> From these spaces, several actions concerning migrant workers of the garment industry were accomplished. Through campaigns that raise awareness about migrant problems (mainly with Bolivians), political and academic documents were produced in coordination with academic circles who conducted action-research.

In this sense, it is interesting to note the author's assertion concerning the experiences of migrant organisations to: 'express the need to surpass traditional frameworks by defining a broader political subject through building 'Latin-Americanness' instead of 'citizenship' (which is a restricted view) and by establishing an integrated relationship concerning migration and labour'. In both cases, their goals extend beyond the workplace and illustrate a significant potential for further development, which focuses on moving forward by incorporating migration and labour as part of their qualitative leap.

In post-Fordist economies, the new model of accumulation implies a rent transfer from labour to capital; that is, a general pauperization of the working class and growing inequalities. But this tendency has not taken place homogeneously among the working class. Although labour segmentation in not a new phenomenon, it has experienced a qualitative leap, deepening into the fragmentation of the working class, with a decreasing core of stable workers in the primary segment and a heterogeneous and growing secondary segment characterized by unstable and precarious jobs, where migrants tend to concentrate.

Castellani and Roca question the division between the primary and secondary labour markets, introducing the concept of "platform capitalism" (Langley and Leyshon, 2017). In the authors' view, the digital platforms that have become widespread globally are not simply a new manifestation of informational capitalism but a radical new feature of market and labour intermediation as well as a new means of capital accumulation. These activities are supported ideologically by the principles of sharing participation and horizontalisation. For them, the emerging terrain of work and organization entails new sources of conflicts and social stratification that influence worker's mobility dynamics and demand new approaches to workers' agency and representation.

A good example of platform economy can be found in Guilia Borraccino's contribution to this book. The author illustrates the case of the mobilisations of logistics migrant workers as representative of the key trends and challenges of labour movement in modern times. Borraccino analyses the logistics sector as a supply chain vertically developed. At the top of this chain are the providers and multi-client companies. At the bottom are the sub-contracted cooperatives managing services related to warehousing. In these cooperatives, the migrants works as porters. The author shows how, behind the ideology of mutualism and participation, lies the fact of workforce exploitation.

The changes in labour markets are addressed by Paula Dinorah Salgado. With regard to the garment industry, the author depicts how, in the past few decades, the gap between intellectual and manual labour has widened. On the one hand, there has been a growing concentration of capital related to big brands; on the other, there has been a gradual erosion of workers' salaries and the conditions in sewing workshops.

Alicia Reigada, Giuseppe D'Onofrio and Jon Las Heras dwell on the agrifood systems. In chapter six, Reigada focuses, on the one hand, on the changes in class positions of farmers, from former day-labourers as employers, and the subordination of the local producer to the large supermarkets chains; and on the other, on the importance that migration acquires as a strategy for achieving the means to a decent livelihood and the costs that it has for the organization of the domestic group. D'Onofrio and Las Heras link the deterioration of working conditions of farmhands with the power and asymmetrical relations between leading firms and small farmers along the Global Value Chain (GVC). The pricing policies imposed by buyers result in a great demand for unskilled, flexible, precarious and cheap labour that is covered by migrant workers from Africa and Eastern Europe, and is linked to the migrants' 'seasonal circuits.' As in the case of logistics porters and the cooperatives that distinguish the Italian case from other ways of running logistics in other countries, the agrifood system presents one specific characteristic for hiring day-labourers: the caporali, a kind of informal intermediary.

Mark Bergfeld outlines how, in the wake of the financial crisis of 2008, German private care companies have been recruiting Spanish nurses to work as care workers for private companies, clinics and care homes. According to the author, the care context in Germany has experienced a significant change within the last 15 years, not only for the move from the remit of 'unpaid work' to 'paid work,' but this work has been outsourced to migrants from poorer countries. As a result of this move, a growing body of research emphasises the exploitation of labour relations and working conditions in care work. Relating to this segmentation, chapter three illustrates how the centre-periphery dynamics can be reproduced by exchanging positions. Every day, or every week, poor women from Morocco cross the border to serve as domestic workers for Spanish households, demonstrating the usefulness of the concept of semi-peripheral countries to explain the relationships within nation-states and the labour transfer in the World System.

On the whole, the chapters in this book show a bleak picture of overexploitation, precariousness and, in some cases, deteriorating living conditions. Castellani and Roca see a new form of labour activism as a response to the spread of a platform capitalism characterised by precariousness, informality, self-employment, subcontracting and increasing alienation. Likewise, Bergfeld claims that the corporatisation of care and the recruitment practices of state-led initiatives and private companies exacerbate inequalities in the care chain.

Martín-Díaz and Aris-Escarcena underline the precariousness, overexploitation and, sometimes, sexual violence that domestic workers suffer, mostly working without a contract. Borraccino depicts the critical working conditions of logistics porters. Salgado dwells on overexploitation as a conceptual arrival point. The author states that, on the one hand, this concept provides an accurate theoretical model for approaching the particular dynamics of labour-capital relations located on one end of the broad spectrum involved within the concept of 'precariousness'; and on the other hand, it allows for an analysis of these dynamics as stable events without defining them as exceptional. Finally, Reigada, D'Onofrio and Las Heras underline the exclusion and dire living and working conditions of seasonal workers in agrifood chains in both Southern Italy and Southern Spain.

This first research question of the book is about trade union policy towards migration. Understanding the cases of migrants' collective action and solidarity described in this book requires paying attention to the regulation of labour relations in Spain, Italy, Germany and Argentina. Trade union policy and performance must be framed within a regulatory context.

The German model of labour relations is characterised by the predominance of sectoral agreements, mostly negotiated between employer organisations and trade unions at the regional scale. Workers are represented in the workplace by works councils, which are elected by the staff and have competences such as negotiating (excluding salary and working time that used to be regulated by sectoral agreements). In Germany there is a clear hegemony of the DGB (Deutscher Gewerkschaftbund), which has approximately 6 of the 7.4 million union members in the country. There are also some minor and independent unions; the main one is the DBB, which organises workers of the public sector. The DGB is structured along industry lines, and the two main affiliated unions are IG Metall, which organises metal workers, and Ver.di, which organises workers in the service sector (including the healthcare and hospitality industries, which are described, at least partially, in this book). While the response of major unions to the Great Recession was effective (Dribbusch, Lehndorff & Schulten, 2017), the coverage of collective agreements and workplace representation have been declining in general terms. Although there are differences between West and East Germany, approximately half of the workforce is not protected by these elements (ETUI, 2019). This leaves certain industries, occupations and subsectors with leeway for informal regulation mechanisms, in which alternative and non-recognised forms of unionism can operate. This is the case of the anarcho-syndicalist FAU (Freie Arbeiter-Union), which has become a reference for many Southern European workers in Germany, especially those more influenced by the far left.

In relation to trade union policy regarding migration, major German unions have tended to focus on information services and legal counseling (generally using resources from a variety of sources, including governmental funds). In addition, there have been several outstandingly successful organising experiences (Meardi, 2013). In this sense, it can be said that German unions have tended to combine the logic of social rights (advocating for citizens and the social rights of immigrant workers) and the logic of class, launching initiatives to attempt to organise migrants as part of the working class.

In the Italian cases analysed by Borraccino, D'Onofio and Las Heras, regarding the logistics sector in the north and the tomato-picking industry in the south, respectively, trade union intervention is conditioned by trade union pluralism. There are three main unions in Italy: CGIL (Confederazione Generale Italiana del Lavoro), CISL (Confederazione Italiana Sindacati Lavoratori), and UIL (Unione Italiana del Lavoro), which are said to have together approximately 6.5 million members in active employment. The Italian system also allows for the intervention of independent unions, frequently inspired by radical leftist ideologies, which can be influencial in certain industries and territories. This is the case of the USB (Unione Sindacale di Base) and SI Cobas (Sindacato Intercategoriale Cobas) described in the chapters about Italy.

Trade unions, together with the state and employer organisations, play an essential role in the regulation of labour relations, mainly through collective agreements at the industrial, territorial and workplace levels (Leonardi, 2017). However, in secondary labour markets of the lower levels of the agrifood and logistics chains, such as the tomato-picking industry and the logistics cooperatives, regulation also takes place by means of informal mechanisms (for example, the caporale, who act as intermediaries between irregular migrant workers and employers). D'Onofio and Las Heras describe how regional collective agreements are systematically ignored, especially in terms of salary and working time, for thousands of irregular immigrants working in agriculture in Southern Italy. Similarly, Borraccino explains how cooperatives in the logistics sector in Northern Italy ignore labour standards that cover other workers. This reality set the ground for the flourishing of alternative forms of trade unionism that put an emphasis on organising.

Concerning migration policy, the major Italian unions, as stated above, have focused on information services, but they have used these services to promote unionization and organising (De Luca, Pozzi & Ambrosini, 2018). It can be said that Italian unions experience strong tensions among different logics, but the logic of social rights tends to prevail over the ethnic and, above all, the class logic (Connolly, Marino & Martinez Lucio, 2014).

Similarly to Italy, Spanish industrial relations are characterised by pluralism. The two main unions are CCOO (Comisiones Obreras) and UGT (Unión General de Trabajadores), which have approximately 900,000 members each and together represent 70% of the workplace , but there are other independent unions that can be very active in certain territories, such as those described by Reigada: SOC (Sindicato de Obreros del Campo), CGT (Confederación General del Trabajo), SU (Sindicato Unitario), and USTEA (Unión de Sindicatos de Trabajadores y Trabajadoras de Andalucía) (see, for example, Roca, 2014). Despite the low rate of union membership, approximately 85% of employees are covered by collective agreements at different levels (mainly sectoral/provincial, but also state, regional and even at the workplace level). Although collective agreements cover all workers regardless of union membership, there are growing segments of the labour market in which labour norms cannot be enforced. This is the case for secondary labour markets in which migrant workers concentrate such as agriculture (described by reigada) and domestic work (examined by Martín-Díaz and Aris-Escarcena).

As several studies have pointed out, the power of the major Spanish unions rests on neo-corporatist social pacts (Las Heras & Ribera-Almandoz, 2017; Köhler, 2018), whilst grassroots and confrontational practices have been displaced to a secondary position. Concerning trade union policy toward immigration, the major Spanish unions CCOO and UGT tend to prioritise the logic of social rights, focusing on the demand and negotiation of institutional arrangements for regulating the social rights of migrant workers (Connolly, Marino & Martinez Lucio, 2019). Their positions have favoured the rise of independent experiences of solidarity networks and community-based unionism at the local scale, as described by Emma Martín-Díaz, Juan Pablo Aris-Escarcena and Alicia reigada.

In the case of Argentina, analysed by Paula Dinorah Salgado, a main characteristic is the high rate of informal work. After 2003, economic growth and political change implied an expansion of collective bargaining, which regulated, among other things, salaries, and, consequently, meant a significant reduction of informal employment. The Kirchnerist reform of that period attempted to reinforce social dialogue by means of the National Council of Employment, Productivity and Salary, in which government, trade unions and employer organisations have collaborated in designing public policies (Senén, 2011). The main unions in Argentina, CGT (Confederación General del Trabajo) and CTA (Central de Trabajadores de la Argentina), which claim to have 2.5 and 1.4 million members, respectively, are formed by the federation of national unions organized along industrial lines. In addition, there are some independent unions. In the garment industry examined in this monograph, there were five different trade unions: SOIVA (Sindicato Obrero de la Industria del Vestido y Afines), UCI (Unión de Cortadores de Indumentaria), STTAD (Sindicato de Trabajadores Talleristas a Domicilio), AOT (Asociación Obrera Textil), and SETIA (Sindicato de Empleados Textiles de la Industria y Afines). This is, thus, a context of inter-union competitiveness, fragmentation and conflicts over jurisdiction.

Regarding immigrant workers, although in Argentina they only represent 5% of the population, and they come mainly from bordering countries, their inclusion in trade union representation structures has followed different logics. As described in the fifth chapter of this book, in some cases the logic of race/ethnicity has prevailed; for example, with the BTM (Bloque de Trabajadores Migrantes) coalition. In other instances, unions have prioritized the logic of class, integrating migrants into their dynamics, structures and actions, promoting solidarity between native and immigrant workers. This was the case for SIOVA and the newly created UTC (Unión de Trabajadores Costureros).

Another objective of the book was studying the relationship between conventional unions and migrant self-organisation. Given the ambivalences and limitations of the approaches of conventional trade union for representing and organising migrant workers, several forms of community-based unionism and solidarity networks have emerged. The cases from Germany, studied by Castellani, Roca and Bergfeld, illustrate the ambiguous relationship between trade unions and migrant workers. In general terms, trade unions oriented toward the logic of action of social rights and that prioritise the strategy of institutional regulation through social dialogue, such as the German DGB confederation, find it extremely difficult to connect with and represent migrant constituencies. However, some of its affiliate unions, local branches and staff can have more inclusive approaches, generally turning toward other logics of action and strategies, as seen in chapter two in the case of certain Ver.di officials.

The gaps between migrant workers and unions in these cases tend to be filled by migrants' solidarity networks and innovative forms of community organising. This is the case for the Grupo de Acción Sindical and the Precarious Office, linked to the Spanish 15M movement in Berlin, and Berlin Migrant Strikers, launched by Italian immigrants with a political background in the autonomist and squatter social movements. These networks act as brokers between, on the one hand, Spanish and Italian migrant workers facing different forms of oppression and discrimination and, on the other hand, German unions and radical organisations such as the anarcho-syndicalist FAU and squatters. These self-organised expressions of community unionism creatively combine repertoires of action and discussions from a variety of sources, including those from radical political traditions and social movements from their countries of origin (the SAT union in Andalusia, the 15M movement, precarious offices in Spain, and autonomous movements in Italy).

In the cases from Italy examined by Borraccino, D'Onofrio and Las Heras, labour-centered forms of community unionism (Fine, 2005) have intervened due to the pluralistic character of the model of industrial relations. In this context, radical political unions (Connolly & Darlington, 2012) tend to adopt a strategy that is more sensitive to migration problems than traditional unions (Ness, 2014) regardless of the prevalence of the logic of class or the logic of ethnicity/race. In Italy, although the major union CGIL developed a strategy to support migrant workers by means of information services and representation in union structures (Marino, 2012), their emphasis on social dialogue tended to distance them from precarious parts of the working class such as immigrants in the logistics sector, who demand more oppositional forms of collective action (Alberti et al., 2013; Marino, 2015).

Regarding the tomato-picking industry in the South of Italy, whilst the CGIL has focused on political advocacy at the national level, at the local level, in the region of Foggia, it has provided information services, 'street union squads' giving labour information and assistance in the workplace, and has created a 'grassroots union representation system' aimed at training migrant workers as union delegates. These initiatives, however, have yielded poor results. In contrast, a radical union, the USB, has been more successful with an alternative community-based approach. The key point of the USB strategy was building an alliance with local workers and farmers at the bottom of the global chain to pressure the firms located at the top of the agrifood chain. The goal of this pressure was improving labour standards in the industry. In this initiative, they have employed coalition-building, strikes, and organising campaigns. Nonetheless, CGIL and USB strategies should not be understood as opposed, but potentially complementary, as suggested by D'Onofrio and Las Heras in their chapter.

In Spain, the oppression and overexploitation of migrant workers in strawberry production in Huelva and domestic service in Ceuta have led to outstanding experiences of community unionism. In the case of Huelva activists in support of migrant workers launched coalitions such as the Platform Against the Immigration Act, formed by non-profit organisations, left parties and radical unions (such as CGT, USTEA and SU). This coalition contrasted with the service orientation of mainstream NGOs (Huelva Acoge, ACCEM and the Red Cross) and the institutionalised practices of the major Spanish unions CCOO and UGT, which gathered at the Migration Board. Whereas the Migration Board of mainstream actors focused on regulating the hiring of migrant workers in the industry, radical unions and progressive nonprofits created an alternative Temporary Migrant Board. This new coalition questioned the demobilizing character of the Migration Board promoted by public authorities and focused on the provision of information, legal support and protest actions for migrant workers. The participation of migrant day labourers in both initiatives has been completely absent.

In the analysis of domestic workers in Ceuta, Emma Martín-Díaz and Juan Pablo Aris-Escarcena highlight the contradictions that the major Spanish unions face when dealing with migrant labour from Morocco. Unions must face the dilemma of defending the national working class or defending migrant workers. Union intervention focuses on advocacy actions in defense of labour rights for domestic workers and the regulation of hiring and employment in the industry. CCOO Ceuta, as an example of representational unionism, has tended to launch awareness-raising campaigns and to undertake dialogue with public bodies. As chapter three shows, in contrast to the CCOO initiative, a different experience of community unionism without labour participation (Fine, 2005) stands out: the Digmun Association. This nonprofit organisation has developed a variety of solidarity actions to support migrant domestic workers: language classes, leisure activities, counselling about labour issues, training on gender and equity issues, and support in cases of physical and sexual violence by employers. The Digmun case illustrates how extra-labour forms of community activism are able to include labour problems in their agenda. In doing so, activists attempt to address the problems of migrant workers in a more holistic way than traditional unions. To this end, processes of bricolage and innovation become fundamental.

Salgado describes the rise of community unions, which have succeeded in representing migrant workers in the Argentinean garment industry. This is the case of the UCEV (Unión de Costurerxs y Empleadxs del Vestido), which contested institutionalised unions such as SOIVA, which excluded immigrants from internal power positions. UCEV was affiliated with the CTA Autonomus confederation and followed a clear class logic based on socialist ideas. A different expression of community unionism created around the migrant workforce is the BTM (Bloque de Trabajadores Migrantes), a community group organized along ethnic lines that mobilises migrant workers for both labour and extra-labour issues. This second experience of community union is characterized by three elements: the prevalence of direct action over dialogue; intervention outside the workplace; and the development of an identity that is close to certain ethnic and religious groups. The manner in which the BTM frame their activism, appealing to Latin-Americaness to justify the demand of social inclusion of migrants from bordering countries (mainly from, Bolivia), is a good example of bricolage.

The chapters in this book show the difficulties faced by trade unions in representing migrant workers and the challenge of developing more inclusive approaches in a context of post-Fordist migrations. The transformation of work, the rise of global chains and the intensification of international migrations are the basis of new forms of oppression, overexploitation and marginalization of ethnic and racial minorities. Trade unions from different geographies and identities experience tensions between different logics of action as strategies when dealing with migrant workers. In situations in which traditional unions fail to response to the needs of migrant workers, alternative community-based forms of unionism and solidarity networks tend to appear that show a significant ability to bricolage and innovate. Recent changes in the world of work, many of them related to what has been called platform capitalism, demand further research on the performance, scope and limitations of community unionism. Since union renewal is a process, research on migrant organising must go on.

References

Alberti, G., Holgate, J., & Tapia, M. (2013). Organising migrants as workers or as migrant workers? Intersectionality, trade unions and precarious work. *The International Journal of Human Resource Management*, 24(22), 4132–4148. https://doi.org/10.1080/09585192.2013.845429

Connolly, H., & Darlington, R. (2012). Radical political unionism in France and Britain: A comparative study of SUD-Rail and the RMT. *European Journal of Industrial Relations*, *18*(3), 235–250. https://doi.org/10.1177/0959680112452693

Connolly, H., Marino, S., & Martínez Lucio, M. (2014). Trade union renewal and the challenges of representation: Strategies towards migrant and ethnic minority workers in the Netherlands, Spain and the United Kingdom. *European Journal of Industrial Relations*, 20(1), 5–20. https://doi.org/10.1177/0959680113516848

Connolly, H., Marino, S., & Martinez Lucio, M. (2019). *Immigrants and trade unions in the European Context. The Politics of Social Inclusion and Labor Representation.* Ithaca, NY: Cornell University Press.

De Luca, D., Pozzi, S., & Ambrosini, M. (2018). Trade unions and immigrants in Italy: How immigrant offices promote inclusion. *Journal of Industrial Relations*, 60(1), 101–118. https://doi.org/10.1177/0022185617723378

Dribbusch, H., Lehndorff, S., and Schulten, T. (2017). Two worlds of unionism? German manufacturing and service unions since the Great Recession. In S. Lehndorff, H. Dribbusch & T. Schulten (eds.), *Rough waters – European trade unions in a time of crises* (pp. 197–220). Brussels: European Trade Union Institute.

ETUI (2019). *Industrial Relations in Germany - Background Summary* (Updated April 2019). Retrieved 26 March 2020 from https://www.etui.org/ReformsWatch/Germany/Industrial-relations-in-Germany-background-summary-updated-April-2019

Fine, J. (2005). Community Unions and the Revival of the American Labor Movement. *Politics & Society*, 33(1), 153–199. https://doi.org/10.1177/0032329204272553

Hochschild, A. R. (2000). The Nanny Chain. *American Prospect*. Retrieved from http://web.stanford.edu/group/scspi/_media/pdf/key_issues/globalization_journalism.pdf

Köhler, H. D. (2018). Industrial relations in Spain – strong conflicts, weak actors and fragmented institutions. *Employee Relations*, 40(4), 725–743. https://doi.org/10.1108/ER-08-2017-0195

Las Heras, J., &Ribera-Almandoz, O. (2017). When Corporatism Fails: Trade Union Strategies and Grassroots Resistance to the Spanish Economic Crisis. *Journal of Labor and Society*, 20(4), 449–466. https://doi.org/10.1111/wusa.12303

Leonardi, S. (2017). Trade unions and collective bargaining in Italy during the crisis. In S. Lehndorff, H. Dribbusch & T. Schulten (eds.), *Rough waters – European trade unions in a time of crises* (pp. 87–115). Brussels: European Trade Union Institute.

Marino, S. (2012). Trade union inclusion of migrant and ethnic minority workers: Comparing Italy and the Netherlands. *European Journal of Industrial Relations*, 18(1), 5–20. https://doi.org/10.1177/0959680111429755

Marino, S. (2015). Trade unions, special structures and the inclusion of migrant workers: on the role of union democracy. *Work, Employment and Society*, 29(5), 826–842. https://doi.org/ 10.1177/0950017015575866

Martin-Díaz, E., & Roca, B. (2017). Spanish Migrations to Europe: from the Fordist Model to the Flexible Economy. *Journal of Mediterranean Studies*, 26(2), 189–207.

Meardi, G. (2013). Unions between national politics and transnational migration: A comparison of Germany, UK and France. Paper for the SASE Annual Meeting, Milan.

Ness, I. (Ed.) (2014). New Forms of Worker Organization: The Syndicalist and Autonomist Restoration of Class-Struggle Unionism. Oakland : PM Press.

Roca, B. (2014). Izquierda radical, sindicalismo y acción colectiva en Andalucía (1976–2012). *Cuadernos de Relaciones Laborales*, 32(2), 439–468.

Roca, B., & Las Heras, J. (2020). Trade unions as retaining walls against political change: A Gramscian approach to remunicipalisation policies in a Spanish City. *Capital & Class*, 44(1), 3–25. https://doi.org/10.1177/0309816818815242

Schiller, N., Bash, L., & Blanc, C. (1995). From Immigrant to Transmigrant: Theorizing Transnational Migration. *Anthropological Quarterly*, 68(1), 48–63. https://doi.org/10.2307/3317464

Senén, C. (2011). Las relaciones laborales en la Argentina actual. *Las Voces del Fénix*, 2(6), 32–37.

Thompson, E.P. (1966). *The making of the English working class*. New York: Vintage.

Ungerson, C. (2003). Commodified Care Work in European Labour Markets. *European Societies*, 5(4), 377–96. https:// doi.org/10.1080/1461669032000127651

Yeates, N. (2005). Global Care Chains: A Critical Introduction. *Global Migration Perspectives*, 44. Retrieved from http://www.refworld.org/docid/435f85a84.html

Index

15M   14, 28–33, 35–38, 4, 52–53, 69, 73, 212
   See also indignados

activism   28, 41, 52, 74, 77, 145, 206, 214
   labour   10, 12, 14, 25, 34, 51–53, 206, 208
added value   167, 189
agricultural industrialization   159
agrifood   154, 156, 166, 174, 208
   chain   154, 155n.1, 159, 168, 196, 205, 209–210, 213
Aldi   168
Amazon   24, 45, 47, 49, 114
anarchist   158
anarcho-syndicalist   34, 209, 212
Andalusia   15–16, 85, 154–161, 166, 212,
Anti-systemic   115–116
AOT (*Asociación Obrera Textil*)   129, 211
APDH (*Asociación Pro Derechos Humanos de Huelva*)   172, 174
Arab Spring   12, 116
Argentina   9, 119, 122n.5, 129, 133, 136, 137n.35, 139n.39, 147, 149, 211–212
ASAJA (*Asociación Agraria-Jóvenes Agricultores*)   165
Asamblea Textil de Flores   134–135
assembly   30, 32n.15, 35, 38–40, 46, 49, 140, 146,
asylum seekers   185
atypical trade   88, 91

Bañez, Fatima   64
Basta!   40, 44
Berlin   24, 27–53, 65–66
Berlin Migrant Strikers   40, 42, 44, 212
Berlin Wie Bitte   30–31, 23n.15
bio-unionism   47, 52
Bloque de Trabajadorxs Migrantes   15, 135, 137, 148,
Board of Migration   172
boundary drawing   6
brain gain   60, 73
bricolage   11, 13–14, 16, 100, 204, 214–215
   unionism   15, 81

broker   12, 39, 40, 47, 50, 53, 212
   brokerage   35, 47, 53
   job   64
BTM   15, 135–137, 148–149, 212, 214
   See also Bloque de Trabajadorxs Migrantes
Buenos Aires   120, 122–125, 134, 140n.42, 149,

Cádiz   157, 160
Cambiemos   131,
CAP (Common Agraricultural Policy)   159, 165,
capital accumulation   1, 24, 157, 181, 207
capitalism   25, 50–51, 82, 89, 117, 155, 163, 176, 181, 183, 198, 205, 215
   cultural history of   154
   flexible   204
   geography of   154
   informational   24
   platform   23–24, 39, 49, 52, 207–208
caporali   185, 188, 208
care drain   60, 71
Carrefour   167
CCOO (*See Comisiones Obreras*)
Ceuta   14–15, 81–100, 205, 213–214
CGIL (*See Confederazione Generale Italiana del Lavoro*)
CGT (Argentina). See General Confederation of Labour
CGT (Spain). See *Confederación General del Trabajo* (Spain)
Church   39, 75
Cisne association   39–40
class origin   156, 159, 176
class-based unionism   105
clothing industry   129, 138, 140, 146
CNT. See *Confederación Nacional del Trabajo*
Central de Trabajadores de la Argentina Autónoma   146
COAG (*See Coordinadora de Organizaciones de Agricultores y Ganaderos*)
Cobas (*See Comitati di Base*)
Colectf de Défense des Travailleurs étrangers Saisonniers dand l'agriculture

collective action 1, 8, 11–14, 25, 29, 33, 35, 45–46, 49, 52, 104, 116, 154–155, 158, 160, 167, 209, 213
  repertoire of 26, 53
collective agreement. *See also* collective bargaining
collective bargaining. *See also* collective agreement
Comisiones Obreras 74, 87, 93, 95–96, 172, 210–211, 213–2014
Comitati di Base 111
commodification 108
  of care 59–60, 62, 76, 204
Communist Party of Spain 38
community
  building 59–60, 66, 68–69, 73
  kitchen 140
  initiative 9
  spaces 131
  unionism 9–10, 15, 131, 148–149, 212–215
Confederación General del Trabajo (Spain) 81, 171, 211, 213
Confederación Nacional del Trabajo 81
Conférération Paysanne 173
Confederazione Generale Italiana del Lavoro 106–107, 183, 190–191, 193, 195, 197–198, 210, 213
consumerist individualism 59
contractors 113, 189, 191–194, 197
  informal 188
cooperative sector 110–112, 116
Coordinadora de Organizaciones de Agricultores y Ganaderos 164
corporatisation of care 59, 61–62, 67–69, 76–77, 205, 208
cosmopolitanism 22–23, 204
criminalisation (of migrants) 171, 198
crisis
  economic 22, 41–42, 86, 91, 109, 162n.10, 204
  of representation (of trade unions) 104–105, 107, 129
critical mass 104, 109, 113
critical political economy 181, 205
Critical Sociology 13
Critical Workers 49
cross-border
  trade 86
  workers 95, 97, 99

CTA Autónoma. *See Central de Trabajadores de la Argentina Autónoma*
CUB (United Rank-and-File Confederation) 112, 115
Cultural Symbiosis Collective 133–137, 148
cycle of contention 108

day labourer 16, 155–156, 159, 161, 163, 166, 173, 176, 185, 188, 208, 213
  unionism 158
Deliveroo 24, 45
delocalisation 4, 83, 113
Democratic Party (Italy) 115n.4
DGB (German Trade Union Confederation) 40, 209, 212
Die Linke 38
Digmun association 93, 96–98, 100, 214
direct action 15, 32n.16, 74, 97, 108, 114, 137, 149, 171, 174, 214
discrimination 61, 95, 133, 144, 145n.49, 146, 148, 212
domestic
  service 88–91, 93, 213
  work 70, 85, 88–91, 93, 96–97, 99–100, 211

Erdogan, Recep Tayyip 115
ethnification 91
ethno-specialisation 45
ethno-stratification 45, 52
European Central Bank 49
Europeanisation from bellow 23
European Union 42, 60, 62–64, 71, 165, 185–186, 204
  enlargement 23, 63,
European Social Fund 71–72
externalisation of costs 71–72

Facebook 27, 33, 46, 47, 61, 65, 74
far left 209
FAU (*See Freie Arbeiterinnen-und Arbeiter*)
feminisation 3, 90, 91, 162
feminism 30, 32, 38, 60, 136n.33,
FILT (Federation on Transport Workers) 111
Foggia 182–184, 186–187, 192,-196, 198, 213
Foodora 24n.7, 45, 50
Fordism 1–2, 6, 9, 28, 46, 81, 83, 181, 204
formality vs. informality 125–127
Franco, Francisco 91, 156

INDEX

Freie Arbeiterinnen-und Arbeiter 14, 37–38, 44–45, 47, 50–51, 74, 209, 212
FresHuelva (*Asociación Onubense de Productores y Exportadores de Fresa Huelva*) 165, 170

GAS (*See Grupo de Acción Sindical*)
garment
   industry 119–124, 128–129, 131, 133–134, 137–138, 141, 147–148, 206–207, 211, 214
   organisations 119
   workers 120, 131, 133, 140–142, 145–146, 148
GCC (*See* global care chain)
GDR (German Democratic Republic) 26
gender equality 173
Germany 14, 21–53, 59–77, 168, 186, 206, 208–209, 212
GFR (German Federal Republic) 26
ghetto 135, 187
Gibraltar, Strait of 161
gig
   economy 24n.7, 49
   work 24
globalisation 2, 4, 6, 61, 83–84, 184
global care chain 4, 61, 82, 84, 205
global value chain 4, 16, 84, 181, 183–184, 194–195, 205, 208
Gramsci, Antonio 182, 190, 205
Grupo de Acción Sindical 14, 32–41, 46–47, 51–53, 61, 66, 69, 73–75, 206
guest worker 65, 155, 161, 162n.10, 168–170, 172–175
GVC (*See* global value chain)

Hartz IV 33, 43, 48
horizontalisation 24, 207
horizontalism 32n.16, 34, 36, 53
housing 7, 27, 30–32, 42, 50, 52, 114–115, 121, 160, 163, 171–172, 176, 196, 198
Huelva 16, 155–157, 159–161, 165, 168, 170–177, 213
Huelva Wellcomes (*Huelva Acoge*) 172
Human Development Index 86
humanitarian organisation 100

identity 5–7, 15–16, 23, 84, 105–106, 119, 134, 137, 148, 156–161, 166, 168, 171, 214
indignados 12, 74

See also 15M
Industrial Workers of the World 108, 116
informalisation of jobs 11
innovation 2, 4, 11, 13–14, 16, 25, 35, 47, 53, 83–84, 109, 214
integration 6, 16, 23, 30, 86, 93
   policies 198
   strategies 204
INTERFRESA (Andalusian Interprofessional, Strawberry Association) 168
International Ogranisation for Migrations 133n.27, 141
International Political Economy of Labour 182
Interventionistische Linke 41
intra-EU mobility 13, 21–22, 25, 51, 204
irregular work 99, 161, 184, 187, 194
Italian Department of Agriculture 191
Italy 22, 32, 41–42, 49–53, 104–112, 181–191, 198, 209–210
IU (United Left) 30, 38, 171
Ivory Coast 160, 170
IWW (*See* Industrial Workers of the World)

Juventud Sin Futuro 30

Kirchnerism 131
Kreuzberg 32, 34

land inheritance 159
lean production 181
Lidl 167
Lista Roja 127, 140, 143–146
logic of action 105, 108, 113, 116, 212
logistics
   porters 104–105, 108, 111–117, 208–209
   services 114
   supply chain 109

Maghreb 170, 184
Mali 157, 160, 170
Marea Blanca 74
Maroon Tide 31
Marxism 116
   Marxist 37, 46, 104, 123
Mauritania 160, 170
mechanisation 160
Mercadona 167
Merkel, Angela 43n.27, 64

methodology of the subaltern   182, 205
migrant labour   1, 25, 45, 52, 126, 184, 192, 214
Migrant Strike   135–136, 148
Milani, Aldo   112
minojob   43
mixed method   120
mobility
   geographic and labour   30, 161–162
   social   23, 157
modernisation   159
Moguer   15, 155, 169
moral
   economy   167–168, 171–172
   framework   155, 168
   values   156, 159, 167, 176, 214
Morocco   21n.2, 86–88, 92, 97–98, 157, 161, 165, 170, 185, 208
mutual aid   9, 15, 61

nanny chain   60
Negri, Toni   32
neoliberal
   citizenship   107, 109
   system of exploitation   107
networks
   community   10, 13
   family   90, 98
   kinship   90
   migratory   161
   online   23
   social   3, 23, 47
   solidarity   10, 15, 115, 211–212, 215
   support   175
   trafficking   121, 127, 132
Nigeria   160, 170
nurses
   Polish   75
   Spanish   34, 41, 59–77, 204, 208

ODS (*See Oficina de Derechos Sociales*)
Oficina de Derechos Sociales   91, 172
offshoring   181
operaismo   32
organising   8–9, 13–15, 25, 35, 38–39, 46, 50, 53, 106, 112–113, 173, 183, 191, 194–195, 197, 210, 212–213, 215
Origgio   111–112
outsiders   6, 9, 81
   vs. insiders   189–190, 198

Outsourcing
overexploitation   15, 119–120, 123–126, 128, 130, 143, 147, 149, 208–209, 213–214

Parque Avellaneda Neighbourhood Assembly   140
Partido Socialista de los Trabajadores   137n.35
Perdiendo el norte   65
piecework   46, 92, 122,124, 158n.8, 187
Platform against the Immigration Act (Huelva)   170–171, 213
platform economy   6, 51, 207
Podemos   30, 38, 53
Poland   63, 155, 162, 168, 185
Polanyi, Karl   166
polarization   159
political culture   111
political economy   12
political exchange   107
political institutions   106, 119, 147
political subjects   131, 149
posted workers   23, 63
post-Fordism   4, 83
   migrations   2–3, 83, 206, 214
Potere al Popolo   51
precarious city   135
precariousness   2, 14, 16–17, 25, 31, 35, 38, 45, 48, 51, 89, 100, 121, 123, 125, 127, 128, 208–209
pricing policy   195
professionalization   89, 159
public pay   187
push and pull   21

race   7–8, 10, 106, 212–213
racialization   16, 91, 182, 198
radical
   left   38n.20, 51, 53,
   See also far left
   unions   15, 17, 37, 51–52, 81, 104, 113, 116, 195, 213
recruitment agency   62–64, 68, 74
refugee crisis   13, 49
regularisation   88, 94, 96–97, 99, 125n.15, 170, 172, 192, 196
repertoire
   of (collective) action   53, 107, 113–114
   of contention   12, 113

protest 149
representation structure 40n.23, 52, 212
repression 115, 160
reproduction 67, 88, 166, 198
  capital 131
  costs 71
  social 88, 90, 155, 163, 167n.15, 176, 205
residential segregation 187
riders 45–46, 50
rights
  citizenship 126
  labour 14, 33–34, 52, 89, 96, 139, 173, 214
  social 7–8, 26, 106, 113, 117, 185, 190, 196, 198, 210–212
right-wing 107, 139, 191, 199
Romania 63, 155, 162–163, 185
Rosarno 107

sabotage 113
SAT (See Sindicato Andaluz de Trabajadores)
Schäuble, Wolfgang 64
Schengen Agreement 87
seasonal circuits 185, 208
seasonal worker 157, 194, 209
secondary labour market 1, 14, 17, 23, 42, 46, 207, 210–211
self-organisation 14, 16
Senegal 160, 170
SETIA (See Sindicato de Empleados Textiles de la Industria y Afines)
Sevilla 33, 155, 160, 170
sex and gender relations 4, 84, 91
sexual división of work 89
SGB (See Sindacato Generale di Base)
shop steward 127, 130, 138n.35, 142–145, 147
SI Cobas (See Sindacato Intercategoriale Cobas)
simulacrum 154
Sindacato Generale di Base 112
Sindacato Intercategoriale Cobas 15, 104–117, 210
Sindicato Andaluz de Trabajadores 33, 52, 81, 172–174, 212
Sindicato de Empleados Textiles de la Industria y Afines 129
Sindicato de Obreros del Campo 160, 172–174, 211
Sindicato de Trabajadores Talleristas a Domicilio 129, 211

Sindicato Obrero de la Industria del Vestido y Afines 129, 211
Sindicato Unitario 171, 211
slave labour 141n.45
smallholding 156
SOC (See Sindicato de Obreros del Campo)
social centers 29, 112
social dialogue 106, 194, 211–213
  See also tripartite bargaining
socially creative entities 14
social media 12, 28–29, 49, 65
social movements 12, 14, 29, 32, 36, 38n.20, 42, 49, 104–108, 114–117, 158, 174, 212
  anti-austerity 12
  autonomous 29, 36n.19, 212
  housing 32, 114
  labour 14, 93, 105–106
  new 105
  non-global 49, 52
  peasant 164
  student 114
  unemployed 136
social relations of production and distribution 154
social security 62n.2, 63–64, 87, 89, 94–95, 192, 196
social tourism 43
Sociology of Labour 127
SOIVA (See Sindicato Obrero de la Industria del Vestido y Afines)
solidarity
  bonds of 66, 68, 77
  class 6, 95, 106,
  international 108, 117
  workers 59, 66, 71, 75
Soli-Pizza 50
squatters 32, 42, 44, 47–50, 53, 212
startup 24, 26,
stigmatisation 126, 132, 135, 137
strawberry production 154–156, 163, 176, 213
street union squads 192
strike 195
  general 112, 115
  hunger 170
  migrant 136–138, 148
  sectoral 112
  social 49
  wildcat 114

STTAD. *See Sindicato de Trabajadores Talleristas a Domicilio*
subcontracting   51, 208
supermarket chains   208
surplus   37, 123n.9, *189*
sweatshops   127, 141n.45, 185
Switzerland   75

Temporary Guest Farm Worker Program   155, 161n.9, 162n.10, 170, 172
Temporary Workers Board   155, 172–174
tertiarisation   110, 113
tomato-picking industry   197, 210, 213
trade union
  confederation   106, 130
  grass-roots   15, 108, 128, 213
  identity   7, 106
  independent   107, 112, 115, 195, 209–211
  interstitial   10, 25, 52, 107, 171
  traditional   46, 51, 74, 104, 111–112, 116–117, 145, 198
  renewal   13, 183, 198, 215
  revitalisation   6, 12, 81, 128–129
Transition (Spain)   32n.16, 158, 164
Transnationalism   2–3, 25, 82–83, 206
transnational social field   2–3, 83, 206
transnational social space   25, 206
tripartite bargaining   107
Trotskyism
  Trotskyite organization   34, 38
Turkey   21n.2, 115

UCEV. *See Unión de Costurerxs y Empleadoxs del Vestido*
UCI. *See Unión de Cortadores de Indumentaria*
UGT. *See Unión General de Trabajadores*
unemployment
  benefit   21, 92, 94, 192
  rate   22, 27, 64, 85
Unión de Cortadores de Indumentaria   129, 211
Unión de Costurerxs y Empleadxs del Vestido   15, 120, 140, 146, 148, 214
Unión de Pequeños Agricultores y Ganaderos   165n.14
Unión de Sindicatos de Trabajadores y Trabajadoras de Andalucía   171, 211, 213
Unión de Trabajadores Costureros   138, 140–143, 212

Unione Sindacale di Base   183, 195–197, 210, 213
Unione Sindacale Italiana   112, 115
Unión General de Trabajadores   74, 93, 172, 210–211, 213
Unitary Trade Union. *See Sindicato Unitario*
UPA. *See Unión de Pequeños Agricultores y Ganaderos*
USB. *See Unione Sindacale di Base*
USI. *See Unione Sindacale Italiana*
USTEA. *See Unión de Sindicatos de Trabajadores y Trabajadoras de Andalucía*
UTC. *See Unión de Trabajadores Costureros*
value   123–124, 167, 189, 195
  creation   4, 83
  market   166
  social   158, 166
  system   175
Ver.di   14, 37, 40–41, 51, 63, 69, 70, 73–75, 209, 212
Via Campesina   164, 173
violence   49, 92–93, 97, 196n.14, 208, 214
vulnerability   2, 25, 51–52, 87, 91, 93, 98, 161

wage
  fair   189, 196
  low   23n.5, 88–89, 143, 160, 182, 185
  minimum   42n.25, 63, 75, 86, 122, 124–125
  sub-standard   198
warehousing   49, 104, 109, 111, 114, 163, 207
welfare chauvinism   14, 25, 43, 45
welfare shoppers   43
work
  devaluation   91
  crowd   24
  gig   24
  irregular   99, 161, 184, 187, 194
  paid vs. unpaid   59–60, 62
  permit   23, 87, 95, 97, 132n.23, 161, 170
working class
  fractions   182, 198
  fragmentation   1, 6, 182, 207
  formation   182, 205
  restructuring   182
works council   40, 75,
World Health Organisation   62

xenophobia   136

Printed in the United States
by Baker & Taylor Publisher Services